SHERLOCK HOLMES
WAS A POMPEY KEEPER

The Extraordinary History of the Early Portsmouth FC

KEVIN SMITH

'Afterwards, I took to association, and played first goal
and then back for Portsmouth FC, when that famous club
was an amateur organisation. I was always too slow, however,
to be a really good back, though I was a long and safe kick.'

Dr Arthur Conan Doyle
Memories and Adventures, 1924

HALSGROVE

First published in Great Britain in 2004

British Library Cataloguing-in-Publication Data.
A CIP record for this title is available from the British Library.

ISBN 1 84114 402 9

HALSGROVE

Halsgrove House
Lower Moor Way
Tiverton, Devon EX16 6SS
Tel: 01884 243242
Fax: 01884 243325
email: sales@halsgrove.com
website: www.halsgrove.com

Printed and bound in Great Britain by CPI Bath.

Contents

Acknowledgements

This book has only been possible through the extensive help of many people. A great deal of assistance was provided by David Garvey and Keely-Anne Storey responding to my badgering to be allowed to spend days lost in time in the archives at the News Centre in Portsmouth.

I am also grateful for the efforts made for me over many years by the librarians in the second floor reference section of Portsmouth's Central Library. More specific help has been given by Kim Adsett, Mick Cooper, Allan Craven, Keith Newbery and Tony Valvona. They have given many hours of their spare time to make suggestions and point out errors in the original draft versions of this book. What you are about to read features many of their ideas.

Michael Johnston, the managing director of Portsmouth Publishing and Printing Ltd, has given me permission to use extensive excerpts from the company's papers. Lin Chaplen, of Portsmouth City Council, willingly provided permission for me to reproduce the instantly recognisable star-and-crescent civic emblem so proudly worn by the first Portsmouth football club players.

The late Commander Geoffrey Stavert MBE generously allowed me to rely on his ground-breaking book, *A Study in Southsea*, on which much of my first chapter is based.

Portsmouth Football Association officials Bert Greenwood and Colin Macey have also given assistance along with Wordsworth Editions from whose *The Original Sherlock Holmes* the illustrations of the detective have been reproduced.

Many of the facts about the output of Arthur Conan Doyle are based upon the book *Teller of Tales – The Life of Arthur Conan Doyle* by Darvel Stashower.

Portsmouth AFC photographed after the momentous Portsmouth Senior Cup finals of March 1891 and posing on a Union flag. The winning players from left to right are: Standing – Private Flannery, AW Cook, GL Pares, Bernard Pares, SR Pike Sitting – D Lever, WE Grant, AH Wood (captain), Basil Pares, H McDonald On ground – GA Garrington with the cup

ABBREVIATIONS

Abbreviations used in the tables in this work:
HSC – Hampshire Senior Cup
PSC/PDC – Portsmouth Senior Cup/Portsmouth Junior Cup
USMG – United Services Men's Ground
USOG – United Services Officers' Ground

The venues could also be referred to as the Men's Recreation Ground or the Officers' Recreation Ground.

Numbers next to a player's position indicate goals scored. Portsmouth AFC's score given first in every game.

Sources for the statistics were:
Evening Mail/ Southern Daily Mail
Evening News, Portsmouth – which is referred to thoroughout as the *Portsmouth Evening News*
Hampshire Post
Hampshire Telegraph
Portsmouth Herald
Portsmouth Times

NOTES ON STATISTICS

Different reporters gave different facts from the same game. Local newspapers around Portsmouth were in their infancy during Portsmouth AFC's existence. With the organised football scene also getting underway, the scene was set for confusion on many occasions. Journalists would stand or sit among the spectators to watch matches. The action often took place on gloomy afternoons when it was wet, cold and always muddy. The players wore no identifying names or numbers and, at times, could hardly be seen, I suspect, at the far end of a pitch. Mistakes were bound to occur in such circumstances. Various papers can report conflicting facts about games. I have usually listed these at the bottom of each season's statistics. I have also given the variations of players' names where different spellings were given. But, on occasions, it has been impossible to decide what a newspaperman saw – or even to guess to fill in any gaps in information.

These statistics can, therefore, only be so complete and so accurate. But the history those journalists reported is well worth re-telling one hundred and twenty years later.

Introduction

This book details the history of the first football club to carry the name of their home town of Portsmouth. The club came into being in 1884. Soccer was a haphazard affair in the naval town. Elsewhere, particularly in the north of England, the sport was flourishing.

The northern pacesetters were starting to embrace professionalism, to the concern of the previously dominant public schools, as Portsmouth AFC was formed. The southern England public school ethos was reflected in the founders of Portsmouth AFC – which I have nicknamed the original Pompey – which was the on-the-pitch identity of the Portsmouth Football Association.

The club was firmly amateur in all its dealings. Among its initial players, at full back and in goal, was a struggling doctor in Southsea. But the literary skills of Dr Arthur Conan Doyle came to overshadow his contribution to football in Portsmouth and his fellow players. None could claim to be household names, then or now, even in Portsmouth. But their legacy, as much as Dr Doyle's, lives on in the form of Portsmouth FC and also inspires passion among its followers.

Sherlock Holmes was a Pompey Keeper is the story of all those players and the story of football's struggles to gain a foothold in a naval port known wherever sailors gather. It is not the story of the time spent by Dr Doyle in Southsea any more than it is a critical look at the stories he wrote while he lived in the seaside resort. Other, more knowledgeable authors, have covered those details in many forms before.

Kevin Smith

This view would have been familiar to Arthur Conan Doyle. It was taken less than 20 years after he left Bush Villas, between the Bush Hotel on the right of the picture and Elm Grove Baptist Church.

Courtesy of Ron Brown

CHAPTER ONE

A pen was in one hand of the Southsea GP and a pad of notepaper was on his desk. An ink bottle was in front of him as he sat down in his rooms on March 8th 1886 to start the latest of his stories.

This one was different. It chronicled the first adventure of a scientific solver of crime.

Sherlock Holmes was the name of the fictional sleuth. *A Study In Scarlet* was the name of the story in which he made his debut. His appearance was heralded with the words:

In the year 1878, I took my degree of Doctor of Medicine at the University of London, and proceeded to Netley to go through the course prescribed for surgeons in the Army.

Having completed my studies there, I was duly attached to the Northumberland Fusiliers as assistant surgeon.

The author was, of course, Dr Arthur Conan Doyle. He possessed a compulsive urge to write. Before he began the opening sentence of *A Study In Scarlet* he would have seen the latest of the steadily increasing number of patients who came to his practice at Number One Bush Villas, Elm Grove, Southsea, for advice and medication, if they had enough money for the latter as well as the former.

But there were still too many empty hours in the day for a man of Conan Doyle's energy and unstoppable desire to communicate to feel happy about. He filled those vacant periods by reading and making notes for his future reference as well as writing. And playing football.

Two days before his opening session creating Sherlock Holmes and his astonishing powers of deduction, Conan Doyle had turned out as a back for the first Portsmouth football club, with his height of 6ft 2in and his 15 stone bulk proving useful in stopping forwards from the opposition.

It was a match, fittingly, far out of the ordinary which preceded the birth of Sherlock Holmes. The game ended in a 13–1 victory for the borough club against their overwhelmed visitors from Petersfield.

Conan Doyle was playing his thirty-first known game for the blue-shirted home team at their ground, such as it was, on the south side of the present Stubbington Avenue and which was a meadow close to Stubbington Lodge.

Readers of the local papers would have struggled to guess the presence of the Southsea doctor in the line-up. Conan Doyle turned out for the club under

Dr Arthur Conan Doyle's lifesize bronze statue on show at Crowborough.

the pseudonym of 'AC Smith'. As the *Portsmouth Evening News* stated after that Petersfield match:

...while he was well supported by the captain, WO Adames, and AC Smith and R Hemingsley who did sufficiently well with the work which fell upon them so that Gibbons had comparatively little to do in goal.

Quite why the doctor and author should choose to hide his identity in this way has remained a mystery. He gave no clues in his autobiography as to why the false name was adopted.

It was only in the match reports that the deceit was maintained. Perhaps it was as the late Geoffrey Stavert said in his history of Conan Doyle's time in Southsea:

Whether Dr Doyle felt that, whereas cricket was a gentleman's game in which he might very properly appear under his own name, the somewhat cloth-cap image of soccer might be offputting to some of his lady patients, or whether it was his own private little joke, we do not know.

It would be interesting to know by what name Dr Doyle's own friends and team-mates referred to him on the field, or in the pub afterwards.

Obviously, they were all in on the Smith joke with him, but we do not know to what lengths he wished to take it.

Even then, the falsehood was only maintained during the club's early years. His mentions with regard to his sporting love – cricket – also featured his true identity.

Conan Doyle had no such reticence, either, so far as

his writing was concerned. The strength of his literary desire drove him to finish *A Study In Scarlet* within two months. By then, he had appeared in a further three games for the original Pompey. Two of them were drawn – separated by a defeat – as he played as a back and the goalkeeper.

He continued to appear in both positions throughout the 1886/87 season that followed, in which he helped his teammates and friends to clinch the first cup won by a Portsmouth football club, and in the early part of the next campaign as he endured a long and frustrating wait for *A Study In Scarlet* to be published.

The manuscript was rejected twice, once with praise and once unread. Originally titled *A Tangled Skein*, it finally emerged in print as the main feature of the 1887 edition of *Beeton's Christmas Annual*.

Its appearance on bookstalls soon after the middle of the November must have been Conan Doyle's proudest moment. The highly coloured cover of the soft-backed book featured *A Study In Scarlet* in large red letters beneath its masthead. His name, Arthur Conan Doyle, was printed in black above the titles of the other contents of the annual, two original drawing-room plays.

The annual was a collection of fiction and short occasional stories founded in 1867 by Samuel Orchart Beeton – the husband of Mrs Beeton, whose famous book of household management came out 12 years earlier. Mr Beeton had been a director of publisher Ward Lock & Co, and ensured his name lived on, as well as his wife's, through the annual.

A Portsmouth magazine of the period, *The Crescent*, reported that the annual sold out within a fortnight. If that was so, it came about without the help of the local press. Neither the *Hampshire Telegraph*, the *Portsmouth Evening News* nor the *Portsmouth Times* set aside any space for Sherlock Holmes's debut, in spite of the author being local.

It was left to the *Hampshire Post* in early December to rectify the oversight. Its edition of December 2nd devoted one and a half columns of one of its broadsheet pages to a review of *A Study In Scarlet*. The thorough critique combined enthusiastic praise and valid criticism in equal measures.

The detective tale was certain to attract a host of readers, the newspaper predicted. Its comment spoke about readers' love of thrillers and detective stories at Christmas, even though it is the season of love and goodwill. They revelled in the murder and marvelled at the detective's worth.

...of breathless recitals of this character we know of no more brilliant example than the little story which Dr Arthur Conan Doyle has just given to the world.

Here then is an abundance of mystery for the imagination to work upon.

Dr Arthur Conan Doyle was described in the article as a novelist with a freshness and novelty bred of conviction and creative fruitfulness.

Such is the enduring interest in this period of Dr Arthur Conan Doyle's life that one of his sketches for *A Study in Scarlet* had a reserve price of £150 000 when it was auctioned in London in May 2004. It was part of a £2 million archive of more than 3000 letters, notes and manuscripts which was discovered 74 years after the death of the author and doctor. A legend in literature had been born.

A Study In Scarlet was issued in 1888 as a separate book to capitalise on its initial success. A few weeks before, Conan Doyle had turned out in goal for Portsmouth and kept a clean sheet in the 2–0 defeat of Portsmouth Sunflowers as the previous year drew to a close.

Over the next two years, several stories and plenty of football games followed for Conan Doyle before Sherlock Holmes next appeared in print, in 1890. And how! The publication of *The Sign of Four* marked a giant leap forward in Conan Doyle's writing career.

The story arose from one of the most celebrated lunches of all time, in August of the preceding year. Conan Doyle found himself at the Langham Hotel in London's Portland Place seated opposite Oscar Wilde, an Irish MP called Gill and the publisher, JM Stoddart.

Sherlock Holmes as he appeared in The Adventure of the Greek Interpreter published in Strand Magazine *1892/93.*

Stoddart worked for the American firm of Lippincott's which published a monthly magazine on both sides of the Atlantic. Its policy was to include a complete story in each edition. Stoddart was searching for new talent. His inquiries took him to *Cornhill Magazine*, where its editor, James Payn, recommended Conan Doyle.

The meal ended with Wilde and Conan Doyle agreeing to each write a new story. Wilde's was *Dorian Gray*. For Conan Doyle, the choice was *The Sign of Four*.

He was to receive £100 for handing in 40 000 words by the following January. It was the first time a publisher had approached him. What a welcome change from having to anxiously approach publisher after publisher with his work.

Hardly a month had passed before *The Sign of Four* was on its way to Lippincott's. The story's opening words are as notorious as those of any fictional crime story:

Sherlock Holmes took his bottle from the corner of the mantelpiece and his hypodermic syringe from its neat morocco case.

With his long, white nervous fingers he adjusted the delicate needle and rolled back his left shirt cuff.

For some time his eyes rested thoughtfully upon the sinewy forearm and wrist all dotted and scarred with innumerable puncture marks.

Finally he thrust the sharp point home, pressed down the tiny piston, and sank back into the velvet lined armchair with a long sigh of satisfaction.

Cocaine was widely available in Victorian times. Indeed, Sherlock Holmes's three-times-a-day habit with seven per cent cocaine could well have been prompted by the British Dental Assocation conference in Portsmouth the previous year, where the effects of the drug were widely discussed.

The Sign of Four was published in February 1890. It became a success in Britain and the USA. Sherlock Holmes was firmly established in the public's mind.

Conan Doyle had played football occasionally in the months which led up to the publication but the book's arrival coincided with the first of several pauses in activity which littered the twelve year history of the club.

Indeed, the Hampshire Senior Cup defeat by the Royal Engineers on December 28th, which was his last appearance for the club, was also their last meaningful game of 1889/90.

Conan Doyle played as a back, as he had done when *A Study in Scarlet* was published.

The 2–3 away reverse was Conan Doyle's first game for a month and followed a spell of three matches in ten days during November. In each, he turned out under his own name. The pretence of being 'AC Smith' had vanished finally in the previous year.

The long and safe kicking of which he wrote more than thirty years later in his autobiography played its part in the clean sheets in those matches. His forwards, by contrast, found their opponents' goals twelve times.

Player or no player, Conan Doyle still presided at the 1890 annual general meeting of Portsmouth AFC, which had come to mean so much to him. He declined to use his growing success as an author as an excuse to miss the important occasion in the outfit's existence.

The meeting took place on September 17th, just after *The Sign of Four* had been serialised in the *Hampshire Telegraph*. The nine-part version of the story had been featured from July 5th in the supple-

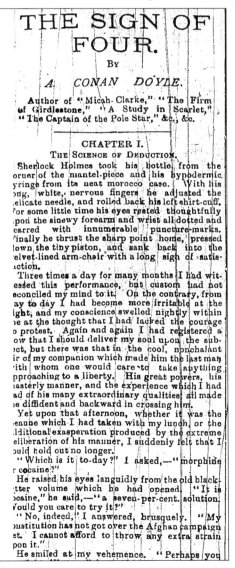

How the Hampshire Telegraph *began its Sign of Four serialisation on July 5, 1890.*

"HOLMES GAVE ME A SKETCH OF THE EVENTS."

Sherlock Holmes complete with his trademark deerstalker hat on his way to solving 'The Adventure of the Silver Blaze' as seen in Strand Magazine *in 1892/93.*

ment which came with the weekly paper.

The *Portsmouth Evening News*, the sister paper, advertised the story modestly and without any reference to its author's links as a GP in Southsea, or as a member of the Portsmouth football and cricket clubs, or of its literary and scientific society.

Conan Doyle was determined to play a full part in Portsmouth's life while he lived and worked in the town. Such activities enabled him to enjoy his leisure pursuits as well as offering the possibility of gaining new patients for his fledgling practice. But the *Portsmouth Evening News* contented itself with saying:

The Sign of Four is the exciting and fascinating history of a crime. It is rich in a number of novel characters and abounds in ingenious situations.

The scene is laid partly in the vicinity of the Andaman Islands and partly in London.

The same edition of the newspaper also recorded how another of Conan Doyle's stories from his time in Portsmouth had gained acclaim, for there was much more to his output while a footballer in the town than Sherlock Holmes.

Micah Clarke was the novel which the *Portsmouth Evening News* had reported as being among the three most powerful historical novels of its generation. The others were *Lorna Doone* and *Westward Ho!*

Micah Clarke was the result of Conan Doyle testing his literary powers on a fully historical work. It appeared in February 1889 during which he played without his alias in Portsmouth AFC's 2–0 Hampshire Senior Cup success over Portsmouth Grammar School and 3–1 defeat of the YMCA in Portsmouth.

Conan Doyle squeezed in the creation of *Micah Clarke* during just six months in which he combined playing football as well as working in his medical practice and studying optics at Portsmouth Eye Hospital.

His initial delight at the book's completion was dimmed by a round of rejections from publishers. *Micah Clarke* made it into print after almost a year following its completion. It was an overwhelming success. The story opens in Havant and concerns a group of English Puritans against the backdrop of the Monmouth Rebellion to overthrow King James II. The *Portsmouth Evening News* of March 4th 1889 stated:

Dr Arthur Conan Doyle has gone at one stride into the front rank of novelists.

His last book – Micah Clarke *– is not only his best; it is* THE *best historical novel that has been published for years.*

A Study In Scarlet was good - Sherlock Holmes being a real addition to the men we know – but both this and its successor, The Mystery of Cloomber, *compared with* Micah Clarke *were studies in fiction, the necessary preparation for a great effort.*

Dr Arthur Conan Doyle has now passed through the initial stage, and has made his first important step in the right direction and at the right time.

The newspaper enthused how much Micah Clarke lit up one of the most romantic periods of this country's national life with Conan Doyle's inimitable character painting and fascinating powers in the descriptions of places and events:

We do not say this because Dr Conan Doyle is a resident of Southsea. A man's own town is generally the last to recognise his own capacity. We are all so much alike that to know a man creates prejudice against him.

Doyle Court is one of a cluster of reminders of the famous author close to Portsmouth AFC's original ground in North End, Portsmouth.

Dr Arthur Conan Doyle's literary output in Portsmouth was prolific. It comprised much more than Sherlock Holmes as this list of his stories written between 1882 and 1890 shows:

1883
J Hababuk Jephson
Crabbe's Practice
The Heiress of Glenmahowley
John Barrington Cowles
The Cobman's Story
The Greek Interpreter

1885
Surgeon of Glaster Fell
The Man from Archangel

1886
John Huxford's Hiatus
The Ring of Thoth
The Physiologist's Wife

1886
Uncle Jeremy's Household
Cyprian Overbeck Wells (A Literary Mosaic)
A Study in Scarlet
The Stone of Boxman's Drift
Corporal Dick's Promotion

1889
The Mystery of Cloomber

1889
Micah Clarke
The Firm of Girdlestone

1890
The Captain of the Polestar
The Sign of Four

It is in spite of the author being our townsman, and not because of it, that we rank his last achievement so high.

The reputation of Dr Conan Doyle as a writer of fiction will be immensely enhanced by Micah Clarke.

The same edition of the newspaper carried a report of the most important football match in which Conan Doyle played as he continued to combine his literary ambitions with lacing up his football boots.

Its outcome, unfortunately for him and for the original Pompey, was much less satisfying than the reaction to his latest book.

The Hampshire Senior Cup final against the Royal Engineers ended in a 1–5 defeat for Portsmouth AFC at Southampton's Banister Park ground in front of a crowd which, at several thousand strong, was larger than any which the borough club had played before.

Rival newspaper, the *Southern Daily Mail*, reported how Conan Doyle had played his part in the blue-shirted defence in repulsing the soldiers' early attacks:

Royal Engineers played at a pace which was astonishing. Conan Doyle's long telling kicks repulsed them.

But the kicks were not enough to save his team from defeat in the only county cup final in which they played. Royal Engineers took the lead after fifteen minutes and never looked back. They built up a 0–3 lead by half-time, though the cause of Portsmouth AFC was hindered by being a man short. Their only goal came from a scramble in front of the Engineers' posts a few minutes before the end.

Conan Doyle recalled the event thirty-five years later in his autobiography *Memories and Adventures*, though he mistakenly connected Portsmouth AFC and the current Portsmouth FC:

(I) played first goal and then back for Portsmouth FC, when that famous club was an amateur organisation.
Even then, we could put a very fair team in the field, and were runners up for the county cup the last season that I played.

He was two months short of his 30th birthday. Unlike his football, his book-writing ambitions and profile continued to grow. But *Micah Clarke* was joined by many other works while Conan Doyle still maintained his playing interest in football. Of these, *The White Company* was the work in which he took most pleasure.

The weeks which led up to Portsmouth AFC's annual meeting in September 1889 saw him decamp to a cottage in the New Forest and focus his mind and imagination on the tale of a group of fourteenth century bowmen during the Hundred Years War.

The story was published during 1891 to great acclaim. By then, Conan Doyle had left his Southsea practice and the friends and teammates he had played alongside.

His final months in the resort were marked by a bout of publications. First to appear on the bookstalls was *The Captain of the Polestar* in March 1890, a collection of ten short stories, many of which had been published previously in such magazines as *Cornhill*, *Temple Bar* and *Belgravia* – which Conan Doyle used to pursue his quest for literary success after he had arrived in Southsea in 1882.

Some predated the formation of the football club, which had stuttered to a halt temporarily at the time of the book's publication. The *Portsmouth Evening News* said of *The Captain of the Polestar*:

When an author takes front rank in fiction by his first ambitious work (Micah Clarke), the minor ventures of earlier years assume a new importance, and are soon disinterred to satisfy public curiosity.

Four days after that review appeared, on Tuesday, March 11th, Conan Doyle kept up his love of football when he presented the trophy to the winners of the 1890 Portsmouth Senior Cup competition after the final at the US grounds. Sadly, for him and other football fans in Portsmouth, the by then famous author did not hand the cup to his former team-mates. They had been knocked out in the second round in a decisive defeat away to Cowes just before the previous Christmas.

Conan Doyle was absent on that occasion but he had been involved when the original Pompey squeezed through against the King's Own Yorkshire Light Infantry in the opening round of the cup a month earlier. He was selected as his team's umpire for the contest in keeping with the usual practice at matches in the pioneering football period in Portsmouth of having one official from each side to help the referee.

He took the opportunity, as he handed over the cup which he had helped to found, to remark on the fact that the cup final for Portsmouth's own trophy was fought between two clubs from Southampton – Freemantle emerging the winners by a single goal against the Geneva Cross side from Netley.

Freemantle's captain, H Maton, accepted the trophy from Conan Doyle who, according to the *Portsmouth Evening News*:

...remarked that he had a peculiar pleasure in undertaking the duty, as he was one of the original players five years ago.

The improvement of the game since then showed the cup had well served its purpose, though as a Portsmouth man, he felt somewhat humiliated that the tie had been lost to two Southampton clubs.

But he was sure, the paper continued, that the mass of young clubs in the Portsmouth area would mean that a home town challenge for the cup would soon be made again and the trophy was only visiting Southampton.

The game that day had been good natured and a partic-

Another literary giant lived and worked in Portsmouth in the early years of Dr Arthur Conan Doyle's arrival in the naval port. Herbert George Wells, however, represented a physical contrast to the strapping 6ft 2in and 15 stone doctor. The frail youth – about 16 when he came to Portsmouth – lived and worked around the corner from Dr Doyle's home, Bush Villas.

But Well's association with the drapery store of Messrs Hyde, in King Street, was a lot more unhappy than the links Dr Doyle established through his medical practice. Wells spent two years at the store after he started there in early 1881. It was a period he hated.

He had previously worked in a draper's and chemist's near to his mother's workplace of the West Sussex stately home, Uppark House. The routine of retail life in Southsea dulled the brain of the teenage assistant. Moving headless dummies around the shop, filling up countless pin bowls and wrestling lengths of cloth provided no mental stimulus at all. Night-times would be spent in the dormitories on the premises he shared with his fellow young workers. Wells would like awake reading by candlelight. The facts of the encyclopaedias caught his imagination with their information about the universe and time.

Wells led this double life – immortalised many years later in his famous novel *Kipps* – until he could stand it no longer. He traipsed the 17 miles to Uppark House where his mother attended the Sunday church services. He told her he would rather drown than continue as a draper.

That episode in early 1883 ended with Mrs Wells promising to do her best for his escape from the world of monotonous work if he would put up with it for a few months longer. He did and the headmaster of Midhurst Grammar School, Horace Byatt, from whom Wells learned Latin during his stint in pharmacy, offered him a job as a student assistant teacher. A year later, and Wells had absorbed enough information to enable him to be awarded a scholarship at the Normal School of Science in London. His literary output developed from there.

ularly fair one, but he could not help saying that if one man more than another was entitled to hold the cup … it was the Freemantle captain.

A novel, *The Firm of Girdlestone*, followed into print the next month. Nearly two years in the writing, and four years in the hiding, the story concerned a medical student at Edinburgh University who worked on an African trading vessel.

Conan Doyle was unconvinced of its merits – its completion predated *A Study In Scarlet* – and it was initially rejected many times. But the success of Sherlock Holmes had, as the *Portsmouth Evening News* stated, ensured that publishers took a more lenient view in later years of Conan Doyle's early works.

To these books from his time in Southsea can be added *The Mystery of Cloomber*, published just before *Micah Clarke* in 1889 and which rapidly disappeared from view, and *The Surgeon of Gaster Fell*. This was another mystery story, this time from 1885, alongside a host of short stories.

This literary success was not enough to prevent a drastic change of mind which saw him announce in November 1890 that he was disbanding his Southsea practice after eight years to train as an eye specialist while keeping his writing as a potentially large source of extra income.

His first wife, Louisa, whom he had met in Southsea, travelled with him while their two-year-old daughter, Mary Louise, remained in England with Conan Doyle's mother-in-law on the Isle of Wight while he left to study the medicine of the eye in Vienna.

His connections with the early days of Portsmouth AFC were ended by his move but not forgotten, as a farewell dinner for him held by the Portsmouth Literary and Scientific Society at the Grosvenor Hotel, Southsea, on December 12th 1890 made clear.

A report in the following day's *Portsmouth Times* was proof of that:

Dr Conan Doyle is essentially an 'all-round' man. During his eight years' residence here, he has steadily made his way in his profession; he has found time to devote to literature, in which he has achieved a national reputation as a writer of sterling and stirring fiction; and, withal, he has gained renown as a cricketer and a footballist.

His love of outdoor recreation is well known, and he will be greatly missed by the Portsmouth cricket and association football clubs, in whose welfare he has taken a practical interest.

That interest received its reward with the only two footballing medals which Conan Doyle won and which sandwiched the eventual appearance in print of *The Sign of Four*.

Both medals came in the Portsmouth and District Challenge Cup, as the Portsmouth Senior Cup was known in its early years, in consecutive seasons. He played in goal for Portsmouth AFC on the first occa-

sion and is sure to have done so on the second as well.

Conan Doyle appeared in the team line up for the latter final but the lack of any team details in the surviving papers which covered the replay means his participation then can only be classed as likely rather than definite.

The first of those triumphs – in 1887 – brought a successful conclusion to the inaugural cup competition for footballers in Portsmouth. Fittingly, Conan Doyle returned the compliment in *Memories and Adventures*:

With its imperial associations it is a glorious place and even now if I had to live in a town outside London it is surely to Southsea, the residential quarter of Portsmouth, that I would turn.

The history of the past carries on into the history of today, the new torpedo boat flies past the old Victory

DR. A. CONAN DOYLE.

The announcement that Dr. A. Conan Doyle is about to leave Southsea for Vienna, where he will continue his special study of the eye prior to commencing practice as an oculist in London, has caused deep regret. Portsmouthians would have preferred to retain the skilled physician, the gifted *litterateur*, and the genial, kind-hearted townsman. Dr. Doyle having, however, after mature consideration, decided to seek a wider sphere of usefulness, the good wishes expressed for his future welfare at the parting dinner at which he was entertained last night at the Grosvenor Hotel, Southsea, under the auspices of the Portsmouth Literary and Scientific Society, will be heartily endorsed by the inhabitants generally. Dr. Conan Doyle is essentially an "all-round man." During his eight years' residence here he has steadily made his way in his profession; he has found time to devote to literature, in which he has achieved a national reputation as a writer of sterling and stirring fiction; and, withal, he has gained renown as a cricketer and footballist.

Dr Conan Doyle, who is 31 or 32 years of age, was born at Edinburgh, and comes from a good stock. His father, Charles Doyle, was an artist, and the son of John Doyle, a celebrated caricaturist (better known, perhaps, as "H.B."). James Doyle, the historian, Henry Doyle, C.B., director of the Irish Academy, and Richard Doyle, formerly of *Punch*, are uncles of the subject of our sketch.

Dr. Doyle was educated at Stonyhurst College, and after a year's study in Germany entered as a medical student at Edinburgh University, where in due course he took his degree of M.D. Then he went on a voyage in the Arctic Seas, following this by a trip to the West Coast of Africa, and eventually, in the year 1882, settled at Southsea as a medical practitioner. But before this Dr. Doyle had given proof of literary talent, for at the early age of 18 he contributed short tales to *Cornhill* and *Temple Bar*, several of which, we believe, were reprinted not long since in "The Captain of the Polestar," published by Messrs. Longman. His first great success was "Micah Clarke," a work in which very many of our readers have doubtless found much to interest them. The *Figaro*, a periodical whose criticisms of the works of budding novelists are not as a rule all honey and sugar, in speaking of the book recently said :— "It must have cost the author an immense amount of labour; for there is not a slipshod passage in it, and the minor details obviously received the same careful attention as the plot and characterisation." The great demand for the book is in itself strong evidence of its popularity; it has now gone through five editions. Since then Messrs. Chatto and Windus have published for him "The Firm of Girdlestone," a more sensational work, in which the character studies are remarkably good, which cannot be said of some of the books of this class which flood the press in the present day. Dr. Doyle's latest great work is "The White Com-

Dr Arthur Conan Doyle's leaving dinner held by the Portsmouth Literary and Scientific Society in December 1890.

with the same white ensign flying from each.

There is a great glamour there to anyone with the historic sense.

Conan Doyle arrived in Portsmouth in early July 1882 on a coastal steamer at Clarence Pier after a voyage from Plymouth. The 'other' naval port in Devon had been the location of his first work as a doctor with a fellow former student, Dr George Budd.

His six weeks with his friend proved to be an experience which Conan Doyle wished to avoid again for the rest of his life. Budd had promised him a partnership in his practice which he had built up by offering free consultations with costly prescriptions to follow.

The unorthodox methods aroused Conan Doyle's anger. The pair fell out and Budd told him to leave. Conan Doyle went first to Tavistock, where he instantly realised he had no chance of becoming established, before Portsmouth came to him next.

The reason was simple. Portsmouth was a naval port and Conan Doyle thought it would offer similar conditions to Plymouth. He had less than £10 in his pockets when he stepped on to Southsea seafront, carrying all his earthly possessions in one trunk. He considered a pound a week would easily cover his personal needs as a twenty-three year-old single man. But he obviously made his priority finding somewhere to stay.

He went into lodgings for a week – at an address believed by the late Geoffrey Stavert to be in Old Portsmouth – and set to work straight away looking for suitable premises in which to set up his practice.

A week passed, as he organised a series of walks around the town to search out the location of existing doctors. Being an energetic person, he criss-crossed the entire length and breadth of Portsea Island. The result of his brisk and long walks was a map marked with the site of every surgery which he had seen and every house.

He detailed the outcome in his semi-autobiographical book *The Stark Munro Letters*:

I found that there was one villa to let, which undoubtedly was far the most suitable for my purpose. In the first place, it was fairly cheap - £40 or £50 with taxes. The front looked well. It had no garden.

It stood with the well-to-do quarter upon one side and the poorer upon the other. Finally, it was almost at the intersection of four roads, one of which was a main artery of the town.

Altogether, if I had ordered a house for my purpose I could hardly have got anything better.

That was Number One Bush Villas.

Conan Doyle again, this time in his autobiography, sets the scene of his early days there:

What with cleaning up, answering the bell, doing my

Bush House in Elm Grove, Southsea, is a post-Second World War replacement of the medical practice occupied by Dr Arthur Conan Doyle between 1882 and 1890.

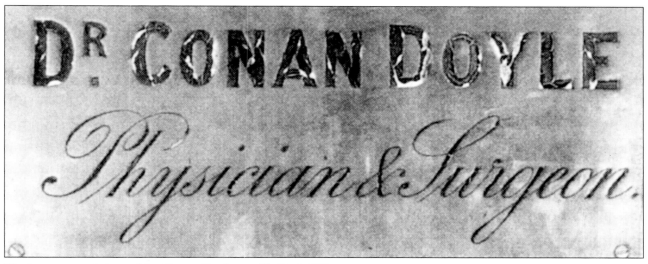

The brass nameplate used by Conan Doyle outside Bush Villas

modest shopping, which was measured in pennies rather than shillings, and perfecting my simple household arrangements, the time did not hang heavily upon my hands.

It is a wonderful thing to have a house of your own for the first time, however humble it may be. I lavished all my care upon the front room to make it possible for patients. The back room was furnished with my trunk and a stool.

Inside the trunk was my larder and the top of it was my dining room table.

There was gas laid on and I rigged a projection from the wall by which I could sling a pan over the gas jet.

In this way, I cooked bacon with great ease, and became expert in getting a wonderful lot of slices from a pound. Bread, bacon and tea, with an occasional saveloy – what could man ask for more?

The fledgling surgery was slow to gather pace. Conan Doyle passed the days after his household

This plaque was unveiled on November 18, 1982, by the Sherlock Holmes Society of London to commemorate the centenary of the detective's creation in Bush Villas, now Bush House, in Southsea.

chores were finished by watching the crowd go by his consulting room window or reading one of the books he borrowed from the library which he had joined.

Literature, though, never beckoned as a career at that stage.

Conan Doyle was joined by his younger brother, ten-year-old Innes, within a month of settling down. In turn, they were joined by a housemaid. The new practice gradually gained strength. Takings amounted to £154 in the first year, £250 in the second and up to £300 in the following year.

In comparison, Geoffrey Stavert calculates the £6 a week of the latter figure compared well the 24 shillings of an insurance collector and the less than 20 shillings wages for a shop assistant. Professional men, however, left Conan Doyle far behind. A vicar would expect to earn an annual salary of £650.

Innes left in 1885 after three years in Southsea. Soon afterwards Conan Doyle married Louisa Hawkins, the sister of Jack Hawkins, whom he had treated for meningitis.

By the time of his marriage, he was well established in Portsmouth's sporting circles. Southsea Bowling Club had been the first outlet for his physical energies, then Portsmouth Cricket Club of which he was a keen and valued member, and captain at one time, and then came football to propel the original Pompey into immortality alongside Sherlock Holmes.

Conan Doyle never forgot his time in Southsea. He wrote in *Memories and Adventures* of his time there:

My life had been a pleasant one with my steadily increasing literary success, my practice, which was enough to keep me pleasantly occupied, and my sport…

CHAPTER TWO

Portsmouth was a slow starter in the development of football. Other south coast towns, such as Bournemouth from 1875 and Southampton - Deanery FC - from 1880, had flourishing football scenes and the makings of representative clubs.

Nationally, the game was well established and spreading by the month. The FA Cup had been started in 1872. Its initial entries of public school and services teams were gradually being usurped by northern working class towns like Blackburn, whose clubs were founded on the wealth inspired by the industrial revolution as the nineteenth century continued.

Midlands giants such as Aston Villa were also establishing themselves. The *Portsmouth Evening News* had reported on January 21st 1884 that three long trains had left Birmingham for Glasgow to take 1,200 fans to watch Villa play Queen's Park. The fervour of the supporters across the three hundred miles which separated the clubs was proof of the increasing popularity of football.

But Portsmouth, an industrial town unlike any other on the south coast because of the huge influence of its naval dockyard, had nothing of any substance to harness that rise in support. Even at the most basic level of neighbourhood clubs, the town was lacking any sort of strength in depth.

There was a Southsea FC and Portsmouth Victorias and a few similar teams. It was rugby union, though, which was the dominant winter sport.

Even the fifteen-a-side game took second billing overall to cricket. The summer game captured most of what sports coverage was given to leisure pursuits

---

A variety of names was used in the press to describe Portsmouth's premier footballing club in the 1880s and 1890s. The town club, the borough club, the Portsmouth association rules club, the Portsmouth Football Association club and a host of variations.

Pompey, it has to be said, was not among them. This had much to do with the fact that the reporting of Victorian newspapers of the fledgling state of football in Portsmouth was far removed from the style of the modern media.

Match reports were strictly that – kick by kick accounts of the 90 minutes of action. The details were relayed in a formal style of prose. Away from games, the reporting of football barely existed. Only accounts of various committee meetings otherwise made it into the tightly packed lines of newsprint which made up the broadsheet pages of the period. Interviews with players, managers and spectators were unknown along with any hint of informality.

Not once during Portsmouth AFC's 12 year history did the nickname Pompey enter into any of the accounts of its activities on or off the pitch. Yet it seems fair to label the first representative football club from Portsea Island as the original Pompey. The distinctive nickname was in existence well before the club's formation and, uniquely, signifies a place as much as a football club.

Portsmouth AFC did, of course, also play in the footballing colours of blue and white which have come to be intrinsically linked with the sport and the city. Indeed, they were the first club to do so – and to wear the civic symbols of the star and crescent – which have been worn with pride by the overwhelming majority of Pompey players over the years.

But why Pompey? For such an instantly recognisable and familiar nickname, its origins are suprisingly vague. Three stories seem to be the most reliable sources for its adoption. Readers can take their favourite choice.

One sees the origin lying with an 80-gun French worship, *Le Pompée*, captured in 1793 which later fought in the battle of Algeciras and went on to become the guardship of Portsmouth Harbour.

A further tale puts the inspiration of the legendary name with a drunk sailor's interpretation of a talk by Agnes Weston, the naval temperance worker. He awoke from the after effects of too much beer during a lecture about the roman Empire only to hear Agnes Weston say that the general Pompey had been killed. 'Poor old Pompey,' he shouted.

Yet another story puts the origin of the nickname firmly in Egypt. In 1781, some Portsmouth based sailors scaled Pompey's Pillar near Alexandria and toasted their ascent with punch 98 feet in the air. Their climbing ability earned them the accolade 'the Pompey boys' throughout the fleet.

But for all the role of the navy in Portsmouth's history the senior service played no role in the foundation of Portsmouth AFC nor of the clubs which followed to take Portsmouth to the heights of the English footballing world.

The reason for that absence is simple. The amount of time sailors had to spend at sea ruled them out of any shore-based activity which demanded their presence week after week.

in the fledgling local press.

Every sport was centred around the United Officers' and Men's sports grounds. The sites on both sides of Burnaby Road were the key to the development of sport in Portsmouth. In Victorian times, as much as now, the town lacked the space enjoyed by Bournemouth, Brighton and Southampton just a few miles away.

Recreational grounds were at a premium and the services – both the army and the navy – controlled most of the acres which existed. The issue was to be a recurrent theme of the history of the original Pompey.

Such was the backdrop to the announcement in the *Portsmouth Times* of October 1st 1884 of a football club for Portsmouth under association rules. The weekly newspaper hinted that the influence of the services was behind the decision by a group of enthusiasts of the game to set up a civilian outfit. The page five article read:

Association players of football will learn with satisfaction it is proposed to start a borough club, under the association rules which are in favour at Hilsea Barracks with the Royal Artillery, so that no difficulty would be experienced in finding opponents willing to start practice games, whilst there are several association clubs in the district.

Those willing to co-operate in this movement may address Mr J McDonald, Chichester Road, Kingston Cross, or Mr F Kent, Stubbington Lodge, North End.

Those eleven lines of newsprint were the start of Portsmouth AFC. That same day, the *Evening Mail* reported the threat of a potential ban on civilian football clubs at the US grounds. This would mean the clubs being denied the chance to play at a venue for which they had paid to appear in the past without collecting a penny of gate money. The *Portsmouth Times* of three days later revealed that the ban had been put in place.

Only those civilians who were playing service teams would be allowed past the gates. The paper's editor was unimpressed by the tough stance:

Under proper conditions, representative cricket and football clubs ought not, unless their presence interfered with service arrangements, be denied the use of one ground. At present, they appear to be treated in nothing less than a churlish spirit.

Nevertheless, a spirit of optimism was present when supporters of soccer met at the Blue Anchor Hotel in Kingston Cross on Wednesday October 8th to form Portsmouth's first representative football club. A turnout described in the *Portsmouth Evening News* as well representative of Portsmouth gentlemen

Report in the Portsmouth Times *on October 11, 1884, telling of the formation of Portsmouth AFC.*

interested in the sport took part. Between twenty and fifty of them – the true pioneers of football in Portsmouth – enrolled on the night of the birth of the club.

They included J Nathan, W Pate, A Bramble, J Lillywhite, J McDonald, and Messrs Vincent and Adames. The paper was encouraged by the occasion:

…by the tone of the meeting and the business capacity exhibited by the committee, it was evident that there was a full intention to make the club thoroughly successful.

R Hemingsley was elected to the chair to become a key figure in the club's formative days. He explained that the absence of a good association football club in the borough contrasted with the situation in rugby where several good clubs existed. He felt ample room existed, and indeed there was a necessity, for such a football club.

There was a likelihood that a meadow which belonged to Alderman GE Kent – the father of football player and prime mover in the new club F Kent

– at his North End home could be made available for home games to overcome the general lack of public open spaces.

Formal resolutions readily agreed by those present established the new club's name as the Borough of Portsmouth FC. Only association football matches would be played. The subscription was fixed at 3s and 6d (17.5p) a year and the club colours would be a dark blue jersey with the borough arms of a star and crescent in white on the chest. The crest, apart from its top line, is exactly the same as that of the present club, and indeed, Portsmouth City Council. That continuous sporting thread runs back one hundred and twenty years to that decision. It was a truly historic moment in the development of football in Portsmouth.

No discussion about the colours was reported but, of course, the dark blue comes close to resembling the uniform of sailors, a frequent sight around Portsmouth, and is the colour of the sea which surrounds Portsea Island

Provisional plans were put in place for the first practice matches to be played by the club. It was agreed by those at the inaugural meeting to leave the arrangements and those for other routine matters with the committee. A nine-strong body was initially elected. They were – Captain: J McDonald, sub-captain: Mr A Guy; secretary: R Hemingsley; treasurer: J Lillywhite and members RE Davis, F Kent, W Pate, G Hayter and Vincent for whom no Christian name initial was given.

Everyone agreed to a further meeting five days later on Monday October 13th at 9pm at the same venue to finalise arrangements for the club as quickly as possible before the season, which had begun in Portsmouth at the end of the previous month, September 1884, began to slip away too much.

More prospective members turned up at the second meeting to fill the hotel's room. They wasted no time in fixing the date for the first practice match at 3pm the following Saturday. The location, as expected, was the meadow that Alderman Kent had agreed could be loaned to the club without charge. It was sited on the southern side of Stubbington Lane. The occupiers of the large terraced houses which currently occupy the land, about halfway along the current road, can be said to be living on the birthplace of organised football in Portsmouth. It was, in 1884, part of the large site around the Alderman's home of Stubbington Lodge.

Mr Kent's crucial generosity was acknowledged with a hearty vote of thanks proposed by Lillywhite, who chaired the meeting, and seconded by McDonald. Alderman Kent was also chosen as the club's first president at the original committee

meeting twenty-four hours later.

A further vote confirmed the player's uniform, as it was called, of a dark blue jersey with the borough arms in white on the chest, dark blue stockings and white knickerbockers and a velvet quarter cap with a peak.

Those present also agreed that members should be chosen for teams ahead of outsiders. Those matches were being arranged by the honorary secretary, R Hemingsley of 13 St Mary's Crescent, Kingston, whose address was included in the hope that it would prompt enquiries.

By the close of the meeting, forty members had been enrolled in the club. It is unknown if Arthur Conan Doyle was among them. His name does not feature in the press reports of either of the initial two meetings, though his keenness for sport makes it a distinct possibility.

CHAPTER THREE

The size of the task of putting Portsmouth on the map as a footballing centre was evident in the same edition of the *Portsmouth Times* as the coverage of that second meeting at the Blue Anchor

> MISSING.—Jonas Cabel, of Portsea, went out fishing in Stokes Bay on Thursday morning last about half-past nine o'clock in a small boat, about 15ft. long. She was under a sprit sail and jib, and has not been heard of since.
>
> PORTSMOUTH FOOTBALL CLUB.—A practice match was played in the club ground, North End, on Saturday, the sides being respectively captained by Mr. J. McDonald and Mr. F. Kent. McDonald's team scored three goals to their opponents' one.
>
> DETAINED AT SEA.—The French sloop N. D. de Perros, Alammat master, came into Portsmouth Harbour on Saturday evening for provisions. She had on board a cargo of twenty tons of cement, but on her journey from Boulogne to Pontrieux she had been kept at sea for five days by stormy weather. The vessel sailed again the same evening.
>
> SUNDAY was the day annually set apart for universal prayer on behalf of Sunday-school work, and reference was made to the occasion at most of the churches, chapels, and Sunday-schools in Portsmouth, special services being held in some instances. In the evening, at 8.30, a united prayer meeting of Sunday-school teachers was held in Elm-grove Chapel, Southsea.
>
> ACCIDENT.—On Tuesday afternoon considerable excitement prevailed in Queen-street, Portsea, in consequence of the escapade of a pony which had been left standing outside a greengrocer's shop, in Cross-street. The animal, which was attached to a light cart, from some unexplained cause suddenly bolted, and before it could be stopped it came into collision with a hand truck laden with furniture. The truck was capsized, and its contents were much damaged, but fortunately no personal injury was occasioned.
>
> HARVEST FESTIVAL SERVICES.—Harvest thanksgiving services were held on Sunday at St. Agatha's

Quickly into action - Portsmouth AFC's first practice match as reported in the Hampshire Telegraph *on October 18, 1884.*

Hotel. The majority of the football reports were devoted to rugby football. The column which reported Portsmouth FC's latest meeting contained the news that several hundred people had watched the US versus Portsmouth rugby union fixture at the US Officers' ground. Crowds of that size would have overwhelmed the football games between the likes of Hayling and Southsea, Southampton Avenue and Portsmouth Rivals and Southsea versus Victoria.

Southsea, it had been reported in the *Evening Mail*, were expecting a successful 1884/85 season. Matches were apparently in prospect against leading clubs around the country. The outfit slipped into oblivion, however, as the original Pompey gathered strength.

The club's playing debut took place at Alderman Kent's meadow on Saturday October 18th at 3pm. Unsurprisingly, perhaps, one of the sides was captained by the host's son, F Kent, who had reported his father's offer of the site at the club's meeting five days earlier.

Paternal influence was not enough to win the game for the Kent team. They lost 3–1 to a side captained by McDonald. With an evident desire to waste no time, further warm-up games were fixed for the next Wednesday, October 22nd, at 4.15 pm, and the following Saturday. The Stubbington Lodge meadow was about to come in for a lot of use.

A single goal won the second of those matches for a side led by W Pate. An advertisement for Pate, Tailors and Outfitters, at 149 and 151 Commercial Road, Landport, had appeared in the *Evening Mail* a few days earlier to give a clue to the player's occupation.

Meanwhile, further evidence of the primitive nature of football around Portsmouth which the new club had entered was evident from a plea by 'The Spectator' in the *Portsmouth Evening News* of November 7th:

...nearly every Saturday lovers of the game – football – are put to great inconvenience through not knowing where matches are to be played. This could be easily remedied if the secretaries of our local clubs would forward us a list of their matches and we published them on Friday nights. Whilst obliging us, they would be obliging themselves as a match is played with more spirit when there are a good many onlookers.

But it was the *Portsmouth Times*, the employer of Portsmouth's secretary Hemingsley, which was the keenest chronicler of the new club's early days. Their first fixture against another club took place on Saturday November 8th.

They got off to a winning start in a match 'which excited some interest', according to the paper. Those initial opponents were the Royal Lancashire Regiment. The original Pompey were eager to get off to the best possible start. They quickly went two goals up and carried on to add another couple. The servicemen managed to pull back two goals. They further narrowed the gap in the last minute with a header from a corner kick. But the home side held on to record a momentous victory of 4–3.

Hayling Island were the next visitors to the meadow a week later for a game at 3 pm which followed a practice match that afternoon. The islanders lined up to face a goalkeeper known publicly as Smith but to his team-mates as Arthur Conan Doyle. Yes, the GP and soon-to-be-author was named for the first time as being involved with the football club. He helped his side to a convincing 5–1 win with his 'free kicking' the subject of praise from the *Portsmouth Times*. The paper's match reporter commented:

Portsmouth are to be congratulated upon the marked success with which they have inaugurated their season.

He also praised centre forward T Simpson and R Davies on the right-wing for their pluck and skill. P Russell and W Adames, the full backs, were singled out as well for their contribution to the one-sided affair. Davies and Simpson opened the scoring after useful assistance from the centre forward, McDonald. The half time lead was built upon by halfback J Poole and a headed own goal from a corner by Davies. A shot by Denny provided the blemish on 'Smith's' performance of the afternoon with the Islanders' only goal. Simpson added his second of the game to restore Pompey's four goal advantage.

Elsewhere in Portsmouth, North Lancashire Grasshoppers and Royal Artillery Ramblers along with Southsea and Chichester were providing alternative football fare. But the original Pompey were on their way with more than forty members involved. Their progress, however, was hindered by the semi-organised nature of football in the town.

Back they went to having to be satisfied with practice matches. The one which took place on November 22nd saw McDonald's team victorious once more by 3–1 against an XI led by Russell. The players were back in action the following Saturday when McDonald's team took on a side captained by P Dancer.

Competitive football, of a sort, resumed with Portsmouth AFC travelling to their first away game.

Havant was the destination for the ground-breaking occasion on December 13th. The journey failed to stop the blue-shirted visitors from notching up another victory.

'Smith' was again in goal, though his initial was 'W' on this occasion, and he kept a clean sheet. His goal was rarely threatened by a home side which played the first half without two of their regular players. Pompey were quick to take advantage. They took the lead courtesy of an own goal after just ten minutes. McDonald doubled the score soon afterwards. That remained the size of the victory as a strong wind and a heavy ground took their toll on the players. But the *Evening Mail* was convinced Portsmouth's initial away fixture should have ended in a more convincing win:

Only bad luck stopped them scoring more goals. They hit the post more than once and one or two near kicks by Simpson deserved to be converted into goals.

Marlboroughs succeeded in gaining five goals to one made by their opponents. The goals were obtained by O'Neil 3, Carnt 2, and Carruthers 1.

PORTSMOUTH v. HAVANT.—An Association match was played between these teams on Saturday at Havant, and a well contested game terminated in a victory for the visitors. During the first half of the game Portsmouth succeeded in obtaining two goals, but no other scoring took place, the high wind and heavy ground rendering effective play most difficult. During the first half Havant played with two of their team absent. The teams were composed as under:—Portsmouth; Centre forwards, J. McDonald and Russell; right wings, Simpson and Vincent; left wings, Dancoy and Hemingsley; half-backs, T. Huddy and Lillywhite; backs, Adames and F. Kent; goal, W. Smith. Havant; Centre forwards, F. Jones and J. Turner; right wings, W. Butts and E. Stallard; left wings, E. Softly and J. Stallard; half-backs, H. Nightingale and A. Carrot (captain); backs, J. Freeston and the Rev. — Thompson; goal, H. Pentoe.

ISLE OF WIGHT

The Portsmouth Evening News *report of the first away game played by the original Pompey - at Havant - on December 13, 1884.*

CHAPTER FOUR

Tucked away in the sports pages the next week was the result of a game that was to have great significance eventually on football's development in Portsmouth – Royal Artillery's first game which ended in a 6–0 rout over Sandown. There were no ground worries for that services' team as they went on to take soccer in the area to new heights as the 1890s progressed.

There were no ground worries for the original Pompey in the immediate future, either, as the Stubbington Lane meadow was pressed into action twice around the Christmas of 1884. The first of those games involved a clash with a team formed around the most influential individual in the overall early rise of football around the naval port.

Mr Pares's side defeated the fledgling borough club by three goals to nil on December 20th. His victory, of which only scant details were recorded, was the first time he and the original Pompey had encountered each other. There were to be many more such occasions as the family of the Justice of the Peace became closely involved in the new team's fortunes. His four sons were described by William Pickford, the leading pioneer of Hampshire football, as 'the fathers of soccer in Portsmouth'.

One of seven brothers, the Reverend Norman Pares was the first to play for the town club the following month, as a back. He was already an FA Cup winner, having been a member of the famous Old Etonians side which defeated Clapham Rovers by a single goal in 1879. The school team knocked out Nottingham Forest on their way to the final. The victory was secured on an outfield of Kennington Oval and was the last match in which Lord Kinnaird, the founder of the FA, skippered the Etonians. When the game ended, he celebrated the victory by standing on his head and clapping his heels.

The Reverend Pares, the curate of St Jude's Church in Southsea, had his winner's medal made into a brooch for his wife. He and his brothers went on to form Portsmouth Sunflowers. They enlisted footballers from among their friends in universities and public schools, then the source of many of the country's most talented players, as the Old Etonians had proved with six appearances in the first twelve FA Cup finals.

Sunflowers secured a pitch on Governor's Green in what is now Old Portsmouth and turned out in olive and green colours. The club also produced a hectographical magazine – *The Sunflowers* – which was edited by the brothers and one of their sisters. This publication was said in later newspaper reports to have extended its readership to several European countries.

It was into this rarified atmosphere that the emergence of the original Pompey was such a shock. As the *Portsmouth Evening News* wrote in 1966, the Sunflowers were seen as aristocrats compared to the working class members of the town club. The teams' clash just two months after Portsmouth AFC's formation had an edge to it and, on the day, Conan Doyle's team-mates must have had their spirits raised when they saw just eight of their opponents turn up. The other three players were busy with exams, just to emphasise their privileged backgrounds, but they were clearly not needed, as it was the borough club who had a lot to learn on the football pitch. That comfortable win helped the Sunflowers to finish their first season as the top team around Portsmouth with a creditable record of: P13 W10 D2 L1.

Another of those wins was achieved in the return clash with the original Pompey on January 17th. Taking place at the East Hants ground in Southsea, on the sites of Worthing and Taswell Roads, Norman Pares led his team to a 2–0 victory. Conan Doyle was the keeper in that clash of the classes. It was a matter of just a further week before he and Pares were on the same side for Portsmouth AFC.

The Sunflowers continued on their distinctive way for several years to come. Yet they were increasingly out of step with the more and more organised world of football. One episode demonstrated this widening divergence. They entered the Hampshire Senior Cup in 1886 only to find out that its first round clashed with their players' studies at universities or public schools. Even worse, the Sunflowers were drawn to meet Woolston Works – composed entirely of ruthless Scots who were rumoured to train on whisky. The Sunflowers managed to field eleven players on the day and were thrashed 6–0 for their troubles.

Smarting from this defeat, they arranged a return match over the Christmas holidays. The precise date was January 1st. Unsurprisingly for a team of Scots, Woolston Works had other pleasures on their minds and failed to show up. They apologised and the Sunflowers turned to the Southampton-based side later in the season for reinforcements. The Woolston players turned up on that occasion, reeking of alcohol.

CHAPTER FIVE

The Sunflowers began to fade, probably because of the restrictions created by combining studies with soccer. But the Pares brothers' influence remained with Portsmouth AFC well into the following decade.

A lasting legacy of the Sunflowers survives to this day with the existence of the Hampshire FA. The county had been joined with Dorset when the organisation of football was in its infancy, but the situation had become unrealistic as the game grew rapidly during the 1880s. In 1887, Bernard Pares led a delegation to a meeting in Wimborne of the joint organisation. He succeeded in having his resolution that Hampshire should secede adopted. By then, Sunflowers were a dying memory. As the *Portsmouth Evening News* poetically stated in 1966:

If the Sunflowers had taken root, they might have been the parents of Portsmouth FC. They were the top team long before Royal Artillery emerged into prominence. But it was not to be. Sunflowers allowed themselves to be transplanted into the proletarian compost created by the Portsmouth town club and that was the end for them.

Compost or not, the original Pompey were getting nicely established as they prepared to welcome their first visitors from across the Solent for their closing piece of action of 1884. Cowes were the opponents who travelled from the Isle of Wight to North End on December 27th.

The game was the precursor to a regular series of clashes between the island club and amateur teams from Portsmouth which were always fiercely contested. A brace of first half goals by C Huddy, one of Portsmouth AFC's forwards, set the home side on course for victory. His first strike was through effective passing and dashing play, and the second came from a successful shot. But Cowes fought back and reduced the deficit before half time. They obtained the equaliser in the second period and the game ended with honours even at 2–2.

It rounded off Pompey's initial two months, which they had survived well. They had played five games against recognised opponents. Three had been won, one drawn and one lost. A total of thirteen goals had been scored and nine conceded. All those involved with the new outfit must have been encouraged by this start to look to the future with confidence.

The positive outlook, however, received a setback as 1885 began. The club's first match of the year saw them three players short for their initial visit to Fareham. They obtained the use of substitutes to fill the gaps but they were punished for the absences by the home team. Portsmouth AFC's forwards were appreciably weaker than usual and they generally missed the strong defence and hard kicking of their regular keeper, Conan Doyle.

His place between the posts was taken by H Cook. He let in one goal in the first forty-five minutes and a further three after the break. Two of the efforts were disputed but his team-mates had no answer to them. The *Portsmouth Times* reported:

Fareham had the decided advantage in physique and played a fine game in excellent form.

It was the borough club's turn the following week to take advantage of a weakened side. Only six of the Southsea team turned up for the scheduled fixture at North End on January 10th. A scratch match was hastily arranged between those players who were present to ensure their Saturday afternoon was put to some use. Portsmouth AFC won 2–1.

Sunflowers were next and then came another defeat – against RA – and the return clash with

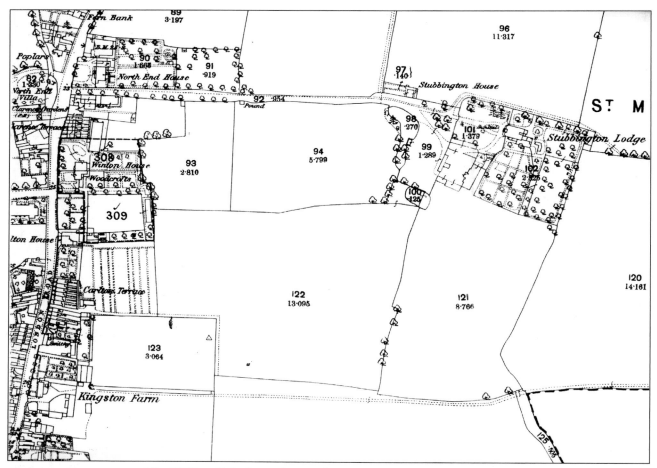

Ordnance Survey map of the 1890s which shows the meadows around Stubbington Lodge in North End, Portsmouth, where Portsmouth AFC originally played. London Road runs along the left hand side of the extract.

Havant. That fixture put the original Pompey back on track for a successful season. They romped to a win, helped by the striking skill of the club's first hat trick scorer, T Simpson. According to the *Portsmouth Times*:

Simpson has never appeared to better advantage.

But more attention was focused on his fellow forward T Nugent. He scored two of his side's goals. One was stunning. *The Portsmouth Times* again:

Nugent splendidly dribbled one ball half the length of the ground up to the Havant goal and he put it between the posts to applause.

In goal, Conan Doyle was rarely threatened and the original Pompey's victory would have been even greater if the Reverend R Thompson, one of Havant's backs, had not possessed such powerful kicking. The match, unusually, was played with twelve men on each side. Havant had turned up with a dozen players and both sides agreed to field the additional man.

CHAPTER SIX

The eve of the game had been notable for a speech by another reverend, the Vicar of Portsmouth. The Reverend EP Grant used a public meeting to criticise the lack of a recreation ground in the borough. He told the audience it was a universally acknowledged fact that such a facility was required. 'Portsmouth was alone,' he said, 'of large towns in England in that respect.'

It was something of a disgrace that such a ground did not exist but the greatest difficulty in providing one was the lack of suitable space within the borough's ever more-crowded boundaries.

Portsmouth AFC travelled outside them to the cathedral city of Chichester for their following fixture. It was an unhappy journey back for Conan Doyle. He suffered his worst display in goal in his debut season and the worst in his football career in Portsmouth.

His tally of four goals conceded could partly be blamed on the freak conditions on January 31st. A strong wind was joined by a terrific flash of lightning and peal of thunder just before half time. Chichester were then three goals ahead with the wind behind them. Conan Doyle's colleagues did their best to make up for his disappointment at his poor showing. Russell scored in fine style, Armstrong kicked another and Simpson added a third, though hands were called and, to the surprise of the players, the local umpires allowed the objections.

The second half was much more evenly contested than the opening forty-five minutes. Conan Doyle's misery, though, was completed when the home side strengthened their lead towards the end of the game. His only consolation could come from the fact that one of the Chichester goals was claimed to be offside.

The next away trip – to Hayling Island on February 7th – proved more satisfying for the GP. He kept his third clean sheet in seven games to play a leading role in his team's 3–0 victory. The *Portsmouth Times* reporter was suitably impressed by his display:

The Portsmouth goal was hardly seriously threatened and when it was their goalkeeper was fully equal to the occasion.

Another clean sheet followed, the first time Conan Doyle had managed the achievement for two matches in a row. His display in the local derby with Southsea was again favourably commented upon, on that occasion by the *Portsmouth Evening News*:

Southsea put forth several good efforts to score. They were frustrated by the strong defence of Portsmouth backs and halfbacks and the coolness and hard kicking of their goalkeeper.

Conan Doyle's play helped to secure a single goal victory for Portsmouth in a tightly-contested game. The deciding effort reflected the nature of the match held at North End. It also says everything about the disorganisation of football during Portsmouth AFC's early days.

The ball was centred from the right-wing and W Adames kicked it just between Southsea's posts. But the decision of the umpires was not heard. A regular 'bully' took place in the goalmouth to decide the matter. The defenders held firm and sent the ball back a few yards. It was promptly returned low by the Portsmouth attackers and, after another goal-mouth struggle, they managed to bundle the ball and their opponents between the posts.

It was to be another three weeks before Conan Doyle was again tested in goal. There was to be no clean sheet on that occasion as Fareham became the first club to play home and away fixtures against the borough side and avoid defeat. The result of the return game was 2–2.

Conan Doyle was first beaten by a fluke effort soon after left-winger C Pinford had given his side a brief lead in the first half. The keeper was beaten by a shot which deflected off a Fareham forward. Dancer, another left-winger, put the original Pompey back in front after half time as the team had the best of the play but Young soon drew Fareham level with a heavy kick during a goalmouth tussle.

Next came Chichester on March 16th and a chance for Portsmouth AFC to gain revenge for that four-goal haul conceded two months earlier.

They were unable to gain the satisfaction of a clean sheet but could still rejoice reaching a decisive 5–1 victory. Two goals from team captain McDonald and one each by Nugent, Armstrong and Davies sealed the easy win. The match was also notable for marking the Portsmouth AFC debut of right-winger A Kindersley, declared by the *Hampshire Telegraph* to be one of Southsea's best players before his switch of allegiance. The visitors' man of the match was Shippam, presumably of the family of fish and meat paste fame.

An initial journey to the Isle of Wight brought the original Pompey's debut season to a close. The fixture on March 21st against Cowes saw Conan Doyle in imperious form once more. The *Evening Mail* and the *Portsmouth Times* were united in their praise:

The hard kicking of the goalkeeper was most serviceable.

Conan Doyle possibly again kept a clean sheet as his team mates wound up their onfield action with a 3–0 or 3–1 win, according to different press reports. New boy Kindersley contributed some excellent runs to a competent display by the blue-shirted side in front of a crowd of excited onlookers. J Williams opened the scoring with a long and well-judged shot. A second goal was added by Davies before half time. The right-winger, who played with brilliant dash throughout, kicked Pompey AFC's final goal after the break. They 'scored' twice more only to see the strikes disputed for offside. That apart, the credits included hard work by T Huddy and Simpson, and McDonald always having the ability to be where he wanted to be. All in all, it was a satisfactory way to round off the first season of Portsmouth's own football club.

It was a feeling which permeated the club's initial annual meeting just over a month later on April 29th. The *Portsmouth Evening News* reported the honorary secretary, R Hemingsley, as saying:

In closing their first season, the members of Portsmouth AFC may fairly congratulate themselves upon the measure of success they have achieved.

In little more than six months, the club had grown to match any other in the area, had avoided getting into debt and had proved equal on the pitch against the best sides the district could offer. This had enabled its objective of spreading the popularity of the association game - as opposed to the rugby union version played by many neighbouring clubs - which was less dangerous to life and limb. McDonald, the club's captain, declared:

Equal skill in dribbling and smartness in effort and judgment for shooting for goal being required. The association game is, in short, proper football with the arms and hands of players being absolutely disqualified from use.

Near neighbours Southsea FC had been the first club to recognise the new Portsmouth AFC. Following their breakthrough, only two games were lost in the home and away fixtures against Southsea, Hayling Island, Chichester, Havant, Fareham and Cowes. But a couple of strong defeats had been inflicted by the powerful teams put out by Bernard Pares.

Scratch matches had also taken place with the North Lancashire Regiment – which was won – and RA (Hilsea), which was lost.

A total of sixteen games had been played with nine of them won, two drawn and five lost. The goals column read 39 for and 28 against.

Most of the defeats could be put down to weakened teams being fielded because of misunderstandings which had caused three players to be absent and replaced by indifferent substitutes. The club had rotated players where possible to ensure members got preference. More than thirty had appeared during the season.

'Thus it will be seen that the club has a sufficient record', the *Portsmouth Evening News* reported from Hemingsley's speech, 'especially when it is considered that it was originally intended for the first season at all events, only to engage in friendly matches amongst ourselves. We departed from that intention because we found ourselves stronger than our modest beginnings had led me to expect.'

Hemingsley was quoted in the *Portsmouth Times* as saying the members had never thought they might be forming a borough club, so modest were its beginnings. Their immediate problems of getting a ground were solved by the club's president, Alderman Kent, who chaired the meeting. The meadow they had used on his land had been the making of the club,

PORTSMOUTH FOOTBALL CLUB.

On Wednesday night the above Club held their first annual meeting and dinner at the Blue Anchor Hotel, Kingston-cross.—A highly satisfactory report was presented by the Secretary, from which we take the following :—In closing their first season the members of the Portsmouth Football Club may fairly congratulate themselves upon the measure of success they have achieved. Started in October last, the Club is numerically almost as strong as any in the immediate neighbourhood, has kept itself free from debt, and has won a decided majority of its matches, though meeting some of the best Clubs in the town and district. The Club was, it need hardly be explained, established in no spirit of antagonism to any of the existing Clubs. They play under Rugby Union Rules, and our object was to popularise the Association game, which, strictly followed, may be regarded as less hazardous to life and limb. Out and home fixtures have taken place with the Hayling Island, Havant, Southsea, Chichester, Fareham, and Cowes Clubs, and of these only two have been lost, but we twice suffered defeat at the hands of strong teams captained by Mr. Bernard Pares, who had, however, the advantage of the services of some of our best players. Scratch matches also came off with the North Lancashire Regiment and the Royal Artillery (Hilsea), the former being won and the latter lost. The most severe reverse sustained by the Club was due to three of the team being absent through a misunderstanding, and to our being handicapped by two indifferent substitutes. In all, however, we scored forty goals against twenty-five made by our opponents. Thus it will be seen that the Club has a satisfactory record, especially when it is considered that it was originally intended, for the first season at all events, to only engage in friendly matches amongst ourselves. We departed from that intention because we found ourselves stronger than our modest beginning had led us to expect. The promoters of the Club had the moral courage to pass a rule that outsiders should not be selected to play in preference to members, even though the latter might not compare with the non-members for skill in football; and, notwithstanding this rule is more honoured in the breach than in the observance by some other Clubs, it has not been found to operate disadvantageously. The report having been adopted, and other business transacted, the members adjourned to the dining-room, where a highly creditable dinner was served by Mr. R. Buckle. The chair was occupied by the President, Alderman G. E. Kent, J.P., and there were also present the Mayor (J. Moody, Esq.), Dr. Doyle, Dr. Snowden, Messrs. A. L. Emanuel, W. J. Tuck, T.C.; A. R. Holbrook, E. Hall, J. W. Boughton, G. Peters, B. Pares, G. F. Green, Harris, Hardy, Chinnock, W. Adams, Towers, T. James, J. Warne, J. Portway, Philip J. Dancer, J. W. Moody, Pearson, H.W. Fisk, Gorsuch, Sherwin, Mason, G. Hayter, Tilly, Lillywhite, Moore, Allen, R. E. Davies, jun., &c.—Mr. R. Hemmingsley, the Secretary, read a letter of apology from Major-General Sir F. FitzWygram, in which he stated that he was afraid that port on of the Seats Bill which concerned South Hants would not be got through in time for him to attend the dinner. Letters of apology were also read from the Rev. J. H. Anderson, the Rev. T. Briscoe, Alderman Pink, and the Borough Coroner.—The loyal toasts having been duly honoured, Mr. B. Pares proposed "The Army, Navy, and Reserve Forces." In doing

Report of the first annual meeting of the original Pompey held on April 29, 1885, as seen in the Portsmouth Evening News.

Hemingsley added.

Conan Doyle backed the positive sentiments with his thanks for the club's initial success. He toasted the health of Alderman Kent, by saying he had given the club material as well as moral support. When the club was in its infancy, he had come forward and given them the use of a field and in future, whatever success the club might achieve, they were indebted to Alderman Kent for that start.

Conan Doyle was inspired to speak by the Alderman's offer of a ground for the following season. It would be in the same location but it could be a different meadow, he said.

TB Hayter, it seemed, had also played a significant role with his provision of a movable dressing tent.

To add to the good news were the donations of two trophies. The first came from one of the most prominent Victorians in Portsmouth, Leon Emanuel. The one-time councillor and mayor had promised a two guinea (£2.10) challenge cup to provide an extra incentive to the players for the next season. The host for the annual meeting – Blue Anchor Hotel licensee Mr Buckle – had also put up a guinea for a cup.

The bonhomie continued with a speech by Portsmouth's current mayor, J Moody. He captured the ethos of improvement which characterised the spirit of the times. He spoke of the usefulness of the public library and the attractiveness of Victoria Park. Both had recently opened. The zeal of public enterprise for the general good also stretched to a recreation ground, which would solve the football club's ground problems instantly. But on that aspect the news was less positive.

Two or three meetings had been held at the George Hotel in Old Portsmouth, he reported, to make preliminary arrangements for securing a suitable piece of land, but he was unsure if any progress would be made beyond the work on the matter by Sir George Willis MP, who was anxious to do everything he could to help them.

Some forty-one people attended the annual meeting, including a representative of the North Lancashire Regiment and three members of Southsea FC, alongside the original Pompey committee of their honorary secretary, captain and treasurer – Hemingsley, McDonald and Lillywhite – as well as A Moore, G Hayter, LJ Allan and RE Davies, who was described as a junior.

The report in the *Portsmouth Evening News* of the meeting occupied 153 lines of solid type. The coverage took up almost a complete column in the broadsheet paper to demonstrate how important the club had become in such a short space of time. But what sort of borough was the paper reflecting and the club making its way in?

CHAPTER SEVEN

The population had expanded rapidly to 133 000 – 6000 of them sailors – in 1884 as the historic built-up area around old Portsmouth grew to take in the previously isolated settlements of Fratton, North End and Hilsea.

The borough boundaries were stretching from Tipner in the west to Great Salterns in the east. Percy Boulnois, the borough engineer to Portsmouth, told the Portsmouth Literary and Scientific Association in December that year that the population was accommodated in 24 022 homes to make an average of five and a half people in each dwelling.

According to the Reverend Robert Dolling, the entire area was degenerate morally. He arrived in Portsmouth in 1885 as the priest in charge of the Winchester College mission of St Agatha's Church situated in the slums of Landport. He said of this time 'There were few worse streets at night in the whole world than Queen Street, Portsmouth.'

He had gained experience of slum life in the East End of London. Portsmouth, however, was something else.

Sailors, everywhere, sometimes fighting, sometimes courting, nearly always laughing and good-humoured... I remember well how... their uniforms and rolling gait redeemed from its squalor and commonplace this poor little district, with its 1,100 houses and its 52 public houses.

Charlotte Street was, from end to end, an open fair, cheapjacks screaming, laughing crowds round them, never seeming to buy; women struggling under the weight of a baby... then some horseplay... many a cuff, and many a blow, but hardly any ill-nature.

The Reverend Dolling certainly practised what he preached. He gave shelter, food and help at his Clarence Street mission to the sick, the down and outs, and the drunks. He offered healthy exercise, talk and dance in his club and gymnasium as an alternative to the pubs. His two sisters and other devoted ladies cared for and befriended girls who sought their help.

His work earned the Reverend Dolling admiration and respect among the poor Portsmouthians. Not so popular were his comments – such as comparing naval towns to 'sinks of inquity' – which were featured in the national press. The Reverend Dolling set up links with the emerging trade unions and Labour movement. He believed the working classes could only improve themselves in the long run through self-help.

No such worries existed among the wealthy residents of Southsea. The few miles between Landport and Portsea and the emerging holiday resort represented a world of riches. According to the Reverend Dolling, Southsea 'was the favoured infant of the corporation'. The previous thirty to forty years had seen the creation of the architect Thomas Ellis Owen attract the gentry with naval connections to its large opulent houses which opened on to tree-lined groves. An excellent water supply and an efficient drainage system sealed the area's reputation as one of the healthiest places in the country. South Parade Pier had recently been opened along with a railway line from Fratton Station to add to the attractiveness of the seafront streets.

But much of Portsmouth fell between these two extremes of the haves and the have nots. During the 1880s, a vast number of houses were being built in areas such as Fratton, Buckland, Eastney and Milton for the better paid artisans, the office workers, the naval petty officers and the non-commissioned officers who were to be found in large numbers in Portsmouth. A total of six new schools were built in the period to cater for the growing population as well as other services to provide them with some quality of life.

But Portsea Island's increasingly widespread inhabitants were dominated by the dockyard. By 1876, the area of the yard was nearly three times that of a century earlier after an extension of 261 acres was completed. Some 6300 workers were employed in the naval base in the late 1880s to make up more than four out of ten of Portsmouth industrial workers of both sexes.

For male workers, the figure was close to seven out of every ten. Spoil from the excavations to build the yard's extension was carried away on a light railway on piling and used to join Big Whale Island with Little Whale Island, with the formation of the naval gunnery school as a result.

The ships built in the dockyard were growing suitably bigger. The largest of the period was the *Royal Sovereign* – a battleship of 14 150 tons. She had four 12-inch and ten 6-inch guns and was protected by eleven inches of waterline armour. But the dockyard's work provided little incentive for outside companies to develop. Government policy was for all its yards to be self-sufficient in every material possible.

Commercial boat builders, with the exception of Vosper, similarly found it hard to prosper in the latter decades of the nineteenth century. One industry, however, which did thrive off the naval presence was clothing. Staymaking in Portsmouth, in particular, was the speciality of the borough, along with seamstresses and dressmakers. The three sectors made up

Houses on the southern side of Stubbington Avenue, North End, Portsmouth, in the 21st century where Portsmouth AFC played their first fixtures.

between 21 per cent and 33 per cent of the borough's industrial employment in the sixty years from 1841. As RC Riley commented in *The Industries of Portsmouth in the 19th Century*:

Moreover, stay and corset making exhibited the kind of localisation in Portsmouth associated with carpets in Kidderminster, straw hats in Luton, shoes in Northampton and cottons in the Lancashire towns. Yet, curiously enough, the association has never been properly recognised, probably because it has always been easier to link Portsmouth with naval shipbuilding.

The reason for the preponderance of the industries was the availability of female labour. Such large numbers enabled employers to peg wages. Women went out to work in Portsmouth because of the poor pay their husbands received in the dockyard and the frequent pruning of the dockies in times of peace. Sailors could also be laid off or even killed – or at the very least be away from home for up to ten years – making a second income a necessity in many homes.

Many of these issues also applied to the large number of Army households in the town. Almost 6000 troops were stationed on Portsea Island and manning the Portsdown Hill forts at the time. The tailoring industry had arisen in the first place because of the need to supply the dockyard and the garrison with uniforms, and benefited directly from the dockyard, unlike other trades.

Third in the list of industries, and a long way behind, were those of food and drink. Bakers and confectioners grew in numbers as Portsmouth expanded. But their individual size was small compared to other businesses. Only the Pimco bakery, run by the Co-op in Fratton Road towards the end of the nineteenth century, was comparable to commercial premises elsewhere.

If size mattered, then brewing ruled Portsmouth's commercial industrial world. Every factory with a rateable value above £300 in 1885 was a brewery. There were six of them. They were centred around Old Portsmouth and Portsea. Pike Spicer was the most famous. But the place at the head of the brewers' table was taken by Brickwoods in 1910. The firm founded by Fanny Brickwood in 1851 underwent rapid expansion throughout the following five decades.

Unfortunately for Portsmouth's economic affairs, the extent of the breweries failed to generate many jobs. The business was one orientated around production space rather than the number of employees. It was also only indirectly linked to the fleet. Sales of beer to ships were virtually non-existent. It was a different matter, though, when sailors were ashore. As RC Riley stated:

They did their utmost to match the town's brewing capacity.

All the housing and commercial usage left space for recreation at a premium on such a small island. The dominant sport of the time for those who could find the room to play in was cricket. Each April to October saw sports coverage locally given over to various matches between cricket clubs, with some reports of horse racing elsewhere. In the winter, it was the turn of rugby union to hog the newsprint. Association football was very much the interloper in the columns.

CHAPTER EIGHT

Not much changed in that respect as Portsmouth AFC's second season got underway even though the 1885/86 campaign contained a fuller range of fixtures than the late-starting initial season. Twenty-eight games were played in all. Many more were won than lost – nineteen compared to four – but the overall nature of the fixtures was parochial. Every match was conducted against a club within a twenty-mile radius of Portsmouth. Only one was of a competitive nature.

The home tie with Wimborne in the Hampshire Senior Cup's first round marked the cup debut of any Portsmouth soccer team. The trophy had only been in existence for a year and the game on December 5th 1885 at the Garrison Barracks or the US Recreation Ground, depending on which newspaper was read, took place just three months to the day of Portsmouth AFC's election to the Hampshire and District FA.

That decision marked the blues' arrival as a recognised footballing entity as well as the increasing enthusiasm for football. Christchurch and Andover were also elected to the association at the same meeting. In somewhat breakneck fashion, a mere three days had passed since a special committee meeting of the original Pompey – at the Blue Anchor Hotel – had agreed to join the association. The decision entitled its players to compete for the 25 guinea trophy which had been claimed by Bournemouth Rovers in a single goal inaugural final victory against Ringwood Hornets. But Portsmouth AFC's historic cup tie – in which 'AC Smith' appeared at full-back – brought only disappointment for the club's followers.

As the first drawn club out of the bag, they had the choice of ground, while Wimborne could choose the date. But being at home brought no joy for the borough side. Their great cup adventure lasted only as long as extra time against their Dorset visitors. The deciding goal, however, could have left the home players feeling disgruntled at their 1–2 defeat. Doubts existed as to whether the ball had gone behind the tape, which was the forerunner to the crossbar, before it was headed in by an unidentified Wimborne player. The goal's time in the half-hour of extra time was similarly unrecorded but the home players had long enough left to rally in the search for an equaliser.

The *Portsmouth Evening News* was sure the match, if not the result, had proved a good showcase for football in Portsmouth and for Portsmouth AFC:

Their play did credit to the town, even if they did not happen to be victorious in this, their first entry into a cup competition, and the match is calculated to further popularise the association game in our midst.

In this respect, the game lived up to its reporter's ravings as 'one of the best association games ever seen in our midst' in spite of the wretched weather in which it was played. The *Evening Mail* was similarly impressed with the performance of the original Pompey. The paper's reporter wrote:

The home club has only been established as many months as the visiting club has years. But it has to be congratulated upon the gallant struggle its representatives made.

Portsmouth AFC were weakened for the game by the absence of two of their forwards but the sides were generally reckoned by those present to be evenly matched. That only lasted until a first-half injury to the home left-winger H Brooks, who strained a tendon to his right leg, proved to be a turning point of the game. Brooks went in goal rather than leave the pitch and reduce his side to ten men. But his lameness hampered his ability to make saves. Wimborne soon took advantage. Two of their forwards attacked with the ball, one of them shot and scored with the stand-in keeper unable to clear.

The home side retaliated and a series of attacks ended with an equaliser after a series of rapid passes, in which T Huddy and Lieutenant T Nelson played a major role, led to Davies kicking between the posts at the ground's Railway End. This description suggests the US Recreation Ground was used.

The sides stayed level throughout the second half, although just before the final whistle, AH Godfrey wasted a golden opportunity to put Portsmouth into the second round. Having taken the ball past the visiting backs and to within a few yards of their goal, he failed to score by over-reaching himself. The centre-forward's blunder signalled the need for extra time to ensure the tie was completed on the day – the deadline for first round matches to be completed. Of his team-mates, Davies was praised in the press for his part in some effective attacks, while Huddy and Lieutenant Nelson were also reckoned to have shown some dashing form on the wings. The half-backs were said to have stuck to their tasks throughout, while the Reverend Norman Pares distinguished himself at full back. Grudging respect was also shown by the *Portsmouth Evening News* to the Wimborne keeper, Wallingford, who:

...relieved his goal several times with no little adroitness.

The significance of the game was celebrated in an after-dinner evening of jollity. The hosts entertained their conquerors at their headquarters of the Blue Anchor Hotel. The catering by the host, Mr Buckle, satisfied their appetites with a meat tea. General Harward, one of Portsmouth AFC's vice presidents, made a genial chairman of the occasion and both sets of players swapped banter about the afternoon's contest before the Wimborne team left for Dorset.

Anchor House at Kingston Crescent, Portsmouth, is the modern occupier of the Blue Anchor pub which served as the headquarters of the original Pompey.

CHAPTER NINE

The season had begun three months earlier. Portsmouth AFC held its second annual meeting in four months, again at the Blue Anchor Hotel, on September 3rd 1885. Kindersley, the club secretary, announced that Alderman Kent had extended his generosity into the coming season. The JP had sanctioned the continued use of the meadow upon which the club had made its debut twelve months earlier. Mr. Hayter had also agreed to the continued use of the movable dressing tents for the players to use before and after home games.

There was less continuity on the playing side. McDonald declined to stand for re-election as the club's captain, despite ably filling the role in the debut season. Left-winger Davies was chosen in his place. Adames, a half-back, was elected as his sub-captain. And, in what must have been the easiest decision of the night, Alderman Kent was re-appointed as the club's president. Without him, the outfit would have been unlikely to survive past its earliest days.

The club's committee was agreed as: LJ Allen, RE Davis, F Kent, G Hayter, OJ Dancer, W Adames, A Moore, P Russell and W Lillywhite.

Most of the evening's discussion centred round how to make the best use of the valuable trophies presented at the previous meeting by Messrs Emanuel and Buckle. It was finally decided that the winners should be determined by a vote of members at the annual meetings for the best general play throughout the season. A restriction of ownership would ensure that the cups would not become the possession of a particular player of the year unless he won them twice in succession or three times in all. At least fifteen members had to take part in the vote to make it valid and a player had to compete in six or more matches to be eligible for the cups.

The first of those games took place at the end of the month, when a practice match at Hilsea against the Hilsea Ramblers got the original Pompey's season underway. The *Portsmouth Times* looked forward to the action in the coming months:

An encouraging season is expected by this young and flourishing club.

A powerful list of supporters had been enrolled by the club's founders to ensure that the outfit had a respectable place in the rigidities of Victorian society in Portsmouth. Besides Alderman Kent as the president, the notables included as vice presidents General Sir Frederick FitzWygram Bart, soon to be elected MP for South Hampshire, the Honourable TC Bruce MP and Sir H Drummond Wolfe MP.

CHAPTER TEN

Their names might have survived, but the result of Portsmouth AFC's initial practice session of the 1885/86 season has failed to last the years. But there was no mistaking the clean sheet kept by 'AC Smith' when the campaign proper got underway

the following week with the short trip to Havant. The keeper's display helped the Blues to a 3–0 win on October 3rd, a year after their formation.

The *Portsmouth Evening News* reported that he 'adroitly relieved his side' on the only occasion when his goal was seriously threatened by the home forwards. He had, though, survived several close attempts at scoring by Carrell, on the right-wing, and the home side's centre forward Dr Strong. Kindersley proved his skill on the pitch as well as in his minuting ability as the club secretary when he opened his scoring for the season with a strong shot. An effort by Williams survived an offside appeal to double the visitor's lead before halftime. They continued to press forward and a third goal duly arrived courtesy of W Packham or J Freeston in Havant's team.

One of those unfortunate Havant backs diverted the ball through his own goal as he tried to kick it away from the visiting forward, Davies. The right-winger had taken the leather right up to the Havant keeper in his attempt to score. The goal was a stroke of ill-fortune for Packham, if he was the scorer. He had prevented the original Pompey from scoring on several occasions when their forwards displayed some superb play, both individually and collectively.

The next week saw the players of Portsmouth AFC on their travels again, this time to Hayling Island. They managed a three-all draw in a game full of incident. Boisterous weather set the scene for the match. The visitors were lacking two of their regular members who had been unable to find the ground from the instructions they had been given. This failed to stop T Huddy and Godfrey kicking two fine goals alongside the effort of an unnamed team-mate. The last of the goals was strongly disputed by the home players. They claimed the ball had been handled before it crossed the goal-line.

Godfrey was one of two Portsmouth AFC players singled out by the *Portsmouth Evening News* for their fine display in the second half. Kindersley was the other man praised. In the first half, C Pearman, T Huddy, Poole and Russell were said to have provided valuable service to their team.

Hayling, in contrast, were judged lucky to have ended with honours even. The most outrageous of their pieces of good fortune came when the visiting keeper, unidentified in the match reports, kicked the ball out of his goalmouth only to see it rebound off one of his players to end up between the posts.

The rest of the season went on in a generally more positive style. A fixture list printed in the *Portsmouth Evening News* on October 13th displayed the rapid organisation of the club and football as a whole. Return matches were lined up with eleven clubs, alongside the Hampshire Senior Cup tie with Wimborne and a solitary home game the following March with the Hampshire cup-holders, Bournemouth Rovers.

Portsmouth AFC's secretary, Kindersley, was revealed to have been living at 62 Chichester Road, conveniently close to the club's ground at Stubbington Lodge and its headquarters at the Blue Anchor at Kingston Cross.

The first of those series of return games took place very quickly with Hilsea Ramblers lined up as the next opponents, on October 17th. 'Smith's hard and safe kicking proved most serviceable', according to the *Portsmouth Evening News'* comments about his side's return to winning ways.

A brace of goals from the sharp-shooting Godfrey – one in each half – secured the win, though it took twenty minutes of early pressure before Portsmouth AFC went in front. The credit for one of the goals had to be given to half-back Poole. His splendid corner kick dropped in front of the cross-tape and Godfrey smartly scored at his second attempt after the initial effort had rebounded off a post to him.

The original Pompey's constant pressure deserved further goals as Poole, Pinfold, T Huddy and Russell put in some skilful work.

But the town club was brought back to earth a week later when they suffered the heaviest defeat of their short history. The eight goal rout was inflicted by the 93rd Regiment without reply during a one-sided affair at Parkhurst on the Isle of Wight.

The regimental side for the Argyll & Sutherland Highlanders contained some of the best players from the Army's southern counties' representative side. And it showed. Their systematic training and combined play gave them superiority over their civilian visitors. The team from the mainland also suffered on a pitch made heavy by days of constant rain.

The soldiers were unaffected by the conditions as they ran rings around their opponents. This was sign of the future of the sport, glimpsed by the *Portsmouth Evening News*:

(The Army side) had the double advantage of daily practice and same XI for all their first class matches. They made the play exciting and fast, their passing was faultless and while Thompson, among others, punted the ball with his head with power and dexterity, McLaren on the right wing kicked four goals in exciting style.

'AC Smith' was given some consolation by the *Evening Mail* as playing a losing game with good spirit among a weakened side. Similar praise went to HJ Smith, T Huddy and Pinfold.

On the same day as the routing, which was severe enough to be the second worst Portsmouth AFC ever suffered, their home meadow was the setting for a

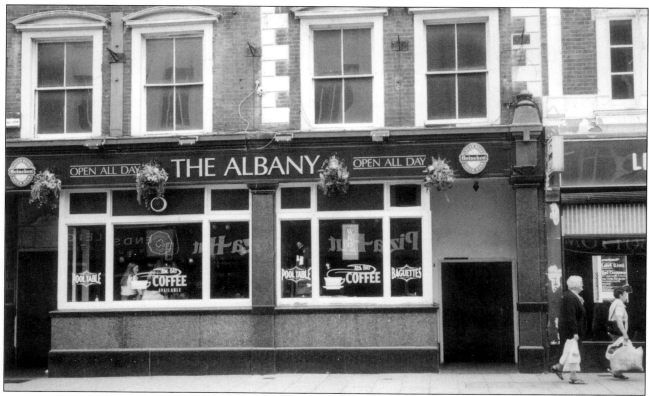

The Albany still stands in Portsmouth's Commercial Road having been used by the Portsmouth FA for many crucial meetings during football's formative years in the naval port.

scratch match between A Moore's team and Southsea Wanderers. The Wanderers fielded nine men against their opponents' seven and predictably won by two goals to nil.

Two weeks passed before the original Pompey had the chance to put their Isle of Wight debacle behind them. They were determined to make no mistake of a repeat when they travelled once more, to Chichester. They pressed straight from the kick-off and Dawson opened the scoring after a good run and shot. His team was undeterred when the home side drew level later on in the first half. The blue shirts had the best of the play after the break and forced Chichester back on to the defensive. A mixture of dribbling by their forwards and some good kicking by their backs put them firmly in front for a 4–1 triumph. The other goals were scored by Brooks, Lieutenant Nelson and Pearman.

Portsmouth AFC's second XI also made their debut on the day in a match at North End with Southsea Wanderers, paying their second visit in as many weeks. A goalless draw was the outcome, showing how far ahead the town club had come in such a short space of time compared to their local rivals, with their reserves the equal of other teams' first XIs. Portsmouth AFC dominated the game, had a 'goal' disallowed for hands and deserved to have won.

A further game also took place on the ground that day. Another original Pompey side drew with Chichester Reserves in spite of being unable to field a full team.

For the first team, another victory followed with a rare defeat inflicted on Stubbington House. The school team had not been on the wrong end of a scoreline for a remarkable three years. That staggering run had to end one day – and that day was November 14th 1885. Godfrey was again the man who did the damage. He ended a bout of rapid passing with a first half opener for Portsmouth AFC. He neatly registered a second goal after the interval before Lieutenant Nelson rounded off the scoring with an adroit kick with his left foot to make the original Pompey 3–0 winners. 'AC Smith' kept a clean sheet for the second time in his two appearances between the uprights that season.

Portsmouth AFC had Godfrey to thank again for their next win. His fine runs from the centre forward position enabled the club to make light of the absence of one of their players when they faced Midhurst away on November 21st. An unnamed substitute had to be called upon to go in goal to fill the gap in the line up.

Godfrey's opening goal ended a spell of give and take play. He made one of his brilliant runs to take the ball up to the Midhurst goal before he neatly kicked it home. Godfrey again used a similar tactic after Midhurst had equalised. His shot was saved by the home keeper but the ball rebounded only as far as T Huddy. He had backed up Godfrey and gained his reward when he calmly put the loose ball into the empty goal. Midhurst drew level for a second time in the second half and had a goal ruled out for hands as both sides tried hard to go in front.

What turned out to be the winning goal was notched, of course, by Godfrey. He rounded off a move of rapid passing with a splendid shot. Godfrey was included in the *Portsmouth Evening News*' praise of the visitors' forwards for their creditable display. At the back, 'AC Smith' and Poole were deemed worthy of special mentions for their contributions to the hard-fought win.

The game was an ideal warm-up for the cup tie with Wimborne, though Portsmouth AFC could not translate their winning fortunes into the competitive fixture.

Consolation, if there was any in the cup defeat, came in the news the following week that Davies, who had occupied their right-wing as the side's captain during the tie, had been selected in the same position for a Hampshire side to take on Dorset at Dean Park in Bournemouth on Boxing Day.

On the opposite wing would be his Portsmouth AFC clubmate, Lieutenant Nelson, who also turned out for the Portsmouth Sunflowers. Portsmouth AFC's recognition was boosted by the selection of Pinfold as a reserve halfback for the county side, while the Sunflowers' Reverend N Pares and his brother, GL Pares, joined him among the reserves as a back and a left-winger.

CHAPTER ELEVEN

On the pitch Portsmouth AFC returned – four days after the Wimborne game – to the winning ways which they had established in the early part of the season. Horndean were the hapless visitors for the resumption of the friendlies. The midweek fixture ended in an easy 4–1 victory for the home side. They were restricted to a single Kindersley strike in the first half by a fine show from Horndean. But they established their class after the break with further goals from Armstrong, Godfrey and Edmonds. It was a display which left the *Evening Mail* purring with delight for the second time in a week:

The forwards, whose individual and combined play left nothing to be desired, were well supported by the backs.

The Christmas fixtures continued the good run of form. The original Pompey played two games in a day. They won both, without conceding a goal. 'AC Smith' played his part in the triumphs, firstly as a keeper and then as a back, for which he and his fellow defenders were said in the match reports to have distinguished themselves.

The Boxing Day double header started with a morning fixture against Fareham at Fareham recreation ground and a 2–0 win. C Huddy opened the scoring with a neat goal after some good dribbling. Soon afterwards, a bout of rapid passing ended in McDonald doubling the score.

A few hours later, and Portsmouth AFC were playing the Worcestershire Regiment at the Garrison recreation ground. A large number of spectators turned out as the civilians kicked off, with just eight men. This failed to stop them going two goals up within the opening forty-five minutes, after being hard-pressed before the vacancies were filled. Edmonds kicked both goals. One was the result of a build up between Davies, GL Pares and Basil Pares. The other came from a bout of good combined head play between the Portsmouth AFC players. GL Pares sealed the win in the second half with a hard shot which went past the soldiers' keeper off one of his own backs.

The matches had been quickly arranged to fill the gap left by Southsea's inability to fulfil their December 26th fixture with the town club.

Two days later, and Portsmouth AFC doubled the score of their previous match. The 6–4 win against Havant was their first match in which the combined score reached double figures. An extraordinary first half saw the original Pompey go six goals up to take advantage of the strong wind in their favour. Centre forward C Huddy kicked four of them in quick succession in a splendid display before his brother, T Huddy, on the right-wing added a fifth. A further goal, likely to have been scored by T Huddy again, followed.

The brothers were to the fore again in the second half when their opponents strove to salvage some respect from the game. They had served notice of their intentions in the closing minutes before half time when the wind dropped, though they were unable to find their way through to goal. The second half was a different story as they pulled back the deficit. They couldn't quite close the gap completely against a defence in which 'AC Smith' was one of the full backs on his way to an ever-present record for the season.

Portsmouth AFC had their moments of threat as well. Nicholson, in particular, had a beautiful shot which just cleared the crosstape. This after the left-winger had seen a goal disallowed in the first half for offside. Havant were handicapped by playing the game two players short, while Portsmouth AFC were reduced to ten men soon after the kick off. A Harward, who was T Huddy's fellow right-winger, had to leave the pitch when some dirt became lodged in an eye when he was struck in the face by the ball.

Portsmouth AFC rounded off 1885 in the most emphatic style possible. Their goal tally reached double figures for the first time as they brushed aside the Royal Marines Light Infantry (RMLI) in a December 30th fixture for a 10–0 win. The Marine side was recently formed and was no match for the comparatively slick civilians. C Huddy opened the floodgates with a fine dribble and a pretty shot, as the *Evening Mail* described his goal. Others followed rapidly. His brother, T Huddy, splendidly headed home a couple of goals from corner kicks. Next to get himself on the score sheet was Edmonds as he smartly chested a ball past the RMLI goalkeeper. In all, the trio each claimed hat tricks. The scoring was rounded off by Nicholson. But a large slice of the credit for the routing had to go to Poole. His corner kicks again played a decisive part in the victory. As many as five of the goals came from the half-back's centres which he crafted to drop straight in front of the posts. Two other 'goals' claimed by the original Pompey were disallowed by the officials as RMLI were overwhelmed. C Huddy was said to have been in brilliant form and was well supported by McDonald. Among the halfbacks, the side's captain, Adames, and Poole in his defensive role, were equal to everything. The full backs, particularly 'AC Smith', did brilliantly whatever work they had to undertake. They enabled Williams's game in goal to become a sinecure. The ball only went near to him once and he relieved the situation with a running kick. His opposite number, Irvine, was good enough to save several shots in spite of being beaten twelve times in all. The result remained the original Pompey's best score for just three months.

It took the club's goal count from their four immediate post-Christmas games to 21 in just five days, with only four goals conceded. Of this tally, the Huddy brothers scored twelve goals between them.

CHAPTER TWELVE

Their side's scoring continued as 1886 began. Portsmouth AFC were soon back in action on January 2nd with a 2–0 win over possibly their closest rivals on Portsea Island, the Sunflowers. The foundations for the latest win were laid by the town club's defenders. 'AC Smith', Hemingsley and

PORTSMOUTH AFC CUP TIES				
1885/86				
Hampshire Senior Cup				
R1	Wimborne	Garrison Rec Gd	L 1-2	5.12.85.
			Aet	
			1-1	90 min

Adames worked tirelessly in repelling the Sunflowers' determined attempts to break through. Their names were among the roll call of ten players commended by the *Portsmouth Evening News* for their part in the victory. The paper omitted to name the crucial goalscorers but it did detail the team's record to date. What a fine record it was: P15 W11 D2 L2 F48 A20.

The record withstood its closest challenge in months seven days later. Cowes were the visitors and, to the surprise of their mainland opponents, included half the redoubtable team of the 93rd Regiment in their side. To further shorten the odds in their favour, the Islanders also travelled with their captain as their umpire for the fixture. The last time the original Pompey had faced the soldiers they had endured a humiliating defeat. Not on this occasion, however. They confounded the pre-kick off expectations generated by their weakened XI facing three crack forwards from the Argyll & Sutherland Highlanders supplied by the safe and hard kicking of McGinnick, among others, at full back.

The borough club could, indeed, have won instead of drawing 2–2, if they had not failed to take their chances mainly as a result of the icy ground. They opened the scoring with Godfrey's dribble and neat shot. JH Smith smartly headed goal number two from a scramble after a corner kick. The home side was forced on to the defensive after half time as the Cowes/93rd Regiment forwards displayed fine passing and dribbling. They sent in several fine shots but it was two lucky efforts which enabled them to draw level as the game progressed. Praise was handed out by the *Portsmouth Evening News* to 'AC Smith' and Hemingsley,

...for sticking to their work at full back, the heavy kicking of the former being particularly serviceable.

The match report was finished by the details of a members' match at their club ground the next Saturday which was to be followed by a high tea and smoking concert laid on by General Harward. Fittingly, the practice match was won 4–1 by

Harward's team against a side led by RE Davies. It was a competitive affair for a friendly occasion. Dr Conan Doyle, his real name in use for club matters apart from match reports, afterwards led the tributes to the General's generosity in arranging the post-match entertainment at the Blue Anchor and for his genial interest in the club. The praise, which showed the doctor's leading role in the club, closed in time-honoured fashion with three cheers for the General after the national anthem had been sung. The evening ended at 10pm and was enlivened by the piano playing of Adames and the singing accompaniment of Pearman. Among the others who took the chance to relax away from the football pitch were Davies, Pinfold, Kindersley, Godfrey, JH Smith, McDonald and Dawson.

The euphoria was wiped away the following Saturday, January 25th 1886, with the visit of the feared 93rd Regiment of Argyll & Sutherland Highlanders, some of whom were making their second trip in two weeks across the Solent. The military side rightly had a fearsome reputation, not the least of which concerned their ability to score more than a hundred goals in a season.

Portsmouth AFC's fears for the encounter were made worse by the unexplained absence of their regular keepers. Dawson had to step in at the last minute for his first appearance in the position. Portsmouth AFC tried to make light of the problem by going on the attack straight from the kick off. T Huddy capped a fine run by putting them in front.

They were pulled back by a lucky goal for the visitors from across the water when the ball rebounded from a clearance by Dawson off an opposing forward and into the goal. The setback failed to see the home side's heads drop. Huddy turned provider as they regained the lead when his shot was firmly headed home by Davies to

The Highlanders soon hit back when play resumed. Their stamina gained by regular training enabled them to hit three further goals without reply, though one was an own goal from the luckless Dawson as he kicked the ball past himself by mistake. The stand-in keeper did, however, redeem himself with several fine saves to restrict the score to

2–4 after the civilians had failed to hold on to a 2–1 half time advantage. He was beaten again in the final minutes only for the effort to be ruled out because the officials judged that the ball had previously just gone out of play over the crosstape. It must have been difficult to tell. There was an inch of snow on the grass to cause the ball to look like a snowball at times.

All in all, though, the display pleased the *Portsmouth Evening News'* man at the match for representing progress of sorts:

Portsmouth AFC, having been defeated at Parkhurst 8–0 must be congratulated upon the highly creditable manner in which its representatives acquitted themselves against such a crack team as the 93rd Regiment. They were not wanting in individual dash or combined play and if they had only had Gibbons in goal they might possibly have made a draw of the match.

January 1886 continued on a much more positive note for Portsmouth AFC against another military team – Hilsea (RA) Ramblers. The 6–0 win was the town club's fourth highest of the season. The highlight was a first hat trick for Godfrey on his way to becoming the club's top scorer for the season. He claimed the place of honour for the victory with a series of mazy runs which delighted the spectators as the far stronger borough XI took a weakened Ramblers side to pieces to achieve another double.

Horndean were next on the fixture list and the away game on January 30th 1886 was notable for yielding 'AC Smith's' only goal of his original

Pompey career. He was able to go forward and contribute to the decisive four goal victory because the village side were overrun.

To quote the *Portsmouth Evening News*, 'AC Smith' and his fellow full back, W Peters, 'were so safe in their dribbling and tackling, they were never once passed so as to put the Portsmouth AFC citadel in danger.'

To make the side's superiority even greater, the team consisted of only ten players on a pitch that was swampy and which made play slow and the ball treacherous. Horndean fielded a side missing some of their regular players, but even so there was little excuse for the town club's keeper to pass the entire game without having to handle the ball. Godfrey continued his goal-scoring form in the victory with a single strike.

He was on target once more as a large crowd gathered at the Garrison recreation ground to watch him help his team to notch up their fifth double of the season with a 3–1 win over Stubbington House School. Godfrey scored the final goal in the victory with a fine shot to make the game safe after the school had pulled back a goal past 'AC Smith', who was unable to repeat his clean sheet of the original meeting between the sides.

Portsmouth AFC had taken the lead through Leader's fine shot. They then agreed to forego a further goal when Stubbington Lodge's claims of offside against Lieutenant Nelson when he sent the ball between the posts could not be decided by the umpires. There was no doubt after half time when his fine run down the right-wing and centre led to his side's second goal from a goalmouth scramble.

The prolific Godfrey was on target for the fourth game in a row when he helped his team to a 6–0 triumph in the February 20th match with the Royal Marines at Forton in Gosport to add to their double figure haul against the same opponents two months earlier. He scored twice in a distinguished display against plucky opponents.

It took twenty minutes for the civilians to open the scoring. More goals followed soon afterwards. The only real threat posed by the home side came when 'AC Smith' had to stop one attack smartly. The *Portsmouth Evening News* had words of encouragement for the vanquished team:

The Royal Marines were much improved in their play and have the makings of a good association team but they were at a disadvantage by reason of the speedy combined play of their opponents.

Godfrey scores a hat-trick as Hilsea Ramblers are defeated 6-0 in January 1886 - *from the* Portsmouth Evening News.

CHAPTER THIRTEEN

Another week, another game and another brace of goals from Godfrey followed. His teammates went one better than the previous Saturday by hitting seven past Hayling Island in their next home fixture, on February 27th 1886. Extraordinarily, though, they went a goal down in the first few minutes. The town side had begun the match a player short and were caught napping. But once they had settled down, the fine style of play, fine dribbling and neat passing among their forwards as well as the strong defence of the backs easily gave them the best of the game.

The headlines were dominated by a player other than prolific goalscorer Godfrey. Williams spent the first half in goal but swapped positions at half time to score after the break. He had enjoyed an easy time of things during his spell between the original Pompey's posts, apart from Hayling's goal. His place was taken by an unnamed player for the second forty-five minutes. Between them, they only had to handle the ball two or three times because of the excellent work of their backs, 'AC Smith' and Peters, whose tackling and punting was described in the match reports as a treat.

The emphatic win took Portsmouth AFC's goal tally to 76 scored from 21 games and 29 conceded as February ended, while the visit of Bournemouth Rovers on March 20th was already being keenly anticipated. Rovers were the oldest association club in Hampshire and Dorset as well as being the Hampshire Senior Cup holders.

What better way for the original Pompey to warm up for the clash than with their biggest win of the season? Petersfield were the hapless victims of the 13–1 thrashing on March 6th. That man Godfrey was the main architect of the victory. His five-goal haul topped his run of six games of scoring as the original Pompey continued their hot streak in front of goal.

The goals kept coming in the home fixture even though Portsmouth AFC willingly ended the game with nine players against the 12-sided visitors in an attempt to even up play. The loans during the match did nothing to help Petersfield. Matters had started to go wrong for them even before the kick off. They turned up at the Stubbington Avenue meadow with only half a team. Portsmouth AFC lent them a centre-forward, Armstrong, and two good backs, Anthony and Williams, just to get the game underway.

Petersfield started with a strong wind behind them but found themselves three goals down before Armstrong pulled a goal back against his usual team-mates. That stayed the scoreline after forty-five minutes.

The restart signalled a deluge of goals for the home side. The scores arrived at an average of every four and a half minutes as they completely overwhelmed their outclassed and outsmarted opponents. Godfrey was joined on the lengthy score sheet by T Huddy with four and Lieutenant Nelson and Edmonds with two goals each to complete their side's biggest win of the season and second biggest in their history.

Again, Gibbons in Portsmouth AFC's goal was spared the necessity of doing much between the posts. The stage was well and truly set for Bournemouth's visit. Or so it seemed. But football fans who had keenly looked forward to the clash were to be disappointed. As the *Hampshire Telegraph* briefly reported, the Rovers were were unable to keep the fixture. No reasons were given.

Replacement opponents in the shape of HMS *Marlborough* were laid on to fill the empty Saturday. The sailors from the naval training base took on a Portsmouth AFC side firing on all cylinders - and won.

To make matters worse for the original Pompey's supporters, HMS *Marlborough* were regarded more as a rugby football team than one which played the association game. Just to rub further salt in the fans' wounds, the game's only goal was netted by none other than T Huddy. He just got a touch to send the ball past his usual colleague 'AC Smith' from a second-half corner by Carruthers to round off a display in which the scorer showed his characteristic dash.

But splendid stamina and dashing pace laid the foundations for a win made all the more surprising by the reasonable strength team which the supposedly all-conquering Portsmouth AFC fielded. Their forwards' combined play was lacking compared to their recent victories, while uncertain shooting wasted the advantage of having the wind in their favour in the first half. Even after half time, Armstrong on their left-wing ought to have done better with a wasted easy chance, while another goal should have resulted from a corner from JH Smith. Consolations for the beaten home side were hard to find. 'AC Smith's' heavy kicking was among them, along with Kindersley's distinguished display and the hard work and hard kicking of the Reverend Norman Pares and Peters at full-back.

The defeat was sandwiched between a pair of one-all draws. The first was at the Hilsea ground of Portsmouth Grammar School. The home side were better than expected from their previous displays and, with Portsmouth AFC purposely resting several players, the academics were more than worthy of the draw. This was thanks, in part,to the contribution of the Reverend Pares. He was a tower of strength and played with his characteristic energy and smartness.

Only a late leveller by Poole, a Portsmouth AFC half-back, from a scramble in front of the posts pegged back the school side. Poole also displayed his usual skill with corner kicks, while Pearman and Kindersley worked hard and AH Godfrey battled well. The heavy kicking of 'AC Smith' was useful to his side as usual. But overall, his team lacked the combined play which had brought them 'a singularly successful season', to quote the *Portsmouth Evening News*.

It was brought to a downbeat close with a journey to Petersfield on March 27th. The market town's Heath was no place to be on a dismal day. To describe the conditions as wretched weather would be a euphemism. Heavy and persistent rain rendered the ball heavy and greasy and the grass slippery as the teams struggled to a 1–1 draw. Add in a gale which blew across the ground and good play was impossible as the visitors sought to add to the humiliation caused by their recent 13-goal drubbing of their hosts.

Petersfield struck first thanks to the weather as they battled to avoid another large-scale setback when Williams fumbled the ball in the visitors' goal after a corner kick. Godfrey (who else?), pulled the visitors level a few minutes later with what was called by the *Portsmouth Evening News* 'a pretty goal' after a neat bit of play among the borough team's forwards. 'AC Smith', as well, received his usual mention because of his heavy kicking in the full-back position especially in the first half, in what was called a hurricane, in a game which completed his ever-present record for the season. T. Huddy, Kindersley, Leahy, McDonald, Poole, Adames, Turner and Hemingsley also received varying levels of praise in the match report.

All that was left of the season was to hold the club's annual meeting. The *Hampshire Telegraph* and the *Hampshire Post* paved the way by reporting their statistics for a second season beyond the imaginations of the founders just eighteen months previously. The outcome of the campaign according to the press was: P28 W18 D6 L4 F94 A31.

Elsewhere, the club's growing stature could have been seen a few weeks earlier. Two MPs, Major General Sir W Crossman and PH Vanderbyl, joined their list of vice-presidents. Mr Vanderbyl marked the occasion with an announcement at the meeting of the gift of a challenge cup worth a guinea to be presented annually within the club.

The meeting was held on April 21st at the usual venue of the Blue Anchor Hotel. Those present had their thoughts fixed on furthering the cause of football as much as the running of the club. The establishment of a trophy for amateur clubs in the borough and district was seen as one way of widening the interest in the sport.

The *Hampshire Post*, writing before the meeting, was sure the cup idea was a winner:

A cup of the value of 10/12 guineas, would doubtless induce local and district clubs to enter the lists for the honour of securing its temporary or permanent possession and by those means much would be done to encourage a pastime demanding skill and developing many qualities.

Donations for the cup (the one from Mr Vanderbyl was presumably too small) were to be kept open until December 15th 1886 to allow the silverware's value to climb to £30. Clubs within an area of Winchester, the Isle of Wight, Hayling Island, Petersfield, Lymington, Romsey, Chichester and Midhurst would be invited to participate.

Alderman Kent's generosity in allowing the use of one of his meadows was noted, along with the resourcefulness of the club's officials in gaining permission to use a field next to St Mark's Church in North End as well as being fortunate enough to induce the committee of the US recreation ground to extend the privilege of its use to them and also to other football clubs as a matter of course rather than as a special favour: a breakthrough for the sport in the town.

CHAPTER FOURTEEN

But the issue of a dedicated sports ground for Portsmouth's growing civilian population was one which was not going to disappear however much the town's councillors might wish otherwise. The *Hampshire Telegraph* reported in April that the council's roads and works committee wanted to take up the possibility of buying twelve acres of land at North End from Winchester College for a recreation ground. The college would only sell the land for that purpose. The cost to the council would have been £6000 – about £450 000 in today's money. A further expense of £3000 would have been incurred by the laying out of the site and building a lodge to serve its users. But permission to borrow the money was turned down by the spending supremos at the Local Government Board in Whitehall to ruin the hopes of Portsmouth's sportsmen.

April also saw Conan Doyle add his voice to the public demands for such a sports site. He took a

Dr Arthur Conan Doyle led the efforts for a civilian sports ground in Portsmouth but it is in Crowborough, where he lived the final years of his life, that he is given pride of place.

leading role at a meeting of representatives of athletic clubs in Portsmouth. Held at the Grosvenor Hotel in Southsea, he chaired the gathering on behalf of his other sporting love of cricket. The issue had united the cricket clubs in the town, of which he was a member, and those in Southampton as well as the Hampshire Rovers and YMCA outfits. Portsmouth AFC was also represented, through Hemingsley, along with Portsmouth Antelopes and the Wanderers and Havant football clubs. Portsmouth Swimming Club, Portsmouth Harriers Athletics Club, Southsea Rowing Club, the cycling clubs of Portsmouth Antelopes, Port of Portsmouth, Fareham and Portsmouth and Southsea Rangers were there also along with Southsea and Albert Tricycle Club.

Conan Doyle and Hemingsley were elected on to the committee which would work with the borough council to plan the desired ground and make all necessary arrangements to bring it about for the coming summer. They were joined on the campaigning group by cycling's JG Smith, who had addressed the meeting, BE Totterdell (rugby union), B Oliver (athletics) and Constable (lawn tennis). Smith was selected as the committee's secretary.

The committee had been chosen to provide a representative sample of the sports which were played in Portsmouth, many of which would benefit from a new ground. Its members were armed with the following resolution, backed unanimously by those present at the hotel:

Ourselves, the representatives of athletics bodies of the town, having long felt the want of a recreation ground, wish to express our satisfaction with the town council in acquiring the site at North End as a recreation ground and will, at all times, endeavour to assist the council in the proper control and management of the ground.

This resolution was to be signed by Conan Doyle and Hemingsley on behalf of the meeting and forwarded without delay to the council.

So, football in particular and sport in general was beginning to move forward in Portsmouth. But the developments were still too few to stop football in the naval port lagging behind the growth of the game elsewhere in the country.

Football had just ended its first season as a professional game. The introduction of payments for players had been sanctioned at a special meeting of the Football Association the previous July. This vote had followed several years of allegations of enticements being made to players to turn out for particular clubs. None of that activity was apparent in Portsmouth, however, or even the rest of Hampshire or the neighbouring county of Dorset.

All the initial professional clubs were based north of Birmingham. Most were sited in the industrial powerhouses of Victorian England in urban areas as diverse as Newcastle and Accrington. This geographical dominance was shown by the feat of Blackburn Rovers in becoming FA Cup winners for three years in a row in the 1880s.

By contrast, those turning out for clubs in Hampshire paid for the privilege. The South Hampshire and Dorset FA made good any financial shortfalls by having collections at its committee meetings. And that after the delegates had paid their own way to get there.

Players chosen to play for the county, such as Portsmouth AFC's Pinfold, had to find the money to get to venues as far away as Walton-on-Thames and Reading. They also bought their own team shirts.

The South Hampshire and Dorset FA had only been formed two years before that meeting of Portsmouth's sports clubs had taken place and just six months before the town football club came into being in October 1884. The association agreed its rules by the September, having sought guidance from the more established Lancashire FA. The regulations included details such as the size of the ball and the size of the pitch upon which the county cup competitions had to be played.

Ensuring the rules were upheld was more difficult, as the countless examples of disputed goals in Portsmouth AFC's games show. No trained officials existed in those early days of the sport. Officiating at matches often fell to county secretaries. By 1886, the two counties' FA had compiled an official list of umpires from names submitted by its member clubs. They were in charge of a game which was lacking a lot of the features which define the sport's 21st century version. Crossbars, penalty kicks and goal nets were still several years away as, indeed, was the replacement of umpires by referees and linesmen, or assistant referees.

The two-handed throw-in was a recent innovation at the time of Portsmouth AFC's formation. Such milestones as goalkeepers being able to handle only in the areas around their goals, the ten-yard rule for opponents at free kicks and numbers on players' shirts were decades away still.

CHAPTER FIFTEEN

But there was the FA Cup, the oldest cup competition in the world. Its success and growing reputation – 126 clubs competed in its first round in 1886 compared with the initial batch of fifteen in 1872 – prompted Will Grant to arrange the Portsmouth and District Challenge Cup competition for 1886/87.

The trophy chosen for the contest was described in the *Evening Mail* as 'exceedingly handsome and massive'. Weighing nearly twenty-five ounces and worked in silver, it was goblet-shaped with decoration in the reponsée style, while there were ovals on the bowl.

The reverse had a football scene in bas relief. The inside of the bowl was gilded and the entire trophy stood upon an ebony plinth.

Fittingly, Portsmouth AFC were its original winners. The final was the first example of the everlasting rivalry with Southampton, and enabled the naval port to gain the initial bragging rights.

The game, as was to be expected, was keenly fought. Hants and Dorset Cup holders Woolston Works were the opponents and had been defeated only once that season – by Bournemouth Rovers. The venue was the US Recreation Ground in Portsmouth, giving the town a slight edge. The date was March 26th 1887.

The *Portsmouth Evening News* set the scene on the eve of the final with a rare example of a pre-match line-up and the news that the valuable trophy was on display in the window of AH Hancox, outfitter, in Commercial Road.

Portsmouth AFC's team for the most important and historic match they had yet faced was: 'AC Smith', W Peters, T Simpson, AE Kindersley (c), FJ Seddon, H Mack, W Boyle, GL Pares, S Diplock, P Ashby, TB Huddy.

An attendance of eight hundred fans, huge for the time, lined a pitch in good condition for the big match. They had plenty to cheer in the first half as Ashby put the home side in front. He scored from Diplock's splendid pass following a corner midway through the half. As the *Portsmouth Evening News* match report in the 6.25 edition that evening commented:

He was lustily cheered by friends of the team.

The Portsmouth Times *sets the scene on March 26, 1887, for the first Portsmouth District Challenge Cup - or Portsmouth Senior Cup -final.*

The lead came after the original Pompey had dominated a game which they kicked off with the wind in their favour. The opening minutes saw Woolston forced to defend after smart work by Seddon, Mack, Ashby and Diplock led to a corner. Portsmouth AFC also went close to increasing their lead just before half time when a good shot tested the visiting defence.

Woolston resumed their attacks straight after the interval and were only denied an equaliser by the width of the crosstape as a sharp shot bounced back into play. On another occasion, it took a sharp save by 'AC Smith' to keep out the visitors. Portsmouth AFC were put under further pressure just into the second half when Kindersley was forced to leave the pitch. The captain had slipped and strained the muscles on his right side.

His injury forced his team mates to struggle on a man short. They managed to hold out until referee H Sandford, from Gosport, signalled the 90 minutes were up. The cup was theirs!

It was presented straight after the game to the victorious team. General Harward, one of the club's vice-presidents, performed the honours to cheers from the waiting crowd who had gathered in front of the pavilion. He handed it to Kindersley, who in turn put the credit for the win entirely over to Hemingsley for whom he asked the crowd to give three loud cheers to show they appreciated his efforts.

As well as Kindersley, Conan Doyle – not the 'AC Smith' of the pre-match line-up – Diplock, Ashby, Pares, Seddon, Mack and Huddy were named by the *Evening Mail* as the winners' best players in the noteworthy triumph. The team had covered themselves in glory by defeating a Woolston side recognised as the best in the county. They should feel proud of the fact, said General Harward. He told the players and spectators that the cup had been bought to popularise football in Portsmouth in line with a growing trend around Britain. He was delighted with the idea's success and the trophy, which was a work of art.

He considered football to be a manly pursuit, which demanded skill and physical training. In keeping with his military background, he continued that he always found that men who were fond of athletic exercises were generally courageous and were able to fight their way through the world. Men fond of such sports made great soldiers in the field, he added, in a speech which typified Victorian values of the virtues of sport.

The *Evening Mail* joined in the congratulatory mood, and football, for the first time, entered its comment column in suitably praiseworthy style on March 28th:

In Hampshire, as in other parts of the country, football has in recent years become exceedingly popular and the final stage of the contest for the challenge cup which took place at Portsmouth on Saturday produced some capital association play and resulted in a victory of the home team. Well done, Portsmouth!

But Woolston had other ideas. What was described in the *Portsmouth Times* as a 'technical' protest against Portsmouth AFC's win was lodged by the Southampton club with the umpire, only to be withdrawn in an abrupt U-turn. The development was revealed to relieved Portsmouth AFC fans on March 30th. No reason was given for the sudden change of heart but the Woolston secretary, unnamed in the press reports, was anxious to smooth over the disagreement. He said Portsmouth AFC were wished every success and added:

I also wish to apologise on behalf of my team for any unpleasantness that may have occurred on the field towards your team, also to the umpires and the referee.

In a response which echoes through the decades, the *Portsmouth Evening News* replied:

We are glad this apology has been sent for, irrespective of any question of rough play, umpires and referees in the discharge of their honorary duties of a thankless but responsible nature, are at least entitled to courtesy from all of the players.

The *Evening Mail* concurred with those views.

A month later, and Portsmouth AFC's players were fêted at a smoking concert at which they received silver medals 'of a neat design and appropriate inscriptions', as the *Portsmouth Evening News* reported, in recognition of their achievements in becoming the town's first football cup winners. The celebratory occasion took place at the Blue Anchor Hotel and General Sir F FitzWygram MP performed the ceremony. It was held on the Monday evening of April 25th.

He handed over the medals in the shape of a Maltese Cross above an inscription in the centre with the title of the cup and the name of the winning club to each of the players. No praise for them was too high for the MP for Portsmouth. He set his sights for the club on no less a prize than the English, or FA, Cup. He wished them the health and strength to play many stout-hearted games and, if they ever aspired to secure the national trophy, he trusted that they would prove victorious. He said no doubts could exist about the difficulty of the contest for the Portsmouth Senior Cup and he congratulated the

Portsmouth AFC team upon their efforts.

He waxed lyrical about football in general to follow the comments of his fellow military man, General Harward. The game required considerable skill, a quick eye, fleetness of foot, agility, strength and pluck to play. It also had the advantages of being suited to any climate at any time of the year, large towns or fields, the torrid plains of India or the frozen regions of the Arctic zone. It was also cheap and within reach of every Englishman, he stated, with a campaigning zeal and a glance no doubt at rugby union with which association football was constantly battling for recognition.

General Harward chaired the triumphant gathering. He concentrated his comments on the winners. They had distinguished themselves and fully deserved the commendations bestowed upon them. Woolston had arrived as the Hants and Dorset Cup holders but were brought low by the prowess of a Portsmouth AFC side who had played pluckily from the beginning to the end of the contest, he eulogised.

This, in spite of having to stand up against a novel kind of play of a rougher and different nature than that to which they had been used. Their players had been forced to labour under many disadvantages from their opponents and therefore deserved the greatest credit. Overall, he hoped the club would seek to retain the cup whose establishment had enabled football to make worthwhile progress in southern England.

Those present included Portsmouth AFC's captain, Kindersley, and J Mason, the captain of Southsea FC as well as their counterparts from the Chichester and HMS *Marlborough* teams. Basil Pares was also there, representing Lancing College FC. The crowd also included Mr Hancox, who had loaned the use of his window for the pre-match display of the trophy.

CHAPTER SIXTEEN

The cup was only a few months old. Its purchase was one of the first acts of the Portsmouth Football Association following a suggestion by Mr Grant, the honorary secretary of Portsmouth AFC. The association's committee agreed to sell the two cups donated to the football club two years earlier and replace them with the one trophy which the club was about to win. The cup's purchase reflected the closeness between the club and the association which had followed it into existence.

Mr Grant inaugurated the new association in 1886 to take account of the emergence of clubs at Horndean, Petersfield and Fareham alongside the

WE Grant, Portsmouth AFC player and secretary, whose suggestion led to the Portsmouth Senior Cup being started.

town club and Portsmouth Sunflowers. The first cup tie and, therefore, the first match organised by the Portsmouth FA took place on October 30th 1886. Fittingly, it resulted in a 6–1 away win for Portsmouth AFC over Petersfield.

The market town's Heath was the location for the historic game, which once more featured 'AC Smith' in goal. His colleagues won easily enough, though they were unable to repeat the free-scoring endeavours of the clubs' last but one clash. It took thirty minutes for them to break the deadlock. GL Pares secured the opening goal and his partner, centre forward J Boyle, soon added a second to enable the visitors to change ends with a comfortable lead. The pair doubled their tallies in the second half as their team upped the pace. Godfrey added a fifth goal and Brooks rounded off the scoring from an excellent side shot.

Appeals for offside were twice made by Petersfield in response to goals but the referee, H Sandford once more, ruled in their opponents' favour each time. Petersfield could only gain consolation from a goal by their centre forward, Widdowson, from a high and fast shot.

That apart, 'AC Smith' had an unblemished game. His satisfactory goal keeping was complemented by

Action from the Portsmouth Senior Cup in 2003 when Hampshire League side Fleetlands knocked out Grant Thornton, from the Portsmouth League, in a resounding 7-3 win.

his skill at heavy kicking, again commented upon in the press, this time by the *Hampshire Telegraph*. The praise for his play was mirrored by that for the rest of the side:

All the Portsmouth AFC forwards worked well, Boyle dodging and shooting cleverly. Pares and Brooks made some dashing runs and worked admirably throughout. Godfrey dribbled in pretty style, while Simpson rendered valuable service. The halfbacks were equal to requirements, the energetic captain (Kindersley) particularly distinguishing himself and also taking corners with marked success.

The hard and clean kicking of Peters at full back proved useful.

The cup trail of history had begun for the blue shirts. The other first-round ties were completed in the following month. Woolston gave early notice of their intentions with a 7–0 win against Cowes. The other opening ties were equally high scoring – Hilsea RA 7 Hayling Island 0, Portsmouth Grammar School 7 Horndean 1. Portsmouth Sunflowers handed their match to Freemantle.

The Southampton side immediately found them-

selves in the semi-finals when they were given a bye in the second round draw held at the Blue Anchor Hotel. There was no such luck, however, for Portsmouth AFC. They were matched with the rampant grammar school.

They subdued the pupils in a tie which took place on December 18th at the Garrison Recreation Ground, emerging 3–0 winners. It was described as a well-contested game in which Boyle, usually to be found at centre forward, proved particularly difficult at halfback for the grammar school forwards to get by. Of his team mates, GL Pares put in some rattling good shots, Godfrey dribbled well and Pearman and the other forwards made some dashing runs. The energetic Kindersley and Seddon were eminently useful at halfback and the backs, including 'A C Smith', did their work excellently. All the school players were said in the *Hampshire Telegraph* match report to have played creditably.

Portsmouth AFC's next opponents, Freemantle, had to take to the pitch for the first time in the competition on February 5th 1887 at the US Officers' Ground where they lined up to face Portsmouth AFC. Their involvement lasted just 90 minutes.

The visitors held out in a first half of give and take

play to cling on to a 0–0 draw at the change over. Both keepers were busy in the opening period. Newton had to fend off the home side's succession of sallies into his goalmouth, while Adames was forced to use his hands and feet on several occasions in the Portsmouth AFC goal.

With the wind in their favour in the second half, the game changed dramatically for the home team. Their forwards immediately pressed the Freemantle defence – and kept on pressing. They pinned down the visitors so much in their half of the pitch that Adames was unemployed after the restart.

The first goal for Portsmouth AFC arrived via a boot of Kindersley whose shot, after some useful headers and passes from his wingers, was too hot for Newton to handle. However, the keeper recovered to pull off save after save to restrict the home side to a single goal until the closing minutes.

Simpson succeeded in rushing the ball between his posts from a scramble in front of the goal. An appeal by Freemantle for alleged handling of the ball was dismissed to leave the town side well in control for the final minutes. 'AC Smith' was again praised for his heavy punting of the ball, while the rest of the team was above criticism. The forwards displayed good combinations and passing which left little to be desired, especially in the second half. The back division tackled well and hardly made a mistake, while the halfbacks proved difficult for Freemantle to crack.

Next for Portsmouth AFC were Woolston who had received a bye in the semi-finals after they had thrashed the outclassed Hilsea RA 8–0 in the second round to create a high scoring record for the cup's first season. But they were out of luck in the final.

CHAPTER SEVENTEEN

Further cup excitement for 1886–87 was provided by Portsmouth AFC's success in the Hants and Dorset Cup. They had to travel to the Dorset town of Blandford, at some eighty miles each way the furthest journey the club had embarked upon. They made the return trip in high spirits, a 3–2 victory before a large attendance made sure of that.

The December 15th fixture was just three days before the Portsmouth Senior Cup tie with Portsmouth Grammar School, and had the *Portsmouth Times* drooling with delight. It was, the paper declared, one of the best games in which Portsmouth AFC had taken part:

Their play left little or nothing to be desired.

The forwards ran and dribbled well and put in some fierce shots, and the back division were said to have tackled in fine style and been hard and true in their kicking, with 'AC Smith's' contribution again receiving special recognition. The visitors went in front in the first half with what the paper termed a 'pretty shot' by left-winger Pearman. An attempt by his companion on the left-wing, Simpson, to double the lead, was ruled out for offside after he had followed his shot by charging the Blandford keeper over his goal-line.

But the original Pompey did go two up. Seddon put the ball finely through the home posts after his corner kick had been returned to him. Blandford pulled a goal back before the interval. They equalised after half time only for visiting halfback Seddon to restore his side's lead. He forced the home

PORTSMOUTH AFC CUP TIES 1886/87				
Portsmouth Senior Cup				
R1	Petersfield	a	W6-1	30.10.86
R2	Portsmouth Grammar School	Garrison Rec GD	W3-0	18.12.86
S-f	Freemantle	USOG	W2-0	05.02.87
F	Woolston Works	USRG	W1-0	26.03.87
Cup winners				
Hampshire Senior Cup				
R1	Blandford	a	W3-2	15.12.86
S-f	Wimborne	a	L1-3	29.01.87

keeper into his net. This was the signal for an all-out sustained attack by the Dorset hosts. They did everything possible to get back on level terms. Their combination play was excellent and their stamina was splendid but the visitors proved equal to the task. The list of praise in the newspaper read like a team sheet: Boyle made some clever dodging runs, Godfrey dribbled splendidly, Bentley showed a fine dashing style, Pearman was in admirable form and Simpson was said to have been as useful as ever.

The halfbacks were congratulated for working with their characteristic energy. Seddon, who was switched from his usual forward role, was especially distinguished and was entitled to the highest praise, in the *Portsmouth Times'* opinion, for his safe tackling and reliable kicking. Peters, meanwhile, was in a grand condition. Six of those players were missing for the semi-final on January 29th which involved a repeat trip to Dorset. The game offered Portsmouth AFC the chance of revenge, for the opponents were Wimborne, who had inflicted a defeat in their first ever cup tie the previous year. But it was an opportunity which went begging. The original Pompey were defeated by their strong opponents more comprehensively than on the original occasion. The *Hampshire Telegraph* had warned that the club faced a tough, though not impossible, task in making the final:

> Wimborne are unbeaten but if the borough club are to put a strong XI in the field they have a fair chance of being left to try conclusions with Woolston in the final.

That was not to be, however. The home side proved too strong in spite of a terrific shot by Lieutenant Nelson from the extreme right of the pitch. The expectations raised by that effort were dashed by a series of second-half accidents which ruled out the hopes of that pre-match comment.

Godfrey suffered from a nasty kick, Seddon was partially lamed and another half-back had his boot split in half. The outcome of the misfortunes was a 3–1 win for Wimborne giving them a final date with Woolston, who had received a bye in the other semi-final.

Consolation, if any was to be gained by the original Pompey, came in the words of the football correspondent of the *Bournemouth Guardian*. He was fulsome in his praise of the blue-shirted team with the following tribute:

> No one could deny who saw the game that the players for the navalseaport are up to all the dodges and wrinkles of the game. In fact, they rather surprised me with

> their skill and combination. Pearman is a smart little forward who crosses well, while Lieutenant Nelson was brilliant.

> Commend to me a more unselfish and safer half-back than Kindersley while Bishop, the Worcester Regiment back, carried away with him the praises of the field for his perfect display.

> Portsmouth AFC appear to have been without their regular backs but Bishop they could hardly have improved upon.

Only three visiting players failed to meet the reporter's approval:

> Boyle seemed rather clumsy. I have seen Brooks and Godfrey play better.

The defeat ended a run of ten wins which had taken Portsmouth AFC to new playing heights as a club. That cup setback aside, 1886/87 was a triumph overall.

CHAPTER EIGHTEEN

It opened on September 18th with an unremarkable one-all draw in a practice match with Hilsea Ramblers. McDonald kicked the borough side's goal.

The first fixture of any intent arrived on October 2nd when Woolston picked up a win at the original Pompey's expense. The next week saw another defeat as the 2nd Worcester Regiment departed 3–1 victors from the Garrison Recreation Ground, presumably at one of the many Army barracks around Portsmouth.

Fareham were the next opponents in another match at the ground and became the initial victims of the borough club's revival as the 5–0 scoreline reflected the original Pompey's superiority.

The *Hampshire Telegraph* was highly delighted by the contrast between the games:

> Portsmouth AFC's combined play showed a decided improvement. Fareham won the toss and decided to start with the wind in their favour. But the passing of the Portsmouth AFC forwards and the defence of the backs prevented Fareham from threatening their opponents' goal at all.

On the same day, the original Pompey's strength in depth was shown by the fact that the club could field a second XI to take on Portsmouth Grammar School at the school's Hilsea playing fields and win 5–2, in spite of being two men short.

Original Pompey stalwart GL Pares kick-started a year-long run of success in 1886/87.

Lancelot Pares, another member of the famous footballing family, turned the game into a personal affair. He kicked all of Portsmouth AFC's goals. Useful service was also provided by Cook, A Stimpson and Grice, though the defence of the school was reported to have played a reasonable game. Some of the boys showed excellent promise on the pitch.

The first team of Portsmouth AFC repeated their five-goal haul the following week when the 2/1 Welsh Division RA were dismissed on October 23rd 1886 with a minimum of effort.

Petersfield were dispatched next in the cup by the newly rampant original Pompey before the upturn in their fortunes was brought to an abrupt halt in a game arranged at short notice.

They agreed to play a scratch Garrison side on November 3rd to encourage football in the ranks. The soldiers didn't seem to need encouragement. They were good enough already to inflict a 3–2 defeat on the civilians.

Three days later, and the original Pompey faced the might of the Worcester Regiment, again at the Garrison Recreation Ground, and succumbed to a defeat which allowed the soldiers to achieve the only double against them that season.

Portsmouth AFC did have the excuse that they were lacking several of their usual players and the solitary goal which the makeshift team conceded was

scored luckily. It came from Sergeant Peters, the soldiers' captain, from a first-half shot which trickled into the net after it had struck both posts of the visitors' goal. The closest Portsmouth AFC came to scoring saw GL Pares falling on the slippery surface before he could shoot into the Worcesters' goal, which was at his mercy.

That incident proved typical of an interesting and exciting game, which was well contested throughout, in the *Portsmouth Evening News'* opinion. It was the last defeat, apart from the Wimborne setback in the Hampshire Senior Cup, which Portsmouth AFC suffered that season. It was a year later before the next was inflicted, by Chichester, after twenty-two games.

The amazing run of success kicked off on November 13th 1886 at the Hilsea sports ground of Portsmouth Grammar School. That 5–2 win was the fourth time in six matches that Portsmouth AFC's players had hit at least five goals. They were soon in control against the school team. Godfrey opened the scoring after he had made several good shots. The second goal was kicked by GL Pares. Boyle claimed the third after the school had pulled back a goal. 'AC Smith' gave the school side a glimmer of hope when he netted an own goal as his attempted header back to his keeper went wrong. But the borough club rallied and Godfrey kicked his second goal of the game. Boyle did likewise in a storming finish.

But all the borough club's forwards played their parts in the success, with rapid and correct passing and generally accurate shooting.

They were well supplied by Kindersley and his fellow half-backs and the heavy kicking of 'AC Smith' also proved a plus point.

A midweek fixture against the Royal Irish Rifles followed, with a one-all draw. The original Pompey recovered well from going a goal down after twenty minutes. Godfrey levelled for them in the second half after a good run in a situation which demonstrated the still haphazard nature of the game.

His goal was disputed by the soldiers and it was left to the Portsmouth AFC umpire to rule on the matter as the spectators claimed the goal. Relentless pressure was then applied by the civilians with eight corner kicks won but without any further goals.

Matters were different on November 20th when the club ventured to south Hayling to take on the island team.

They made light of a heavy ground and a greasy ball to hit four past the islanders, though the conditions might have stopped them from scoring even more. Godfrey hit the first goal, and T Huddy and GL Pares added to their side's lead with headers from corners by Wilson. An own goal rounded off the scoring, as a

Godfrey shot cannoned off home half-back Gregory as he rushed in to relieve his goalkeeper.

The match was a successful debut for the Reverend AW Plant, who showed good combination in Portsmouth AFC's forward ranks. Hayling threatened their goal on occasions but Adames was equal to the attacks in the visitors' goal.

A first double of the season was on the minds of Portsmouth AFC's players the following week and was accomplished in the 3–0 win over the military side of 2/1 Welsh Division, or the Royal Artillery Second Battalion First Brigade, depending on which description suited the newspapers which reported on the November 27th clash in 1886.

The soldiers were defeated thanks to a hat-trick by W Boyle. He was in excellent form throughout the game and put in a lot of strong shots. The Reverend Plant also confirmed his place in the side with some conspicuous service among the forwards with a satisfactory display and admirable centring from the left-wing. 'AC Smith' kept a clean sheet.

Portsmouth AFC's reserves also had an outing that afternoon. The nine-man side failed to be daunted by being outnumbered and defeated Portsmouth Grammar School 2–1, to follow the example of the first XI. Leahy and Stimpson were the scorers.

Further recognition of the original Pompey's advancement came with the selection of Kindersley and T Huddy for the Hants and Dorset side in the county fixture with Buckinghamshire and Berkshire on December 11th. The game was on home territory for the half-back and right-winger with the US Recreation Ground in Portsmouth hosting the clash.

The outcome was a 1-1 draw which was played out in front of 'a limited number of spectators', to quote the *Hampshire Post*. That apart, Portsmouth AFC's only footballing activity in December consisted of the cup ties against Blandford and Portsmouth Grammar School. Both were won, to set up the team perfectly for 1887.

CHAPTER NINETEEN

The year started disappointingly, with two Saturdays in a row being disrupted by Chichester's scratching of the intended fixtures. To fill the gap, the town club fixed up their return match with the Royal Irish Rifles. One absentee for the hastily-arranged game was the free-scoring Godfrey, the side's top marksman in the opening half of the season with five goals. He was away playing for Hants and Dorset in a further county fixture against Somerset at Blandford.

His team-mates survived without him to notch up a win by the only goal of the game. Lieutenant Nelson netted the all-important strike with a fine shot from the right.

Just four lines were devoted by the *Hampshire Post* to the win. Most of its attention and news space was focused on the rugby game between HMS *Marlborough* and Guy's Hospital in London. The union game's match report received top billing and filled thirty-two lines of print in its sports columns.

The clash between the XVs had 'been looked forward to with considerable interest by football followers', according to the paper. A large gathering of spectators ignored the cold piercing wind to watch the match at the US Men's Ground. Guy's won by one major point to one minor point, as the scoring system was described.

Portsmouth AFC, meanwhile, prepared for their Hampshire Senior Cup semi-final by carrying on their winning run courtesy of Fareham in mid-January.

Godfrey, typically, marked his return to the side with a goal after another of his skilful runs to make the game safe for his team after Finlay's good shot had given them the lead. Both goals arrived in the second half.

Horndean were next up, before the Wimborne defeat, and GL Pares took over the goalscoring mantle from the absent Godfrey with a hat trick. He quickly equalised after Horndean had gone in front after the opening forty-two minutes and added two more after the break.

His overall performance was outstanding with splendid runs and accurate shots. The second of Portsmouth AFC's four goals was struck by Diplock.

It was a more than competent midweek team performance to set the players up perfectly for two semi-finals in consecutive weeks.

Those out of the way, with contrasting results, it was back to the more mundane business of friendlies. A quick, and third, clash with the Royal Irish Rifles beckoned. What a triumph the ninety minutes were for GL Pares. He achieved the unique feat of scoring all of Portsmouth AFC's goals in the convincing 4–2 win on February 12th 1887. Never before, or since, would a single player fulfil such a dominant role in a scoreline of that size.

The afternoon also saw another run out for Portsmouth AFC's reserves in a well-matched and enjoyable contest with Portsmouth Grammar School – seemingly their only opponents. The school won 1–0 at the third attempt in matches between the two clubs, though the match reports named WO Adames as the scorer at the same time as including him among the best of the town club's players. Stimpson and Hemingsley were other familiar names given an outing in the reserves.

The first team faced Horndean the following week. They swept aside their opponents 7–0, including a further four goals by GL Pares. The high scoring continued when their fifth double of the season was achieved with a 5–1 victory over Portsmouth Grammar School.

GL Pares repeated his feat of the previous games by netting four goals to complete an achievement which none of the dozens of other Portsmouth AFC players could match in the club's twelve-year history.

One-way traffic was the nature of the match in the first half. The original Pompey dominated play. 'AC Smith' set up their opening goal with one of his trademark heavy kicks into the school's goalmouth where it was picked up by GL Pares and adroitly sent between the posts. He quickly scored another... and another... and another, to give his side an over-whelming four goal lead at half time.

He also sent in some tough shots which the school's keeper, Felgate, had difficulty in saving. Into the second half, and the prolific Pares was still torment-ing his opponents' defence. As the *Portsmouth Evening News* reporter wrote:

GL Pares showed splendid form, his dash, dribbling and sure shooting being quite a treat. Indeed, his performances this season fairly entitle him to be regarded as the best forward player.

But he played no part in Portsmouth AFC's final goal of the afternoon. That resulted from a fine centre from the extreme right by Diplock which left Adames with the easiest of tasks to put the ball into the net.

The school's consolation goal came just before the final whistle when an injured Hemingsley, with a

Pride in wearing the Star and Crescent civic badge unites Portsmouth's footballers throughout three centuries.

damaged knee, allowed Hastings to score.

That aside, the town defence was sound. Diplock made some excellent runs and centred well, though he occasionally kept the ball too long, in the reporter's opinion, while Boyle was said to have been hard-working and unlucky not to score. Among the defence, Kindersley, Seddon and 'AC Smith' were singled out for praise.

GL Pares took his tally of goals to an incredible fifteen in four matches with a hat trick against Royal Irish Rifles in yet another game between the sides, as the paucity of Portsmouth AFC's parochial ambition showed in a lack of opponents. It was the teams' third clash in two months and their fourth of the season. The riflemen must have been fed up with the sight of the borough club by the end of the March 10th match in 1887 with its 5-1 scoreline in favour of the borough club.

Just three minutes had passed before the soldiers found themselves a goal down. Armstrong netted with a neat kick from a throw-in. The Royal Irish gave themselves a glimmer of hope with an equaliser. Before half time, Pares had cleverly headed a goal after Seddon had obtained a free-kick in front of the Rifles' goal to give the civilians the lead at the forty-five minutes mark.

They dominated the second period. Pares quickly completed his latest hat trick and Price rounded off the scoring to provide some variety on the score sheet. It was short lived.

Pares, once more, took the game to the opposition when his club travelled to Petersfield for a match on the Heath on March 19th. He rounded off a dribble with his team's goal and had a further two shots which hit an upright. An effort by Ashby also struck a post to leave the away side hard done by with a final scoreline of 1–1.

Just one match was left before the original Pompey's historic appearance in the first Portsmouth Senior Cup final. The midweek warm up slot was filled to perfection by the quaintly named Mr Richard's Garrison Team. Of course, it was GL Pares – who else? – who got his name on the scoresheet twice in the 2–0 win. His goal in each half was the perfect tonic for the rapidly approaching cup decider.

A strong wind dominated the match at the US Recreation Ground with the side put together by Mr Richards, making accurate shooting difficult. Pares eventually sent the ball between the posts to break the deadlock. The garrison men strove for an equaliser and were only foiled twice when 'AC Smith' saved his goal at the expense of corners. But the match was put beyond the reach of the military when a move which linked Ashby to Godfrey to Pares was finished with a searing shot which baffled the opposing keeper, Private Hughes of the Worcestershire Regiment.

The scene was set for the cup final and the euphoria of the success followed – without a GL Pares goal – before a triumphant Portsmouth AFC ended their outstanding season in the most fitting of ways: a 2–1 triumph over HMS *Marlborough*. Appropriately, GL Pares opened the scoring to end a campaign in which he had been the dominant personality of the latter months.

He sent in a fierce shot which left Green standing in the sailors' goal. Another Pares shot went over the crosstape by an inch as HMS *Marlborough* played well for a team with the first choice sport of rugby.

GL Pares was also instrumental in his side regaining the lead when Green failed to hold another of his shots and one of his brothers, the Reverend Norman Pares or Bernard Pares, ran in and sent the ball into the goal to end the possibility of a repeat of the naval team's triumph of a year earlier.

Overall, the town forwards showed more accurate passing than their opponents to help them end the season in winning style. The *Hampshire Telegraph* commented on the finishing of a football season the like of which had been unknown in Portsmouth:

This was the closing match of the season at the US Recreation Ground where the game has, for the last six months, been generally positive as compared with former years and the interest by spectators in particular special matches was keener than formerly. As, however, spring is advancing so rapidly, it has been necessary to suspend football in order that the turf might be properly prepared for cricket of which a series of good contests among strong clubs are in the process of arrangement.

The statistics compiled by the *Hampshire Telegraph* for the season enjoyed by Portsmouth AFC were astounding: P33 W25 D3 L5 F87 A30.

The individual honours went to GL Pares. His twenty-three goals were netted in just thirteen games for an incredible strike rate. Boyle was the only other player to get into double figures, with eleven goals. The rest were spread out among eighteen players, according to the *Hampshire Telegraph*. In all, a remarkable fifty-eight were selected for the home team, giving the impression of a truly amateur side with players becoming available and unavailable week by week in spite of their success.

The *Evening Mail* put the credit for the outcome of the campaign on the captain:

Portsmouth AFC had a most successful season, thanks in great part to their energetic captain, Kindersley.

All that remained was to attend the cup winners' evening laid on at the end of the month. One cup triumph, another semi-final appearance and an overall success rate of more than two out of three games was how the season had ended. That was as good as it could possibly get for a club in only its second full season.

CHAPTER TWENTY

The positive atmosphere extended beyond the pitch into the sport's committee rooms after the last of the goalposts had been taken down and the pitch markings erased. On April 13th 1887 a resolution proposed by Bernard Pares led to the formation of the Hampshire Football Association.

The groundwork for the historic occasion had been prepared by his Portsmouth AFC team-mate Hemingsley. He had gathered the ten signatures needed to call a special meeting of the association. It took place at the Crown Hotel in Wimborne. The delegates backed the view of Bernard Pares:

That the South Hampshire and Dorset FA be dissolved and that the two counties be at liberty to form separate associations.

An amendment to postpone the matter for a review was defeated. A further vote resulted in Bernard Pares's motion being carried by twenty-five votes to three. Separate discussions by the two counties'

Bernard Pares - one of several members of the famous family to play for Portsmouth AFC - proposed the formation of the Hampshire FA.

representatives straight afterwards led to two distinct FA's being proposed. Hampshire's version formally came into being at a general meeting of its members on April 20th at Southampton's Spartan Club.

Hemingsley, the architect of the organisation, was appointed as its initial honorary treasurer. He had proposed the split to enable football's rule makers to cope fully with the growing popularity of the sport. The South Hants and Dorset FA had administered an area which stretched well inland as well as along the coasts of the two counties and covering the Isle of Wight. Travel and communications posed problems within the vast region.

Suggestions by some members had also been made about forming renegade bodies outside the official FA's remit. Something had to be done and Portsmouth AFC had led the way in achieving it.

The pioneers of football in Portsmouth had every reason to be proud of their efforts. They had almost five months before the next season started to begin the planning to build on their early achievements. They were still able to bask in the glory when the original Pompey's annual meeting on September 15th 1887 provided the next footballing news. The *Portsmouth Times* reported that civic luminaries such as a Major General Sir W Crossman MP, General TW Harward and P Vanderbyl, one of the two MPs for Portsmouth between 1885 and 1886, had paid guinea subscriptions to the club with pride.

Others like General Sir F FitzWygram Bart MP, Sir S Wilson MP, General Sir G Willis and Admiral Sir G Willes had also been elected vice presidents.

'Several of these gentlemen wrote that they considered it an honour to be identified with a club which had such a brilliant record last year,' the newspaper noted.

But a major change in personnel was needed. Kindersley had relinquished his role as captain in which he led the club to its early successes because of his move from Portsmouth. Those at the meeting

This road in Havant ensures that the memory of original Pompey vice-president General Sir Frederick FitzWygram lives on.

passed a vote of thanks for the courteous and efficient manner in which he had carried out his duties. His replacement was chosen to be the half-back, F Seddon, with Diplock, a left-winger, selected as his vice-captain. McDonald was re-elected as the club's treasurer, after having reported a healthy balance of funds, and Hemingsley similarly stayed as secretary.

Hemingsley was specially complimented by the meeting's chairman, Conan Doyle, for his efforts which resulted in another formal vote of thanks.

One of the secretary's first jobs following his re-election was to obtain an insurance policy to cover injuries to players involved in club matches. The *Hampshire Telegraph* stated that the remarkable immunity from accidents which the club had enjoyed in its first three years could not be relied upon to continue.

The insurance policy was a further sign of football's increasing organisation, though to pay for it the members of Portsmouth AFC had to agree an increase in their yearly subscriptions from 3s 6d (18p) to 5s (25p). They were also told to pay up quickly to enable the cover to be taken out promptly.

Conan Doyle continued his prominent role in the affairs of Portsmouth AFC by being elected to the committee for the forthcoming season. His fellow members for 1887/88 were GL Pares, T Huddy, W Boyle, J Simpson, WE Grant and Stimpson.

But as they sought to strengthen and progress the club, they found they were already becoming too successful for some. The triumphs of the team frightened off many of the potential entrants for the second season of the Portsmouth Senior Cup. At the cup committee's meeting earlier the same evening, Hemingsley reported that only five of the sixteen clubs he had contacted were willing to enter. The others considered that they were too weak to compete against the borough outfit.

This left the first round draw looking rather sad: Portsmouth Grammar School v Havant and Portsmouth AFC v Petersfield was its total strength, with Hilsea Ramblers receiving a bye.

As omens go, the draw was a good one for the borough club. Petersfield had been their opponents in that first Portsmouth Senior Cup the year before and were swept aside 6–1 as the Blues made their way to becoming cup winners.

How different the second season was to be. The competition had everything – drama, controversy and intrigue. It only ended with the original Pompey retaining the trophy in spite of twice having been defeated in the semi-finals. Football in Portsmouth had never seen such an incident. It probably never has since in the more than a hundred years which have followed.

CHAPTER TWENTY-ONE

But first things first, and that opening tie with Petersfield. Any hopes which Portsmouth AFC harboured of a repeat of the previous year's rout at the Heath in the market town were swiftly destroyed when they had to be satisfied with a draw.

The first half of the replay on November 19th was little better for them. The teams were locked on a goal each. Wasteful shooting meant the home side squandered chances to take an early lead in diabolical conditions of heavy rain and mist at the US Recreation Ground. Even worse, they went behind to an own goal off a full back before a scorer – unnamed in the match reports – equalised following a series of attacks.

Portsmouth AFC continued to press after the break. Repeated corner kicks failed to be turned to their advantage because of the conditions. W Jupp eventually gave them the lead with a beautiful shot and GL Pares made the game safe with a further goal. The final fifteen minutes were played in semi-darkness.

GL Pares hit his highest individual tally of five goals when the Royal Engineers were easily defeated 8–2 in the next round on December 3rd.

Hilsea Ramblers were the opponents in the only scheduled semi-final of the 1887/88 Portsmouth Senior Cup. The kick off on December 17th at the Officers' Recreation Ground along Burnaby Road was the start of 270 minutes of unprecedented mayhem in footballing circles in Portsmouth. The competition might have been short on games but it was big on disputes.

The semi final, though, started in the best possible manner for the original Pompey. The club were two goals up within just six minutes. First to score was Bernard Pares from a good pass by Seddon. Leader was the next to put the team on the road to victory with a goal from out on the left-wing.

The early successes did not continue. The civilians were pegged back by two goals from Whiston and Wardrope, both left-wingers. A further strike quickly followed to put the Ramblers in front at the interval. The second half made the borough club's players grateful for that insurance policy. To quote the *Hampshire Telegraph*:

Play in the second half, although still interesting, was marked by occasional roughness by Hilsea Ramblers, which on all occasions is to be deprecated and it was fortunate no serious injury ensued.

The Ramblers mixed the fouls with playing football as they tried to strengthen their lead. One shot went to the right of Portsmouth AFC's goal, one shot to the left and another was kept out by the ever-watchful borough keeper Glennie. His forwards hit back but team captain FJ Seddon was unable to take advantage of a corner. His side made every effort to rescue the match, and their hold on the cup, as time began to ebb away.

The *Hampshire Telegraph* journalist had already rounded off his match report: 'Time ran out and it was expected Portsmouth AFC were out of the competition' when Seddon embarked on an epic run. He covered three-quarters the length of the pitch according to the *Hampshire Telegraph*, half in the estimation of the *Hampshire Post*, with the ball at his feet. He ended his charge at the Ramblers' defence by laying off the ball to Stimpson whose well-placed shot was parried by Hardy in the soldiers' goal and agonisingly rebounded over the line from his right hand post. 'A right hearty cheer greeted the point,' in the hastily-written words of the *Hampshire Telegraph*. There was just one minute left. Those sixty seconds had enabled the town club to stay in the cup.

But their relief was mixed with apprehension at having to go through the same ordeal again in the replay. The *Hampshire Post* was optimistic that Portsmouth AFC would make the most of their great escape:

It will be noticed that the Portsmouth AFC team were without four or five of their regular team which, no doubt, accounted for the uncombined nature of their play.

If only. The replay was fixed by the club committee back at the officers' ground on January 7th 1888. It ended with the borough club seemingly out of their own cup competition amid conditions of fierce controversy.

Their fury was centred on a first half melée in front of the Hilsea Ramblers' goal. The ball passed between the soldiers' posts. The umpires, Nicholson (Wimborne) and Collins (Hertford), who were brought in from a distance to ensure a lack of bias, ruled Portsmouth AFC had scored.

The Ramblers disagreed and the referee, again Gosport man HW Sandford, overruled his umpires.

The tussle and disputed goal came after sustained pressure by the original Pompey had failed to bring them the lead. They besieged their opponents' goalmouth with a much-improved team from the original tie, though the absence of Norman Pares, one of Hampshire's most dashing players, was a blow. Diplock hit a post as Portsmouth AFC poured

"STEEL TRUE, BLADE STRAIGHT"

Fitting Epitaph For A Portsmouth Author

BY

CHRISTINE REES

TO-DAY is remembered as the 25th anniversary of the death of Sir Arthur Conan Doyle, author of the world-famous "Sherlock Holmes" stories and many other literary works.

Conan Doyle, one of a family of 10 brothers and sisters, was born May 22, 1859, in Picardy Place, Edinburgh: he was the idol of his mother's heart.

He trained to become a medical doctor and came to practice in Southsea. In his spare time he wrote stories. The dining room table, in his grandfather's house, around which sat such literary giants as Thackeray, Scott, Wordsworth and many other writers, all friends of his grandfather, became to him a symbol.

One of his earliest ambitions was to have a story accepted by the editor of the Cornhill Magazine: to his delight he achieved this ambition, and on July 15, 1883, received a cheque to the value of 29 guineas for a short story entitled "Habakuk Jephson's Statement." This early acceptance by no means brought him fame. he had to travel a long and hard road before he achieved national acclamation as an author.

In 1882 he set up in practice at No. 1, Bush Villas, Elm Grove, Southsea. His house, demolished by air attack in World War II, was situated between Elm Grove Baptist Church and the Bush Hotel.

Conan Doyle wore the regulation dress of the professional man of those Victorian days. the frock coat and high hat. He was poor and could afford to furnish his house only in a meagre and spare fashion: but his enthusiasm was unbounded. Among a few articles of furniture he bought a bedstead, but quite forgot to buy a mattress and bed clothes.

He could not afford to employ domestic help. He endeavoured to maintain the dignity of his profession by dressing up his young ten-year-old brother, Times, in the uniform of a page for the purpose of answering the door to patients.

Conan Doyle used to creep out after dark and polish his brass name plate, to avoid the embarrassment of being seen performing such a menial occupation.

He married a Miss Louise Hawkins. The marriage proved to be a happy one. By degrees his practice increased; he was able to send his young brother to school and employ domestic help in the kitchen.

He was able to buy more furniture for his house and he records that he had 14 pictures and 11 vases in his surgery, and so much furniture in the waiting room that there was hardly room enough for the patients.

Arthur Conan Doyle now began to mix about a bit. He proved to be a fine sportsman and particularly good at cricket, regardless of his 15 stone, all muscle and innocent of surplus flesh, which so admirably offset his great height, which was 6ft. 2in.

His greatest satisfaction was in joining the Portsmouth Literary and Scientific Society. of which he later became the Society's secretary.

On the eve of Conan Doyle's departure from Southsea, after eight years' residence, the Society gave a farewell dinner in his honour, which was recorded in the Portsmouth Times. dated December 13, 1890.

Dr. Watson, the President of the Society, after whom he named the famous partner to Sherlock Holmes in his detective tales, occupied the chair.

While Conan Doyle was living in Southsea, in between his medical duties, he wrote the story of "Micah Clarke" in three months. The story contrasts the austerities of the Puritans with Micah Clarke as the hero, and the easy latitudes of the foppish days of the Stuart Kings. The early setting of the story is in the familiar area of Havant.

During Conan Doyle's stay in Southsea he became to know and love the Isle of Wight and sent his children to Sea View for holidays.

Twice he stood for Parliament in Edinburgh and failed to gain a seat; although he was disappointed he was not unduly cast down as his first and great love was his writing.

He was a man with a prodigious memory, a continual flow of ideas and an inexhaustible capacity for work; akin to that he possessed a perfect genius for the mechanic of the art, in his characterization and naming of the people and places.

The popularity of the Sherlock Holmes stories grew, until, at last, Conan Doyle felt the stories to be getting the better of him. In a letter to his mother. he writes telling her that he intends to slay Sherlock Holmes. It was useless, the reading public refused to let Sherlock Holmes die!

Conan Doyle had the plan in his head to write an entirely different sort of story. The editor of the Strand Magazine clamoured for more Sherlock Holmes stories.

In exasperation he offered to write a dozen more for £1,000 in the hope that the offer would be turned down. The editor of the Strand Magazine immediately closed with the offer!

At 40 years of age he volunteered for the Boer War, performing yeoman service in the cause of the sick and wounded. Pro-Boers wrote to the Press bitterly attacking the management of the hospitals in the Veldt. Conan Doyle replied with spirited and fiery articles in their defence, in particular that of the Army orderlies who, he contended, worked so hard with very little public acknowledgement.

Conan Doyle's mother was the presiding genius of his life He always wrote to her as Ma'am. In childhood two of the precepts she taught him were to be "Fearless to the strong; humble to the weak.'

Although brought up as a Roman Catholic, he forsook the religion of his forefathers and for many years, was an agnostic, maintaining, however, a reverent attitude towards religion. In his later years, to the dismay of some of his friends, he embraced spiritualism.

It is as the creator of Sherlock Holmes, the philosophical detective, which was, in reality, himself, that he will best be remembered.

After the death of his first wife, aged 49, who died at Hindhead, he, several years later, married Miss Jean Leckie. He continued to write for some time but failing health compelled him to give in.

Conan Doyle died July 7, 1930, at the age of 71 years, with his wife by his side. On July 11, he was buried in the grounds of his beautiful home at Windlesham; his wife attended the ceremony attired in a light summer dress.

On a headstone made of British oak, by his wife's request, were inscribed his name and the date of his birth and the words: "Steel true blade straight."

A fitting epitaph for a man whose high courage pressed him on to fight with his pen for the rights of the weaker man.

Too often, as in this Portsmouth Times *article in July 1955, Dr Arthur Conan Doyle's part in the early years of football in Portsmouth is overlooked.*

forward soon after a shot by left-winger Plant from the right-wing had been saved by Harding in goal for the Ramblers. A shot by Wood was also held by the keeper before Plant struck the crosstape with another effort.

Having held on for a 0–0 draw at half-time, the Hilsea Ramblers' forwards played better in the second half with a more forceful display which led to half-back MacDonald scoring with a long and low quick shot. Portsmouth AFC desperately tried to get back into the tie. 'AC Smith' sent in a difficult shot which just cleared the opponents' goal in spite of the supporters thinking it had gone in.

The referee's final whistle, with the Ramblers a goal

PORTSMOUTH AFC CUP TIES
1887/88

Portsmouth Senior cup

R1	Petersfield	USRG	D	
R1r	Petersfield	USRG	W3-1	19.11.87
R2	Royal Engineers	USRG	W8-2	03.12.87
S-f	Hilsea Ramblers	USOG	D3-3	17.12.87
S-fr	Hilsea Ramblers	USOG	L0-1	07.01.88
S-fr2	Hilsea Ramblers	USOG	L0-4	25.01.88
F	Portsmouth Grammar School	Hilsea Rec Gd	D0-0	17.03.88
Fr	Portsmouth Grammar School	Hilsea	W3-2	31.03.88

Cup winners

Hampshire Senior Cup

R2	Royal Engineers	no record of tie being played		
S-f	Woolston Works	Bar End Cricket Gd	L0-1	04.02.88

up, was far from signalling the end of the matter. The original Pompey's secretary, Hemingsley, immediately stated that he would appeal to the cup committee against the decision of the referee about the disputed first-half goal. He said the umpires were unanimous in awarding the goal and that Mr Sandford had no right to intervene.

Over to the cup committee members. They held a protracted discussion at a meeting at the Albany Hotel, which was reported in the *Evening Mail* on January 21st 1888. They decided to throw Portsmouth AFC a cup lifeline. The club, though, were clearly fortunate. It emerged in the paper that the facts on match day were incorrectly reported. After the disputed goal was claimed, one umpire ruled in favour and the other against. He changed his opinion to back his colleague. This led the Ramblers to appeal to the referee. The latter account swayed the committee members in favour of the soldiers. Two out of the three voting members clearly said the head umpire had ruled a no goal. But the meeting's resolution was at odds with this view, according to the paper:

It was resolved that in order to uphold the usual custom of sustaining the decision of the umpires the two clubs should meet again and such competition will take place on Wednesday next (January 25th).

But as a lifeline it proved as useful to the civilians as a lifeboat with a hole in its keel. The Ramblers clearly felt they had a score to settle in the enforced replay.

And settle it they did, 4–0.

It was an easy win for the garrison team. All their goals came in the first half in a blitz on the civilians' goal.

The opener arrived after twenty-five minutes through Armstrong (an Army Transport Corps right-winger) when his side smartly counter-attacked after they gathered the ball from a Portsmouth AFC throw-in at the opposite end of the pitch. Two more goals followed within ten minutes.

Both were scored by Myles, of the Scots Greys, with the first being a clever shot. The last goal was notched through right-winger Edmonds (Royal Artillery) in the forty-first minute. The game was already over as a contest.

Before the worst sixteen minute period the original Pompey had yet endured, Hemingsley had displayed much skill and judgment in repulsing the attacks of the soldiers, and 'AC Smith' was also prominent in protecting his side's goal. All that was to no avail. In the second half, Portsmouth AFC played pluckily in the face of adverse circumstances and superior power but their fate was sealed. Or was it?

CHAPTER TWENTY-TWO

Meanwhile, the town club could only look on with envy as Hilsea Ramblers duly took their place in the 1887/88 Portsmouth Senior Cup final against Portsmouth Grammar School on February 18th. Some three hundred spectators watched at the Officers' Recreation Ground as yet another game which involved the Ramblers was cloaked in controversy. They won by the game's only goal, disputed of course, but the victorious team had hardly grasped the trophy before it was snatched away from them again.

The use of a specially imported player from the Scots Greys Regiment at Brighton, infringing the rule of seven days' residence within the Portsmouth district, led the cup committee to award the prize to the school. To make matters worse, the ineligible player had appeared under an assumed name.

But still the fate of the cup was not settled. The competition was turning into a farce in only its second season as the committee suddenly decided to order the grammar school to face Portsmouth AFC to win a trophy which should have been theirs by right as the finalists beaten by a rule-breaking team.

The committee made the decision on March 5th on the basis, reported in the short-lived *Portsmouth Herald* paper, that the town club and the school should have the chance to contest the cup as both teams were wronged by the Ramblers.

The second final was fixed for March 17th 1888, at Hilsea Recreation Ground after Governor's Green was found to be unavailable. The dominant team were again the Ramblers even though they had been kicked out of the competition. Their shadow hung over the drawn game like the darkest of thunderclouds. That presence was in the shape of the supporters of the soldiers rather than the players. Their large number accounted for the 'far more numerous' crowd which the *Portsmouth Evening News* reported had turned up 'in the face of a bitter wind and threatening snow'.

The soldiers' fans believed in being heard as well as in being seen. In the first recorded case of football rowdyism in Portsmouth, the members of the Royal Artillery and the Scots Greys of Hilsea Barracks from whom the Ramblers drew their players maintained a sustained barrage of disturbances during the match. One Portsmouth AFC player in particular, Hemingsley, was the focus of most of their fury. The *Hampshire Post* reported:

Evidently smarting under their club's disqualification, some of these men behaved throughout the game in quite a disgraceful manner. They hooted and jeered the players continuously and appeared more like a set of Bedlamites [in a reference to the mental hospital of Bedlam] than reasonable men.

Particularly was their conduct directed towards the secretary of the local cup committee, any little slip of his being received with a burst of contemptuous laughter and the use of language more vigorous than polite.

Similar condemnation was forthcoming from the *Portsmouth Evening News*, which was adamant the scenes should not be repeated:

A considerable number of Hilsea Ramblers witnessed the match and the continuous hooting and discordant noises in which they indulged culminated at the close of the contest when they threw several clods of earth at members of Portsmouth AFC [for whom Conan Doyle was in goal] as they passed towards the town.

The Ramblers were to say the least guilty of the most discourteous conduct towards their final opponents and let us hope that when the final tie is again played in the course of the next few weeks, steps will be adopted to avoid a repetition of such unseemly and unsportsmanlike behaviour.

The action around the touchlines overshadowed that on the pitch. The game ended in a 0–0 draw in spite of five original Pompey players having the advantage of playing in the previous season's final. The rematch took place on the school grounds' upper goals to allow the spectators, rowdy or otherwise, the best vantage points on the slopes and ramparts of the surroundings.

Portsmouth AFC were kept on the defensive for the first quarter of an hour with 'AC Smith' having to be constantly alert to the dangers to his goal. The school had two good shots and two corner kicks in that period. The town club retaliated, and give-and-take play continued until well into the second-half.

The deadlock was nearly broken as both sides stepped up their efforts in the closing stages of the game. The cup holders sent in a couple of testing shots as they tried to ensure they retained the trophy, while 'AC Smith' was called into action again when the school put in a late strike.

His display earned him a creditable mention in the *Portsmouth Evening News* alongside Huddy, Diplock, Pares, Seddon, Stimpson and Simpson. But the cancellation by the sides of each others' efforts meant a further, and third, final had to be staged. This extended the football season in Portsmouth to its latest point: March 31st 1888.

The entire drawn-out nature of the Portsmouth Senior Cup irritated commentators in the local papers. For the *Portsmouth Times*, enough was enough:

Footballists must be heartily sick of the Portsmouth District Challenge Cup and the series of trumpery little disputes it has engendered.

It railed in its edition of March 24th:

After contest after contest the question of who shall hold the much-prized cup still remains in abeyance and if management have anything to do with it the competition will probably be in a state of 'suspended animation' and the competitors in a state of 'animated expectancy' until football, according to the association rules, has ceased to exist.

There has been a good deal of fault-finding with regard to the action of the committee in selecting the Portsmouth AFC to again play in the final, it being urged that disqualification of the Hilsea Ramblers in the Portsmouth Grammar School match cannot thus outweigh the tremendous thrashing which Portsmouth AFC had previously received at their hands.

The Ramblers and Portsmouth Grammar School faced each other for their final tie. The former were disqualified and common sense would therefore naturally suggest that the latter should be awarded the cup without further ado instead of having to fight a team which, in earlier contests, had been completely routed.

The condemnation was shared by the equally fed-up *Hampshire Post*, which said the cup committee had been shown up by the events of the past few months and should scrap the event:

It's not very clear as to why the borough club should be allowed to compete in the final round at all. If the borough club objected to the victory of the Ramblers when they humiliated them on the US Recreation Ground on the score the Ramblers had infringed the rules as to professionalism, why was not the objection laid before the committee in a reasonable time and then and there decided? If the objection was upheld, what right did the Ramblers have in the final at all?

Or if the borough club were not in a position to prove their case by all the rules that govern sport surely they cannot claim a match by disqualification of a team brought about by another club's agency?

We maintain that, on the disqualification of the Ramblers through the appeal of Portsmouth Grammar School, the school are fully entitled to claim the match and the cup. And this committee, in allowing the borough club to compete again, are guilty of injustice.

It was urged the school should refuse to have the cup unless the borough club met them in friendly rivalry. This is quite fine but in that case the duty of the committee was quite plain. They should have withheld the cup from presentation this season.

The launch of the cup – less than eighteen months earlier – and the mood of optimism which surrounded the competition must have seemed a long time ago to the organisers.

After all the bluster, it was probably a relief to get back to actually playing the game. A full two weeks elapsed before the replay of the second final went ahead on Easter Saturday, with Hilsea again the venue. A remarkable three-goal comeback in the second half ensured Portsmouth AFC ended the convoluted and controversial affair by 3–2 as the only holders of the Portsmouth Senior Cup. All the goals for the winners came in the last twenty minutes as their greater weight and better staying power enabled them to outshine the school team.

The first half had been a different story. The Portsmouth Grammar School team had matters all their own way and displayed vastly superior skill to take a two-goal lead by the interval. However, the original Pompey soon equalised and it was the blue-shirted players who were presented with the trophy by Sir George Willis.

Still, though, the furore about the competition would not die. That day's edition of the *Hampshire Telegraph* contained a lengthy letter from Hemingsley, recovered from his verbal bruising at the tongues of the Ramblers' fans. He revealed from his home in St Leonard's Villas, Queens Road, that Portsmouth AFC had indeed been willing to hand the trophy to the grammar school after they had learnt of the Ramblers being kicked out of the competition. But the school had decided that the more manly course of action would be to play for the trophy. He wrote.

Like most people who do not know the real facts, they doubtless felt that both the spirit and the letter of the game warranted the decision of the committee in placing on terms of equality the teams which had been unfairly defeated, especially as the disqualification was due to neither club.

Hemingsley added that the cup committee had only been able to confirm suspicions of the Ramblers' cheating thanks to inside information supplied by 'A Disgusted Soldier', finding the identity of whom would tax Sherlock Holmes.

It appeared, from the cup secretary's information, that the Ramblers had been guilty of systematic abuse of the cup rules by playing an ineligible player under a qualified man's name. Doubts were raised by Seddon, the borough club's captain, in the soldiers' first tie, the original semi-final against Portsmouth AFC back in the previous December. He withdrew his vocal after-match protest after he had been assured by his counterpart with the Ramblers, Corporal Edmonds, that his suspicions were groundless. The grammar school did much the same. They decided to abandon their initial thoughts of objecting because they wrongly wondered if soldiers were

A challenge to the popular view that Dr Arthur Conan Doyle's time combining his medical work with playing football and cricket in Portsmouth was a failure was made by a fellow doctor.

Canadian-born Dr Alvin Rodin, who taught pathology in the US, compiled a medical casebook of Dr Doyle in 1984. He told the *Portsmouth Evening News* at the time of its publication that Dr Doyle had been more of a success than was commonly thought.

Dr Doyle helped to create the impression of penury in his memoirs. But Dr Rodin took a fresh look at the facts 60 years after the autobiography was issued. His research revealed Dr Doyle's practice at Bush Villas received 20–25 calls a week to visit patients. Each trip would have been worth 3s.6d plus the proceeds of any medicine sale he made to the patient. Rodin states:

He was a very bright, young, well educated physician who appeared to have considerable empathy with his patients. There was the myth that he was struggling because he never made more than £300 a year. But we must remember that was four times what a skilled tradesman made in those days.

From his medical writings and articles in journals, he was experienced and correct for his time.

The reason that people thought that he was a complete failure as a physician is because in his own autobiography he talks more about the first six months he was at Southsea getting the practice going.

He did set the odds against himself. The vast majority of young doctors bought established practices but he started from scratch.

Those first few months were rough and people seem to think it was that way throughout. But seeing 25 patients a week, he could not have been starving, could he?

He left Southsea for two reasons. Firstly, he was getting bored with general practice. And, secondly, he wanted more time for writing, which was really his first love. He wrote manuscripts when he was only six years old.

Dr Rodin, from the Wright State University School of Medicine at Dayton, Ohio, said he admired Dr Doyle as a man. 'Doyle was absolutely honest and always fought for the underdog.'

A new insight into Dr Doyle was revealed in a book published the previous year. 'The Unknown Conan Doyle Essays on Photography' featured twelve articles which the author had written about the new invention.

They were contained in the pages of the *British Journal of Photography* to which Chichester man John Michael Gibson had access at the British Library after he had looked through 60 scrapbooks of material which belonged to Dr Doyle.

Mr Gibson joined with Richard Lancelyn Green to edit the works for publisher Secker & Warburg.

---

spared the usual eligibility rules.

This cleared the way for the committee to present the cup but saw the committee's treasurer question Corporal Edmonds about the allegations. Hemingsley refused to elaborate on the replies but stated it was later discovered from the adjutant of the Royal Scots Greys at Brighton that Private Stewart, who took part in this year's Sussex Cup, played for the Ramblers against Portsmouth AFC and Portsmouth Grammar School in the Portsmouth Senior Cup.

At a further meeting of the cup committee, the secretary of the Ramblers admitted the violation of the rules and voted for his club's removal from the cup. It was also hinted by Hemingsley that the Ramblers had pulled the same trick with other players. And the cup rule in question? It stated:

The cup shall be competed for annually by eleven members of each club, qualified according to the rules of the English Association; or who shall have been duly elected members of the club for at least 28 days; such members to be actually living within the defined area at least 28 days prior to the first round of the cup ties, or the nominal home to be within such area.

CHAPTER TWENTY-THREE

Matters were a lot simpler and shorter for Portsmouth AFC in that season's Hampshire Senior Cup as one of only nine competing clubs. Their involvement lasted just one game after Portsmouth Sunflowers had scratched their first round clash. The game took place as the semi-final when their adversaries were their rivals from the previous season's Portsmouth Senior Cup final, Woolston Works.

This time the Southampton side emerged the winners by a single goal with none of the recriminations of the earlier encounter. Portsmouth AFC were at full strength for the semi-final on February 4th

1888 at Bar End in Winchester as they attempted to better their performance of the previous season by reaching the final.

Woolston, in turn, imported five players from the AMD Netley to show the seriousness with which they treated the competition and their desire to hold on to the cup, which they were wrongly rumoured in the previous November to have mislaid.

They were rewarded in the sixty-seventh minute with the game's only goal which, as the *Evening Mail* claimed, was luckily scored after a combined rush of the Woolston forwards. The score was unfortunate for goalkeeper 'AC Smith'. He played well through-out the semi-final and repelled the rest of the opposi-tion attacks.

But despite their grudging acceptance of the goal, the *Portsmouth Evening News* had to admit Woolston played better as a team against a side which was together for the first time that season. Nevertheless, the original Pompey still carried enough threat to put pressure on their Southampton area opponents.

A shot by Plant rebounded behind off a post after GL Pares and Jupp had taken the ball up to the Woolston goal on the right-wing and Jupp had centred. Woolston replied to end the half on the attack.

Diplock went closest first in the second half with a near miss shot as Portsmouth AFC pressed.

Woolston soon made two fierce attacks. The initial effort was well saved by 'AC Smith' and the second was kicked behind by his defence. A hefty kick by the keeper, one of his trademarks, and GL Pares and Jupp combined again to play a large part in taking the ball right up to the other end of the pitch where a Woolston defender was forced to concede a corner.

Back came Woolston, only for Norman Pares and Simpson to clear. Play continued to be fast on the heavy ground as the blue shirts bounced back again with Diplock and Plant in possession before Diplock sent a splendid shot just over the bar. Seddon, his captain, piled on the pressure straight away. He met a kick out from the Woolston defence with an instant centre which was well fisted out by the opposing keeper.

He was heartily cheered for his attempts, which capped a display of hard work and energy as the perfect example to his team. The cheers came next for the Woolston fans as they went one up. Give-and-take play followed and Portsmouth AFC went close to equalising many times in the frantic closing stages. On one of them, Pares centred to Huddy who nearly rushed the ball through the Woolston goal as it bounced narrowly over.

Of the Portsmouth AFC team, besides the praise for 'AC Smith', Diplock and Plant were said to have shown excellent combination, their first class passing attracting cheers from the spectators. GL Pares and Jupp showed excellent form, with Pares's dribbling being top quality and Huddy having no room for improvement in the centre left position.

Simpson and JH Smith worked energetically and did well but the Reverend Norman Pares and Stimpson were criticised for failing to play together as much as they might have done.

CHAPTER TWENTY-FOUR

So, that was Portsmouth AFC's hopes ended in the Hampshire Senior Cup for another season, and coming just two weeks after the second victory by Hilsea Ramblers in the Portsmouth Senior Cup, the latest defeat seemed the end of all their cup hopes. That was not to be the case, but the rest of the 1887/88 season was a period of faint promise.

Their first players received Hampshire representa-tive honours to bring the club wider recognition. But the campaign, for the most part, failed to live up to the expectations of those which had previously been enjoyed.

It had opened with high enough hopes as the annual meeting of the Portsmouth (Association Rules) Club, as it was called in the press, took place at the Albany Hotel, in Commercial Road, on September 15th 1887. The optimism seemed justified a month later when back Sergeant Peters and right-winger Huddy turned out for the Hampshire FA in their inaugural fixture.

Sometime Portsmouth AFC player GL Pares also turned out on the left-wing in the county's newly-chosen crimson and blue strip, with a badge which showed the white rose of Hampshire and a golden crown, although he was listed in the line-up as playing for Portsmouth Sunflowers.

Hampshire won the historic fixture with Sussex 2–1 at Oaklands Park in Chichester thanks to a late goal from centre forward William Pickford of Bournemouth Rovers. Two Woolston Works players were in the visiting team, with a further two from Winchester and one each from Royal Engineers, Ringwood Hornets, Andover and Banister Court in Southampton.

How the popularity of football had spread, yet Portsmouth AFC's fixture list failed to reflect the fact. They could only manage eighteen fixtures in 1887/88, including the numerous Portsmouth Senior Cup semi-finals and finals.

This compared to the twenty-six games of the previous season which gave the original Pompey the title of the busiest club in Hampshire.

HMS Marlborough *in use as a depot ship alongside HMS* Duke of Wellington *in Portsmouth Dockyard.*

The first of the games saw the club begin 1887/88 with a friendly against the same side as their last game: Portsmouth Grammar School at Hilsea. The school team succeeded in achieving a 4–4 draw in the curtain raiser on October 1st.

The season's opening goal was scored by the school before the town club went into a 2–1 lead by half time. The school soon levelled before some excellent play saw Portsmouth AFC take the lead again just two minutes from the end.

There was still long enough left, however, for the school to grab a further equaliser amid protests from their opponents. Despite the game's opening-day status, both teams were keen for more action. They agreed to play a further twenty minutes in which they each scored a further goal.

A pair of blank Saturdays followed before Portsmouth AFC were on the road. Horndean was the destination and a routing of the village side was the result. The visitors were four goals up after forty-five minutes and went on to win by 5–0. Even more remarkably, they fielded an under-strength side.

Those players who turned out were camped around the home team's goal in the opening period before Diplock kicked the opener. Further attacks brought three more goals, with a brace from Grant and another by Simpson. Horndean, in contrast, could make no headway.

The second half followed much the same pattern, though the town club could have notched up a higher score if stand-in forward Kavanagh had taken any of the chances which came his way. The game was all one-way traffic towards the home goal, though it took the visitors until just before the final whistle to register their fifth, and final goal, through Dickson.

The win was followed by the publication of Portsmouth AFC's first fixture card. It listed all of their notable backers to reflect the club's now established place among the naval port's civic elite. The president was the mayor-elect, Councillor Albert Addison, with the vice-presidents reading like a municipal *Who's Who* of many familiar names: Major General Sir F Fitzwygram Bart MP, Major General Sir W Crossman MP, Sir S Wilson MP, Admiral Sir F Willes, Lieutenant General Sir R Willis, Lieutenant General Harwood, P Vanderbyl, J Pares and Alderman E Kent, owner of their ground.

The committee also included Arthur Conan Doyle, the Reverend AW Plant, W Doyle, AJ Simpson, WE Grant and T Simson, who were all players. Their captain, EJ Seddon, was joined by S Diplock as his vice-captain. The treasurer was J McDonald and R Hemingsley was the secretary.

A grand total of twenty-nine games were detailed from the next Saturday against Hilsea Ramblers to March 24th when HMS *Marlborough* would be the opponents at the US Recreation Ground. But in a mystery worthy of Sherlock Holmes, who was soon to appear in print, the club effectively stopped operating after January, with the exception of the many cup games.

CHAPTER TWENTY-FIVE

The reason for the shortened season went unremarked in the newspaper columns. Its likely cause was a slowing of the club's momentum and the lack of a permanent home. October and

November showed no sign of the drought of games to come.

That was perhaps just as well if the antics in the next fixture were anything to go by. Hilsea Ramblers set the scene for the rowdy cup ties later on with a game that was one long argument from beginning to end.

The soldiers' rough play disabled two of the Portsmouth AFC team and, with the borough club's umpire unexpectedly absent, the Ramblers claimed a 3–1 win, with two of the goals being disputed.

Portsmouth AFC still managed to put the ball between the Ramblers' posts three times, only to have two of the goals ruled out. All that action was in the first half. The second period saw the civilians, according to the *Evening Mail*, make the most of their difficult circumstances:

> With their crippled players and for a team without the best services of their best forwards, Portsmouth AFC pinned the Ramblers down and, beside repeated shots at goal, achieved a number of corner kicks.

No matter. The big football news of the week was revealed in the *Portsmouth Evening News* on November 3rd 1887. It reported that the mighty Preston North End could be on their way to Portsmouth. The Lancastrian team were a season away from the first double in the inaugural season of the Football League and were among the pioneers of professionalism.

Their name alone, and the thought that they might be heading to the South Coast, was enough to excite the newspaper. The intriguing game was being lined up by the committee of the United Services FC 'with their customary enterprise', to quote the report, with the opponents being a strong South of England FC. Portsmouth AFC, the holders of the town's cup, were maybe not considered strong enough to take on the North End. The paper added:

> We are sure the inhabitants of Portsmouth will be much pleased of the opportunity thus afforded of seeing this celebrated club play, and we have no doubt that the match will be of great interest and will give immense impetus to football playing in this district. The date is not yet fixed but will probably be towards the latter part of this month.

Portsmouth AFC's players well and truly staked their claim for places to play the fabled visitors in a 5–1 rout of Hayling, three days after a 0–3 home defeat against Chichester. The town club pressed from the kick off and Grant soon opened the scoring against Hayling.

The islanders pulled level to end the first half on equal terms. That was the last time they were to be in the game. The change of ends gave the original Pompey the advantage of the wind and they dominated the second half. Glennie added to his good performance with some clever shot stopping in the opening forty-five minutes by coming to his team mates' rescue time after time in the visitors' goal after the break.

But Portsmouth AFC got the better of him on four occasions in the forty-five minutes. Two of the goals came from Grant. Diplock and Plant scored one each.

The *Portsmouth Evening News* was full of glowing praise for the scorers for their excellent form, with GL Pares and Jupp also being commended for

> ...playing in a dashing style. Also, the whole of the back division did exceedingly well, the captain in particular being conspicuous for his clean tackling and dashing pace.

Another week and another win followed. For the second game running, though, the borough club played at the Recreation Ground, probably the US Recreation Ground, rather than the Stubbington Lodge meadow which they had used for their first three seasons.

The change of venue made no difference to their fortunes as they swept aside the Royal Scots Greys 3–0 in one of two games at the ground that afternoon, the other being Southsea versus Victorias.

Portsmouth AFC again started slowly, though that was as much due to being a player short at the kick-off against a side with the wind behind them, as to any lack of warm-up. The Greys went straight on to the attack to take advantage of their good fortune at facing understrength opponents, only to find 'AC Smith' in goal and the rest of the blue shirted defence in excellent form. Half-time came and went with the teams, both now at full strength, locked together in a goalless draw. That soon changed.

Original Pompey forward Jupp put in a shot which completely baffled Hardy in the soldiers' goal to give the civilians the lead. They continued to attack and were rewarded when Armstrong netted their second goal. The final goal of the game arrived when Huddy headed home from the last of a series of corner kicks, faultlessly taken by Seddon.

'The game was keenly contested throughout,' said the *Portsmouth Evening News*. 'The pace and combination of the borough team gave them the advantage.'

The mini winning run was abruptly halted by the visit of Winchester on November 16th. Their 6–3 victory was Portsmouth AFC's third defeat of the season, in their seventh game. The town side showed six changes from the previous match but another slow start proved costly on this latest occasion.

According to the *Hampshire Telegraph*, Winchester scored three goals before the original Pompey replied. The *Portsmouth Evening News* put the early deficit at two goals but there could be no denying the fact that the home club were outplayed in the game's initial stages.

They struggled on in the second half but were unable to prevent Winchester inflicting their heaviest defeat in twenty-five months by the time the game ended in semi-darkness.

Portsmouth AFC resumed their successes by getting their defence of the Portsmouth Senior Cup off to a winning start against Petersfield before the Royal Irish Rifles were their next opponents at the Men's Recreation Ground in the final fixture of November, on the 26th. The game finished 2–2 to reflect its even play.

But the football news was again dominated by Preston North End, only this time it was bad news, ultimately. The *Hampshire Post* had opened the weekend by anticipating the Northerners' game

---

One of Britain's most distinguished footballing ambassadors took the chance 60 years on to pay tribute to the pioneering work begun by Dr Arthur Conan Doyle and his fellow enthusiasts in Portsmouth.

Sir Stanley Rous was the guest of honour at the diamond anniversary celebrations of the Portsmouth Football Association. Sir Stanley was at the time the secretary of the national FA and ten years away from becoming the president of football's international ruler, FIFA.

With the exception of Dr Doyle, he must have been the most distinguished person to hand over Portsmouth's very own football trophies, the Portsmouth Senior and Junior cups.

The winners for the anniversary season of 1950/51 were the Royal Ordnance Army Corps of Hilsea, in the senior cup appropriately given the military dominance of football's early years in the city, and Liss in the junior version.

Sir Stanley told the midweek anniversary night of May 31, 1951, he was delighted to be at the dinner:

An association such as this is the backbone of the game in this country. There is a lot of fear, discord and trouble in the world today but we are not worried in the world of sport. And it's meetings such as this which create the fellowship which we all strive for.

He praised the officials of the Portsmouth FA and reminded them that top calibre players such as Peter Harris and Reg Flewin had risen from its teams to join the professional ranks of Pompey and help to bring glory to that club.

JL Fleming, the Portsmouth FA's life vice-president, said local footballers appreciated the work of the city council in providing pitches. But Portsmouth was badly placed, he stressed, in that regard because the Navy and the Army had so much ground for their own uses. It was impossi

ble for the corporation to take full advantage of the possible sites.

His comments could have been made 60 years earlier at the association's inaugural meeting by the likes of Hemingsley or Kent as much as at its special get-together six decades later.

Similarly, the comments of the Lord Mayor, Alderman AE Johnson, could also have been transported from the 1890s. He told the celebratory dinner that the council had tried to make adequate provision for sport. 'They have not done all they wanted to do but I will make a promise,' he assured the officials, 'they are definitely going to do more.'

He joined Sir Stanley in presenting the trophies to the winners from the Portsmouth FA's seven leagues and various cups.

The council was as good as the mayor's promise. The Portsmouth FA's centenary handbook recalled how rapid progress was made in the 1950s with the development of playing facilities. Dressing rooms were improved at Southsea Common, Cosham and Baffins. Pitches were opened at Farlington in 1955 and consultation was carried out at the same time about new facilities as Cosham.

In 1958, Bransbury Park was restored from allotments to make the situation regarding the availability of pitches easier than at any time.

For Sir Stanley, the following years saw him rise to the top of world football for 13 years. He was elected as FIFA's sixth president in 1961. He was a referee in his youth and had written a version of the laws of the game in the 1930s which stood the test of time for nearly six decades.

His spell at the helm of FIFA saw its number of members grow as newly independent nations joined and television transmission increased football's influence. Sir Stanley was made FIFA's honorary president in June 1974. He was succeeded by the Brazilian, Dr Joao Havelange.

against the Swifts, scheduled for the following Wednesday, November 30th:

The lovers of football in Portsmouth are promised an association match of exceptional interest when the celebrated team of professionals known as Preston North End will meet the Swifts, the crack amateur club, on the US Ground. Special railway facilities are advertised.

But the news was bleak just three days later. The *Portsmouth Evening News* broke the story that the game had been called off:

Preston NE having telegraphed on Saturday they should be unable to keep their engagement owing to a cup tie commitment. Much disappointment has been expressed by football players at the match thus having fallen through.

Portsmouth AFC did their utmost to provide consolation for football fans in the town. They battled to their biggest win of the season with an 8–2 success against the Royal Engineers. A fair-sized crowd gathered at the US Men's Ground on December 3rd to witness the borough club at their best. The *Hampshire Telegraph* purred:

Portsmouth AFC were in first class form and their combination in the handling of the leather was all that could be desired.

They didn't have things all their own way, though, despite scoring the first goal after just ten minutes. The soldiers attacked and Glenny in the home goal was called upon to save the ball bravely a couple of times to preserve the original Pompey's lead.

His forwards then moved up a gear. They powered into a 4–1 half-time lead. The same score was repeated in the second forty-five minutes with GL Pares netting Portsmouth AFC's biggest individual haul of the season with five goals. Grant, with two more, and Huddy completed the scoring.

The mood was lightened even more for football fans with the news that Preston NE could be on their way to Portsmouth after all. The *Hampshire Telegraph* of December 7th stated:

The proposed visit by Preston NE players to Portsmouth has been fixed and the date selected is February 7th. It's not known at present, however, if the Swifts will undertake to compete with them.

The game failed to be played. No reason was given in the press. Next came the first of the Portsmouth

Senior Cup semi-finals against Hilsea Ramblers, followed by a Christmas Eve 1887 friendly with the Sunflowers. The original Pompey won 2–0 against a team which included their some-time team mates, the Reverend N Pares at back and Basil Pares at centre-forward.

Their presence, though, was unable to stop the borough club dominating the game and achieving the victory. That rounded off 1887 as far as football in Portsmouth was concerned. Cup ties aside, there was little action which involved Portsmouth AFC in the opening months of 1888.

CHAPTER TWENTY-SIX

The club's fixture card had boasted a plethora of games every week up until late March. Only one took place, according to the five local papers of the time. The absences were never explained.

The disappearing games could be accounted for by the absence of a club ground. All the original Pompey's 'home' games that season were played away from Stubbington Lodge meadow. Practically, this meant they used the variously named US grounds in the town centre. But a charge was made by their management committees for the hire of the facilities. Servicemen also had to be admitted free.

Neither aspect could have been appealing to a strictly amateur club, seemingly yet to attract more than a few hundred fans at each game.

The lone friendly of those barren months in early 1888 saw the US Men's Ground in use for the visit of Horndean on February 1st. The midweek game attracted 'a fair number of spectators', according to the match reports.

They left on that Wednesday afternoon having watched a 1–1 draw. Portsmouth AFC fought back after they went a goal down in the opening half in spite of twice going close to the Horndean goal. In both instances, the shots – the first by Seddon – were just too high.

Their equaliser arrived thanks to a disputed but allowed goal by Leader which followed a couple of well-directed shots by the home players and a corner.

The game served as a warm-up for the Hampshire Senior Cup semi-final the following Saturday. No such luxury was available for the original Pompey's players before their surprise appearance in the final of the Portsmouth Senior Cup.

Lack of games proved no barrier to success for two of Portsmouth AFC's team at the start of the year. Club captain Seddon and PO Ashby were selected for the Hampshire FA team to take on Surrey, at half-back and right-wing. The January 19th 1888 fixture at Winchester ended with the teams level on a goal each. Seddon definitely took part along with GL Pares, also of Portsmouth AFC. The other club player – on the right-wing – was named, possibly wrongly, as WJ Ramsey.

So, the 1887/88 season ended with a whimper for Portsmouth AFC, the Portsmouth Senior Cup eruptions aside, a long way from the promise of the opening weeks of the campaign.

It was the following June – of all times – in the middle of a long, long close season, that some hope was available in the club's need for a permanent base.

The prospect of action revolved around a petition of almost thirty yards, the wardens of Winchester College and a Victorian class war. All three were involved during a lengthy meeting between a deputation of Portsmouth ratepayers and the town mayor, Councillor Albert Addison. At issue was the creation of a North End recreation ground.

This was the land which Winchester College had agreed in 1886 to sell cheaply to Portsmouth Corporation on condition that it was used for a public recreation ground. The price was £500 an acre. But that was £500 too much for the councillors at the time.

They had failed to be persuaded otherwise by that near thirty-yard-long petition of supporters of the scheme. Charles Gillham, on behalf of the ratepayers, promised a repeat show of strength if the corporation needed any more persuading in favour of the purchase. The *Hampshire Telegraph* commented:

He did not know if it was desirable to get up another petition of that kind but, if it was necessary, it would be perfectly easy to do. As to the desirability of providing a place at the north end of the town for the purpose of recreation he thought there could be no question as there was no other suitable site and as the time which the corporation might secure it at a reasonable price had nearly expired, he was persuaded steps should be taken at once.

The deal to which he referred was shelved by the councillors and the college because of the corporation members' unwillingness to pay up. The college's officials had generously agreed to hold their offer and price for two years. Just three months remained when the ratepayers and the mayor got together in midsummer. That was long enough for the corporation to act for the people it represented, according to AW White, another member of the delegation:

At present, Portsmouth was without a recreation

ground where cricket, football and other sports could be indulged in by the working classes, a state of things which was somewhat unique in the history of the other great towns of the kingdom...

...he was quoted as saying by the *Hampshire Telegraph*.

He commented on the 'farce', in which Portsmouth AFC were an unwilling party, where sporting clubs had to go 'cap in hand' to the owner of a field or the authorities who ran the government recreation sites to ask permission to stage a match.

He also held out the prospect of a financial killing for the corporation if it took up the option offered by the college on the land. The site would be worth thirty, forty, even fifty per cent more within a short period if the government went ahead with its proposal to build naval barracks nearby.

Mayor Addison urged restraint on the gathering – there were seven ratepayers in all – at the municipal offices in Arundel Street. The 'somewhat strained condition' of the corporation's finances meant many members would question going ahead with the land purchase, he said.

His support for the scheme was tempered by his inability, under the corporation's regulations, to bring the matter to members' attention. But he advised the ratepayers to speak to their local councillors so that they knew all about the issue, or raise it again with another lengthy petition.

CHAPTER TWENTY-SEVEN

The season of 1888/89 arrived with Portsmouth AFC playing at the US Men's Ground and no public news about a recreation ground at North End. The club had begun the preparations for the new campaign by sending their own delegation to the first annual meeting of the Hampshire FA. Those present also included Cowes, Bournemouth, Winchester, Aldershot and Netley.

They were buoyed by the news that the original membership of fourteen, created when the FA broke away from the Hants and Dorset FA thirteen months previously, had doubled. To spur them on for the coming season, the Hampshire Senior Cup was loaned to the meeting by its holders and Portsmouth AFC's conquerors, Woolston Works, to allow the representatives to appreciate the handsome silver trophy, worth thirty guineas.

A slight deficit of £2 was reported in the association's accounts, though this failed to perturb the delegates and, if it was any consolation to the Portsmouth AFC representative, the Hampshire FA also had to pay to use a ground. In their case, the money was handed to Hampshire County Cricket Club for the hire of the county ground in Southampton.

No such money worries were reported at the Portsmouth FA meeting at the Albany Hotel on September 15th, which effectively launched 1888/89 in the town. The balance sheet was reported to be satisfactory and arrangements for the next Portsmouth Senior Cup were well in hand, the meeting was told. WE Grant, the association's honorary secretary, was ready to receive entries at St Jude's School in Southsea. The closing date was agreed as September 30th. The draw would take place three days later.

Positive news was also on offer at Southsea FC's annual meeting the day after the Portsmouth FA's gathering. The club was said to be playing twenty-four matches in the months to come. Curiously, none were against their borough rivals who kicked off their season by fielding a scratch side to face the United Services on October 6th.

Only six of the players who wore the blue shirt belonged to the club for a fixture which had more significance for the newly-formed opposition. US were making their debut and eased their way to a 2–1 win over the borough team of strangers.

From the form shown throughout by the US, the new club seems capable of giving a good account of itself in the coming season...

...in the *Portsmouth Evening News'* opinion. That said, it was Portsmouth AFC who scored the season's first goal. A Seddon brother, one of the few

regulars on display, crossed from the right following some good passing and Sweetenham sent the ball easily between the uprights with a well-judged kick from the right of the goal.

The strike was against the run of play. The US team equalised before half-time and went on to add the winner in the second half. But the military team were to inflict worse on the original Pompey as the remarks of the match correspondent acquired a prophetic feel just a month later.

The new boys inflicted the most painful defeat Portsmouth AFC had suffered to date. November 3rd was the day and the US Men's Ground the venue for the borough club's first defeat in 'their' cup, the Portsmouth Senior Cup. The club had been defeated before in the competition – most notoriously by Hilsea Ramblers at the start of the year – but the setbacks had always proved temporary.

There was no way back after the decisive three goal mauling at the hands of the US Men's team. Nor did the civilians attempt to find one.

They were poor and deserved to be beaten. The cup triumphs of the previous two seasons, involving a total of eleven games, counted for nothing because of a listless display.

No words were minced by the *Hampshire Post* in its account of the debacle:

Portsmouth AFC's play was very erratic and uncertain, much inferior to that which we have been accustomed to expect from the premier club.

The *Evening Mail* was similarly dismissive:

The Portsmouth FA representive side in 2003.

Portsmouth AFC had only two attempts on goal and both failed...

...it reported contemptuously.

For the *Portsmouth Evening News*, the display by 'AC Smith' at full back was the only plus point of his side's capitulation:

Smith's prompt actions alone kept Services from gaining further.

The military men were just a goal ahead by half time but they had dominated the opening forty-five minutes. They confirmed their victory with two further goals, though the tempo of the game was viewed differently by those watching for the *Portsmouth Evening News* and the *Hampshire Post*.

The former's man at the match was positive in his opinion:

During the second half, the ball was taken up and down the pitch at a furious rate and some fine play witnessed US score two more goals.
Portsmouth AFC's forwards played hard in their endeavour to avoid defeat, Diplock, Smith and FJ Seddon especially distinguishing themselves, but the backs were extremely weak.

Disgruntlement, however, was the feeling of his rival from the *Hampshire Post*. The ground was heavy, the defence of the US team was weak and the general character of play was a disappointment, in his opinion:

Play was very slow after the kick-off. There was little or no energy exhibited and both sides lacked the smartness which alone makes association football interesting.
After half-time, play brightened up a little but at no time were the town men very dangerous.

Portsmouth Grammar School, incidentally, won their first round tie in the cup, 3–2 over Freemantle.

But much better was to come for the borough club, including a goal glut unique in Victorian football in Portsmouth. The 15–0 drubbing of perennial victims Hayling Island was remarkably achieved with only a ten-man team.

The goals flowed for Portsmouth AFC every four minutes on average – and their overrun opponents could do nothing to stem the tide. The rout took place on January 12th 1889 at Hilsea, and Hayling might as well have stayed on their island for all the impact they had on the game.

The *Portsmouth Evening News* kept its comment on the stunning victory succinct to the point of abruptness:

Portsmouth AFC played with one man short but Hayling were quite unable to cope with the passing and dribbling of the borough club.

The reporter at the game dubbed the winning team a moderate one. If that was the case, its undoubted stars were the Seddon family. FJ Seddon led with one of the match's two hat tricks and his siblings, E Seddon and GF Seddon, weighed in with a goal apiece.

In all, the goals were shared around a remarkable eight of the town club's nine outfield players. Never again did that feat ever come close to being equalled.

Only in one other game that season did a Portsmouth AFC player even achieve a hat trick when Wood repeated the feat which had made him the other triple scorer against Hayling.

His second multiple strike came in his side's second biggest win of a campaign drastically shortened by their Portsmouth Senior Cup exit. Six goals to nil in their favour was the scoreline over Fareham as Christmas approached.

Yet again, with a substantial victory by the borough club, very few details were reported in the press. The most words were managed by the *Portsmouth Evening News*:

The Fareham team, many of them second XI players, exerted themselves a great deal but the result proves they were overmatched.

Prominent footballer and official AH Wood who regularly turned out for the original Pompey.

The result was the reverse of the worst game of 1888/89 for the original Pompey in a fixture intended to start their competitive season, except that the team didn't compete when the Royal Engineers journeyed from Chatham on October 13th to take them on at the US Recreation Ground.

Blunt talking was the style of the *Evening Mail* journalist at the season opener. 'A crushing defeat for Portsmouth AFC' summed up his view. The other match reports were more complimentary, just. The *Hampshire Telegraph* blamed the defeat on the original Pompey's lack of combination, the good displays of which had been such a prominent feature of the previous season's play:

> *The visitors, who have some particularly fast wingmen, had matters all their own way.*
>
> *Diplock made some good shots at goal, EH Seddon, Edmonds, Grant and Johnson were conspicuous for their plucky runs. Doctor Doyle also put in some good fine long emergency kicks.*

Note the last name. No longer was the alias of 'AC Smith' used to cloak in anonymity the medical man and author's participation in the game. Perhaps it was his team mates who needed the disguise. Played two, lost two was the tally of their new season when the Hampshire FA team played their first game.

One of the Pares brothers and Prinsep ensured Portsmouth AFC were represented in the goalless draw with Sussex. Prinsep, again, and GL Pares also earned a cap on either wing, along with FJ Seddon at half-back, for the next fixture against Surrey.

Left-winger Prinsep helped to set up the Hants goal by Pickford in a further draw, 1–1 on that occasion.

United Services once more were the opponents for the town club's third game of 1888/89. At least this was drawn, to provide some relief to the gloom of the opening weeks. For the second time in three weeks, Portsmouth AFC took the lead against their service opponents but failed to stay in front. There were signs, though, that the blue-shirted players were rediscovering their ability to work well together.

Winning ways indeed returned a week later with a 2–0 victory against another military outfit, the South Yorkshire Regiment. Making a reappearance as well was the pseudonym, 'AC Smith'. That was far from being the most remarkable aspect of the game. That distinction fell to the side's keeper, Sweetenham, who scored their first goal. How or why was never explained. His effort passed without comment, unlike the state of the ground: slippery – and the weather: raining.

Plant secured the game for the original Pompey in

the second half, with honourable mentions in the match reports for FJ Seddon, 'AC Smith', Jupp, JH Smith and GF Seddon. The midweek fixture falsely buoyed up the club's hopes with an unprecedented three game losing streak about to start with that devastating Portsmouth Senior Cup defeat. Morale must have dropped severely after that setback.

Not only did the team suffer that trio of consecutive defeats, they also failed to score in any of them. Just ten men, apparently, trudged on to Havant recreation ground a fortnight after the cup horror show. They were second best throughout in the no contest of a mismatch with the home side. The *Evening Mail* was unimpressed by the visitors' display:

> *Portsmouth AFC were hard pressed to start with. After Havant scored, they played with more speed. In the second half, Portsmouth AFC tried harder to score, Diplock having a good shot saved by Agate. EF Pares and W Grant were the best Portsmouth AFC players.*

The agony for the Portsmouth side was continued, doubtless with relish, by a Portsmouth Grammar School side eager to gain revenge for previous defeats. That they did to ensure the original Pompey ended a downbeat November on an even more despondent note. The school team were simply all over their rivals in the early stages.

They scored three times in the first half, only to see two of the efforts disallowed. Another 'goal', luckily for Portsmouth AFC, was ruled out because of a misunderstanding by an umpire.

Portsmouth AFC had the wind in their favour after the interval and tried hard, but failed to score. Even the presence of such footballers as the Reverend Plant and GL Pares brought them no joy.

CHAPTER TWENTY-EIGHT

That made it 270 minutes without a goal and counting for the original Pompey to create an air of depression around the club. Their J McDonald chaired the Portsmouth FA meeting at the end of the month at which the second round draw for the Portsmouth Senior Club was made. It was the closest his club got to the later stages of the competition that season.

Another twenty minutes of goalless action had to be endured by him and his colleagues and their fans before their drought was broken to end a spell when going a goal up seemed as elusive as a cup success.

Eventually, some good luck went their way and on December 8th against Petersfield they made the most of it. One of their opposing backs in the Petersfield team, Armstrong, mistakenly paved the way for the elusive opener. He had kept the borough team at bay during a constant siege of his team's goal during the game's opening stages.

Cruelly, he slipped to allow Grant to shoot home for the original Pompey. Few spectators were present to share the moment because of a persistent downpour, the reason no doubt for Armstrong's error on a greasy pitch.

Petersfield proved capable of making a contest of the game with an equaliser, before one of the two Seddon brothers in the Portsmouth AFC side – FJ Seddon – gave the club a half-time lead. Back came the visitors again with a seventy-fifth minute goal and the game seemed to heading for a draw. Grant settled matters with his second goal with just five minutes left to secure a hard-fought victory.

The referee blew the final whistle early to take account of the deteriorating pitch as the rain made conditions poor, but Portsmouth AFC's ten men were pleased for the respite after they had battled against their full strength opponents.

It seemed a bizarre recipe for success – playing a man short in a shortened game – but the result set the team off on an eight match unbeaten run. On and on it went into 1889 to become the club's third best sequence of results to date.

Winchester followed five days later and were defeated 2–0.

Next to fall victim to the original Pompey's surge of form as their season gathered momentum were Fareham, with their mainly second XI team no contest for the more experienced borough men.

Portsmouth AFC were back at the US Men's Ground three days later on December 22. The game with United Services was notable for being one of three matches reported in the fifth edition of that day's *Portsmouth Evening News*, although with only twenty words, in an early version of the still-continuing *Sports Mail*.

Play on the pitch failed to live up even to that brief mention, with slippery conditions ruining either sides' chances of playing well. They slithered to a 0–0 draw. For Portsmouth AFC, Prinsep, Grant, FJ Seddon and GL Pares were credited with putting in some good work.

Borough rivals Portsmouth Sunflowers were the original Pompey's next victims, as 1889 opened with a derby match on January 2nd on Governor's Green. An unnamed player, described only as 'a forward', scored the precious goal which separated the sides. It arrived in the second half and followed a superb run along the right-wing by the brothers Seddon and a pass into the goalmouth.

Portsmouth AFC went in front after they had

survived a sustained bout of Sunflowers' pressure in the first half. Only some good defending kept the Sunflowers at bay. The original Pompey were livelier after half-time and repelled their opponents' attempts to equalise.

The *Portsmouth Times* was clear where the praise should be placed for the hard-fought victory:

Grant and Seddon tackled their forwards before they were within shooting distance. Smith and Hampton played a good defensive game at back and Durell preserved his goal well.

Joy at the success was dulled by the disappointment of the news that Woolston Works had pulled out of their scheduled game with the borough club four days later with a keen and exciting contest in prospect. Regardless of that withdrawal, Portsmouth AFC continued to improve as they opened their Hampshire Senior Cup bid with a four-goal away win over King's Royal Rifles.

GL Pares was the hat-trick hero on that occasion in the second round after the town club had received a bye in the opening stage.

The Reverend Plant opened the scoring on fifteen minutes after a neat pass from Prinsep before Pares shot home ten minutes later. He put his side further ahead from a splendid run after he had been set up by another good pass by Prinsep.

The number nine rounded off the scoring in the second half. Defensively, 'AC Smith' took the honours in the opening forty-five minutes. His long kicks helped to relieve the pressure of the soldiers' attacks. One of the Seddons, probably FJ, was the defensive star after the break, though following the fourth goal, Portsmouth AFC dominated the game. Only their erratic form stopped them from scoring more.

The *Evening Mail* was delighted nevertheless with the side's performance at Aldershot:

The winners showed much better combination than in any previous game this season. All the forwards played a good passing game with Prinsep and Pares doing excellent work with Plant, while the brothers Seddon did well on the right. The long kicking of Hampton and 'AC Smith' was most serviceable.

Durell had an easy time in goal, the paper added. It was his fourth outing in the five matches in which Portsmouth AFC had maintained a cast-iron defence against their opponents. Their remarkable record continued the next week when Hayling Island were overrun in that fifteen-goal landslide.

The onslaught meant some 450 minutes – or more

A. Brook, forwards. Southsea: Pratt, back; Andrews, Mason, and R. Way, three-quarter backs; Whitmey and Davison, half-backs; Allan, Gibbs, Shaw, Pearson, Slade, Woodhouse, Miall, T. Way, and Hicks, forwards.

HAMPSHIRE ASSOCIATION CLUB AVERAGES.—Subjoined are the averages of the clubs named below up to date:—

	Matches.				Goals.		
	Played.	Won.	Lost.	Drawn.	For.	Against.	Average.
Portsmouth Sunflowers I	2	2	0	0	13	1	13
Royal Engineers	16	12	2	2	87	10	8·7
Christchurch Star	7	0	1	0	24	3	8
Portsmouth Sunflowers II	2	2	0	0	13	2	6·5
Cowes I	13	10	2	1	68	13	5·23
Geneva Cross	9	4	1	4	12	3	4
St. Luke's Harriers	9	7	2	0	39	9	4
Fordingbridge Turks	10	8	0	2	34	9	3·77
Fordingbridge Pirates	5	4	1	0	15	4	3·75
Christchurch	10	6	0	4	39	11	3·54
Totton	9	7	2	0	57	21	2·71
Portsmouth Y.M.C.A.	10	7	2	1	48	20	2·4
Bournemouth Arabs II	11	7	2	2	31	14	2·21
Freemantle I	12	5	2	5	26	12	2·16
Portsmouth F.A.	9	5	3	1	17	8	2·12
Fareham II	4	3	1	0	15	9	1·66
Hampshire Senior F.A.	3	1	0	2	3	2	1·5
Cowes II	9	4	2	3	12	12	1·5
Bournemouth Dean Park I	9	4	3	2	21	14	1·5
Winchester I	9	3	2	4	16	12	1·33
Winchester Rovers	8	4	4	0	19	15	1·2
Freemantle II	5	1	1	3	12	10	1·20
Dean Park II	9	4	5	0	30	26	1·15
Lymington	12	7	4	1	27	26	1·5
Winchester II	3	2	1	0	8	8	1
Ringwood Hornets	8	4	4	0	18	18	1
Bournemouth Albion	11	5	5	1	20	20	1
Bournemouth Arabs I	12	3	7	2	22	23	·95
Havant	12	4	4	4	18	22	·81
Hampshire Junior F.A.	1	0	1	0	1	2	·5
Christchurch School	7	2	3	2	11	23	·47
Fareham I	14	5	10	0	19	48	·39
Southampton Artillery Vol	10	1	7	2	6	43	·41

Golf.

UNITED SERVICE GOLF CLUB.—The monthly competition for the Davies Gold Medal...

Portsmouth AFC were 15th in this round-up of 33 Hampshire clubs' 1888/89 performances to January 12, 1889, as listed in the Hampshire Telegraph.

than seven and a half hours – had passed since the town club had last conceded a goal. A further seventy or so minutes went by before an original Pompey keeper had to collect the ball from behind his goal in a complete reversal of their fortunes earlier in the season.

Shutte was the unlucky player, after a free kick. Even then, the goal was allowed by the referee only after he had overruled the umpires' refusal to grant the score. But Shutte's team-mates had already gone three goals up by then against Fareham.

Just a month had passed since Portsmouth AFC had put six past Fareham. The re-match was a more even contest but they still ended it as comfortable winners. They survived the encounter better than the ball, which burst in the second half and had to be replaced.

The leather had been hit with some force by E Seddon who sent in a long shot from a touchline which the Fareham keeper was unable to save. The blockbuster goal followed Lovell's opener from a scrum in front of the home goal.

Portsmouth AFC had all the play before half time and went further ahead midway through the second half as E Seddon's good run up the right-wing and splendid centre enabled Ozzard to notch up the third goal.

The winners' good form was built upon their threatening raids along both wings. The Seddon brothers made several good forays along the right-hand side while Ozzard and Eynott kept the Fareham backs busy on the opposite flank, but the home side began to make some determined attacks on Portsmouth AFC's goal in spite of being three goals down, leading to their lone reply.

CHAPTER TWENTY-NINE

All good things have to come to an end, and for the first time since late November, the original Pompey tasted defeat on January 26th 1889. The Yorkshire Regiment were the victors who ruined that proud run, with a single goal ten minutes before half time.

The match was keenly contested and one goal was always likely to be enough to settle the matter. Early attacks by the original Pompey had come to nothing before both sides settled down to displays of commitment and judgment.

According to the *Evening Mail*, the result failed to do Portsmouth AFC justice:

They all worked with energy and deserved a better reward.

February quickly saw a return to winning ways as the YMCA were sent packing 3–1 even though the match reports detailed a poor performance by the town club. The *Portsmouth Evening News* was curt in its assessment of the display:

Portsmouth AFC played very much out of their usual form, individually and as a team. Play was chiefly in the centre (of the pitch) and YMCA's half but the forwards occasionally broke away.

Enough times, anyway, for Wood, Basil Pares and GF Seddon to grab a goal each. The YMCA keeper also saved his side on several occasions in what appeared to be the original Pompey's only game of the season at their former home in Stubbington Avenue at North End.

The result, if not the out-of-sorts display, was the perfect preparation for the Hampshire Senior Cup semi-final. Portsmouth Grammar School were the opponents. A highly-charged game was in prospect after the Portsmouth Senior Cup escapades of the previous season.

The game's importance can be gauged by the appearance of pre-match reports in the *Evening Mail* and the *Portsmouth Evening News*. They both predicted that the school were the favourites because of their fine form – as if the recent eight game unbeaten run by Portsmouth AFC counted for nothing.

The forecast was also in apparent defiance of the achievement of the borough club in reaching their third Hampshire Senior Cup semi-final in a row. The previous two games had ended in defeats: 1–3 versus Wimborne and 0–1 against Woolston. Maybe that track record led the reporters to write off Portsmouth AFC's chances.

But it was third time lucky for the borough club. They played their way to a 2–0 victory at the US Men's Ground in front of a mass of enthusiastic supporters who lined the ropes around the pitch. Most of the crowd were fans of the nearby grammar school, which seemed to have had the day off.

They had every hope of revenge for the previous year's Portsmouth Senior Cup debacle when half time arrived with the tie scoreless on the cold and frosty afternoon of February 23rd 1889.

Their optimism was dealt a blow on the hour. FJ Seddon latched on to a tremendous kick out of defence by Bernard Pares and scored. 'There was the wildest enthusiasm,' noted the *Portsmouth Evening News*, 'and the Portsmouth AFC goalkeeper attempted the difficult feat of standing on his head'.

The school team played with almost frantic energy in an attempt to draw level but GL Pares put the result beyond doubt with the second goal of the semi-final after a tough struggle in the centre of the pitch. But it was full back Conan Doyle – who had thrown off his pre-match alias of 'AC Smith' – who laid the foundation for the historic win.

He repulsed the grammar school's attacks when they replied to the original Pompey's opening rallies. He also saved a seemingly certain goal as the school poured forward after half-time by relieving the pressure with a tremendous kick.

Two days later, and the details of the final were confirmed. Portsmouth AFC would be facing the Royal Engineers (Aldershot) at the County Ground, also called Banister's Park, at Southampton the following Saturday.

The rush to complete the competition ruled out any sustained build-up to what could be seen as the biggest of games for the original Pompey. The team left Portsmouth on the 12.15pm Southampton train on match day, which meant a tight timetable for the 3.15pm kick off.

Several thousand spectators filled the ground on March 2nd as Portsmouth AFC stepped out into the unknown – and were torn to shreds. The optimism, the good form, the resolute defence of recent months vanished as they slumped to a 1–5 defeat.

CHAPTER THIRTY

The omens looked bad when the blue-shirted players lined up one short at the kick off. Matters got worse. The team had to play without right-winger GF Short until half time, when a substitute could be found. Nevertheless they began brightly.

Centre-forward GL Pares sent in a stinging shot which cleared the Engineers' crosstape by an inch after a good dribble. But that was all as far as his side's attacking initial credentials were concerned. The *Evening Mail* was awestruck by their opponents:

Portsmouth AFC showed sprightly combination but the RE had greater staying power. They played at a pace which was astonishing.

Conan Doyle held them off for a while, in a repeat of his semi-final heroics, with his telling kicks. The Royal Engineers were not to be denied, however. A fast, low shot by their centre-forward, A Grey, put them ahead after fifteen minutes. Mellis, a right-winger, soon added a second. And before the town club could gather their breath they were a further goal behind. Mellis was again the scorer, with a header. That remained the half-time score as:

Royal Engineers displayed some questionable tactics which evoked the displeasure of the spectators...

...according to the *Evening Mail*.

There was no doubting Kilbourn's skill, however, as the back deprived GL Pares of the ball as he was about to shoot following a fine run down the centre of the pitch. The second half saw right-winger F Smith put the Engineers further ahead as the game lurched more towards being a one-sided affair.

Portsmouth AFC became disheartened. They struggled to cope with the fast play of the army side. The *Evening Mail* lamented:

Pares failed to save what looked like several easy shots.

They did manage to piece together some attacks when GF Seddon, GL Pares and Prinsep sent in some fine shots only to see them saved by Breeze. RE, not satisfied with a four goal lead, hit back. Gray rounded off a fine run with goal number five. As the military team prepared to celebrate their emphatic win, GL Pares sent in a magnificent shot in the last minute for a consolation effort for the original Pompey. They had been awarded a free-kick for a foul just off the goal-line. The kick led to a goal-mouth scramble from which Pares scored.

In some circumstances, eighty-ninth minute goals are memorable and a cause for celebration. Not that one in the Hampshire Senior Cup Final. Referee CC Wooldridge, from Winchester, blew the final whistle and all that was left for the afternoon, which must have been getting dark by then, was the cup presentation by the Hampshire Challenge Cup committee secretary, Dr R Bencraft. Portsmouth AFC were congratulated for the plucky fight, as if that was any consolation.

GL Pares had a duty to perform after the match. He chaired a Hampshire FA meeting at the County Ground to decide the details of the Hampshire Junior Cup final the week after, on March 10th 1889.

CHAPTER THIRTY-ONE

The defeat effectively spelt the end of the club's season. Another three games were played. All were lost as the campaign fizzled out. A first fixture with Stubbington House School opened that run of defeats the Saturday following the final loss.

Portsmouth AFC travelled to the school only to receive a 1–2 defeat for their troubles. The scoreline got worse seven days later in another away match – at Havant's athletic sports meadow. The original Pompey turned up with less than a full team, again, and had to rely on substitutes to fill the gaps.

They somehow went a goal up after just three minutes through the previously unknown right-winger Freestone, who could have been one of the replacements. Havant soon equalised, went ahead before the end of the first half and scored a third goal later on. Portsmouth AFC's season might have been falling apart, but for one of the Pares brothers it got a lot better on March 23rd.

The unidentified member of the footballing family scored the only goal of Hampshire FA's win against Dorset with a brilliant shot fifteen minutes from time. Meanwhile, the town club could only look on at the end of March as Geneva Cross of Netley made a raid on the Portsmouth Senior Cup with a 1–0 victory over Portsmouth Grammar School. That was the second tournament of 1888/89 in which Geneva Cross had reached the final.

Portsmouth AFC also had reason to rue them on the occasion of their first triumph. It occurred in the second Hampshire FA six-a-side tournament which

was reported in the *Evening Mail* of January 2nd. The original Pompey were in the middle of their finest form of the season and powered their way through to the semi-final of the event at Winchester.

They brushed aside a weak and late arriving Banister Court in the first round by two goals and one corner to nil. The second round saw Portsmouth AFC pile up the day's biggest score with a 21 points success of five goals and a corner against Bournemouth Dean Park. GL Pares and Prinsep grabbed a brace of goals apiece and E Seddon completed the scoring. The form led the *Evening Mail* to crow:

After these two matches, Portsmouth AFC were installed as the favourites and everyone agreed they were the finest team on the ground.

Pares and Prinsep were very skilful and tricky and E Seddon, the best of the 'crack' halves, showed that he knew the way to dribble and shoot.

FJ Seddon was in demon form at half-back and Grant was both safe and smart.

Next came a third convincing win. The Southampton side of St Luke's Harriers was overcome by four goals and a corner to nil.

But the semi-finals pitched Portsmouth AFC against Geneva Cross. It was a game full of controversy. The Netley side soon went two goals clear but Seddon immediately pulled a goal back and Portsmouth AFC piled forward to obtain a corner and level the game.

A fierce struggle between the two sides developed in the second half. Tempers rose as a fine shot by Prinsep was disallowed as a goal after an appeal by the opposing keeper. A further 'goal' by Prinsep was also ruled out, for offside that time, while a long and lucky shot by the Netley side's back Howarth sealed matters by beating Shutte.

Geneva Cross failed to take advantage of their good fortune when they crashed 10–5 to the home side, Winchester, in the final. The *Evening Mail* was unconvinced of the merits of the eventual winners:

Winchester, as the home team, scored a popular victory but they were not as popular as Portsmouth AFC would have been and in accord with the feelings of most of those present.

But, for all the excitement of the competition, and Portsmouth AFC's achievements in reaching the semi-final, with a Hampshire Senior Cup final as well, the outcome of 1888/89 could not disguise the club's inability to make progress.

Elsewhere in the country, Preston North End had

just won the inaugural Football League championship for which Aston Villa, Blackburn Rovers and Wolverhampton Wanderers had also competed. So great was the enthusiasm for the competition that a rival league – the Northern Alliance – was formed and soon became the league's second division.

Preston NE had also won the FA Cup, soon to reach its twentieth staging, and the Scottish League was about to start further north. Divers innovations such as goal nets and penalties were also on the way as the game entered the modern era.

Off the pitch, Burnley had become established at Turf Moor, Sheffield United were opening Bramall Lane and Blackburn were about to move into Ewood Park. And Portsmouth AFC?

They were virtually homeless and often began games with less than eleven players. They relied on an Alderman's generosity to play their home games with the only alternative being paying to use a military ground. Their opponents were as far removed from the newly professional era as possible. The Havant athletic sports meadow hardly had the same inspiring ring as Villa Park.

Even Portsmouth AFC's triumphs were parochial, with the Hampshire Senior Cup being out of reach. The original Pompey were falling further and further behind the leaders of the game.

Optimism about the club's prospects was expressed, though, by the *Hampshire Telegraph* as it reviewed the local 1888/89 season:

One has only to look back a few years or so and the comparatively few matches which were then arranged with the series of contests brought off this season to be convinced of the growth of the popular feeling in winter games favoured both from the players' and supporters' points of view.

Rugby and association have vied with each other almost weekly in affording to hundreds of brief diversions, particularly on Saturday afternoons.

Portsmouth AFC were mentioned as one of the prime movers in the growth of organised sport along with Portsmouth Grammar School, the Post Office, the United Services and Southsea. The paper also pointed to the numerous improvements at the US Men's Ground as proof that organised sport was on the up in Portsmouth:

The cricket pavilion has been enclosed with ornamental railing, similar to that on the Officer's Ground, and tar paving has been laid inside the rails but it would be a further improvement if the committee could see their way to laying paving outside the railing as well, as far as the end of the turf.

Fine words but they were unable to stop Portsmouth AFC falling to yet another defeat at the hands of a well-organised military team in a six-a-side tournament at the County Ground at Southampton in mid-April of 1889. They went out in the third round to the King's Royal Rifles after a 9-0 win over Winchester A in the previous round and a bye in the opening round among the twenty-eight entrants.

The competition was won by the St Mary's B team against the club's A side in another sign of the times. St Mary's had become a limited company two years earlier with the increasingly organised football set-up in Southampton contrasting with the totally amateur Portsmouth AFC. The red-and-white team along the Solent were also just five years away from turning professional.

PORTSMOUTH AFC CUP TIES
1888/89

Portsmouth Senior Cup

R1	US Men's Team	USMG	LO-3	03.11.88

Hampshire Senior Cup

R1	Portsmouth Sunflowers	h		
	No record of match being played before November 30 deadline			
R2	King's Royal Rifles	Aldershot	W4-0	08.01.89
S-f	Portsmouth Grammar School	USMG	W2-0	23.02.89
F	Royal Engineers (Aldershot)	Country Gd. S'hampton	L1-5	02.03.89

Finalists

CHAPTER THIRTY-TWO

A glimmer of hope for Portsmouth AFC arrived in the *Hampshire Telegraph* of May 4th with a report that work would begin the following week on the levelling and laying out of the new recreation ground at Stamshaw. Tenders were sent out by the town council for the work to be done as soon as permission had been received for the scheme from the government.

In March, the paper had been bemoaning the lack of action of the Local Government Board in allowing the council to borrow the money for the project. Months had passed since a government inspector had given the go-ahead. The paper despaired that the work would get under way quickly enough:

...so that the local football players may at least have home and habitation in the coming winter.

At last, those hopes were being fulfilled. And the price of doing so? £1665.13s.8d was the tender for the work by TP Hall which was accepted by the councillors as the lowest of the six submitted by £151.4s.

The issue of a ground was one of the main matters at the Portsmouth FA's annual meeting on September 12th which heralded the start of the 1889/90 season. The gathering at the Albany Hotel agreed:

...the thanks of the association are due to the committee of the US Cricket Club for kindly assisting them to carry out their fixtures by placing their grounds at the disposal of the association for the semi-final and final matches.

The meeting was the third annual report of the association and its members, according to the *Hampshire Telegraph*, were told about the success of the previous year. Ten clubs had competed for the Portsmouth Senior Cup and it was hoped that every football club in Portsmouth would take part in the competition in the coming season.

There was a fee involved, of course, and the 5 shillings had to be sent to the association's secretary, WE Grant.

Even greater optimism for the months ahead was evident from the Hampshire FA. With the first games of the new season a week away, the association revealed its increasing strength:

The Hampshire FA anticipate a successful season, [the *Hampshire Telegraph* stated]. *It now has more than fifty clubs under its control. In 1886, nine clubs played football. Last year, thirty-four entered competitions. This year, the number will be almost double that. These figures indicate the rapid strides the game is making, which is particularly the case in Southampton and Portsmouth.*

The number of clubs under the county FA's control entitled it to send a representative to the Football Council, presumably part of the national FA, in a further reflection of Hampshire's growing influence in the sport.

Teams had been formed in Winchester and Bournemouth but there was sad news of Portsmouth AFC's old adversaries at Woolston Works. The club had ceased to exist, without a reason being given. They reformed in later years. The original Pompey, meanwhile, received a bye in the Hampshire Senior Cup first round to give them the best possible start in their bid to go one better than their losing finalists' role of a few months earlier.

Four of their players were also picked for the Hampshire FA team versus Surrey: half-back FJ Seddon, who was at the annual meeting, GL Pares (right-wing), Lieutenant Loring (left-wing) and FC Prinsep (left-wing).

But Portsmouth's footballers could be forgiven for feeling jealous of the progress being made by those involved in the rival code of football in the town. To glimpse how matters should be done, they had only to look at the local rugby union club just down the road from their Stubbington Avenue meadow.

No mention of any sporting progress off the field was complete in Portsmouth's papers without a moan at the authorities at the US grounds. As the *Hampshire Telegraph* of October 5th 1889 stated:

Those interested in football will learn with pleasure that Portsmouth Rugby Club have succeeded in securing, chiefly through the kindness of Arthur Brickwood, a ground of its own which will render it independent of the obnoxious terms under which it had played on a certain other ground in the borough.

A meadow, in every way suitable for the purpose, has been secured on London Road, just beyond North End, and is being laid out by Messrs Carter and Co of Cosham, who will have completed their work by the 19th, when the opening match will be played with the Trojans of Southampton. It may be mentioned that this is the first private local club in Portsmouth that has acquired a ground of its own.

Both rugby and football were to feature in another major innovation for sport in Portsmouth to reflect the growing strides that recreational pursuits were making in the Victorian era. They were to be given a paper of their own.

CHAPTER THIRTY-THREE

The football special edition of the *Portsmouth Evening News* made its debut on October 12th 1889. Its birth was revealed in the editions of the previous day:

As from Saturday next a special football edition of the Evening News will be published at 8 pm every Saturday evening and in addition to local matches it will contain the results of all the chief contests throughout the country.

These forty words were the official announcement of the new venture, though the editor thought more needed to be said elsewhere in his publication:

To meet the current demand for prompt information, we have determined as announced in the notice inserted above to issue each Saturday evening a special edition about 8 pm with all the principal matches played throughout the kingdom the same afternoon. Captains of local clubs will kindly understand that we shall be glad to receive results from games the same evening of all matches at which our own reporters are not able to be present, the ground at times being too extensive for our newspaper staff to cover.

On the day itself, the *Portsmouth Evening News'* 5 pm edition made a plea on page three for the co-operation of local clubs if the initiative was to fulfil its potential:

Our special edition at about 8 pm tonight will contain all the latest results of the afternoon's matches. Club officials must forward their details as early as possible after the termination of the contests in which they may be engaged. This will greatly assist us and add to the completeness of the match list.

That earlier version of the paper managed to contain some match reports. Among them were details of Hampshire FA's defeat against Sussex at Chichester. As previously noted four players from Portsmouth AFC provided the club's biggest contingent in the

Doyle Close is suitably close to Alderman Kent's meadow where the first Portsmouth team - Dr Arthur Conan Doyle included - played their initial games.

county side.

No copies of the first football edition have survived and anyway the original Pompey were sitting out the Saturday, the second of the season. Their first game made it on to page three of the following Saturday's Football Special. What better way to celebrate their inclusion than with a 4–1 victory? That historic report began:

Portsmouth AFC kept the ball in YMCA's half for the first fifteen minutes. The pressure paid off when Watts scored a sound goal and Drew added a second a few minutes later after a fierce struggle in front of the YMCA goal. After thirty minutes, Edmonds sought a chance to add a third goal but was ruled offside.

The second half contained more of the same. Prinsep scored after another goalmouth scramble. Drew added his second of the game to put the original Pompey further ahead. He latched on to a ball out from the YMCA defence and immediately sent it back with a long straight shot.

The game at Alderman Kent's farm at North End, a long way in ambition though not distance from the rugby club's new home, was also covered by the *Evening Mail*. Its journalist noted how the home side should have recorded an even bigger win:

In the second half, Portsmouth AFC had the better of the game with the wind at their backs but the good kicking of the YMCA backs and the bad shooting of the forwards meant Portsmouth AFC were still without further goals.

Both the last two strikes came too late in the game to receive more than cursory coverage in the match report curtailed by the deadline of the early evening print slot. But that situation was about to end in that paper.

The next Saturday, October 26th, the *Evening Mail* stepped up its rivalry with the *Portsmouth Evening News*, with the unveiling of its special edition on Saturday evenings:

Football players and those who take a special interest in our game are so numerous that it is our intention to publish a special edition of each Saturday's Evening Mail with detailed accounts of principal matches in Portsmouth and Hampshire during the day.

Correspondents were needed to ensure the coverage was as complete as possible. Reports had to be handed in to the paper's offices in Commercial Road or telephoned over, on a service barely invented, by

5.30pm. In true competitive, journalistic tradition, the *Sports Mail* – as it would evolve into – was being published at 7pm, a full hour before the football version of the *Portsmouth Evening News* appeared on the streets.

CHAPTER THIRTY-FOUR

The battle between the editors was certainly fiercer than any which Portsmouth AFC faced that season. The campaign summed up the club's growing dilemma. They were too good for the local sides but not good enough to take on those outside the borough.

Without a ground of their own, they also lacked the ability to raise funds through entrance fees and social activities. On paper, 1889/90 looked a good one for the club, if a little short.

They won ten out of their fourteen games and scored forty-two goals in the process. A three game spell alone yielded sixteen goals. At the back, their defence went seven games without conceding a goal to create a club record. However, six of the sixteen goals they did let in came in the two defeats which summed up the widening gulf between the town outfit and the rest of Hampshire soccer.

Such thoughts must have been far from the minds of the club's officials as 1889/90 got off to an astounding start. The opening win over the YMCA was followed by a further eight straight successes which stretched until Christmas in a sequence which the club had never enjoyed before or would experience again.

YMCA were followed on to the list of defeated opponents by the Royal Marine Artillery on October 26th. Another four-goal haul by Portsmouth AFC marked their debut in the second of the footballing specials. The opening goal noted by the *Evening Mail*'s version was put through by left-winger Edmonds with a fast and high shot which the Marines' keeper failed to stop. Adams made it 2–0 for the original Pompey before half time.

The second half opened with Portsmouth AFC pulling even further ahead as a 'pretty piece of play' – the *Evening Mail*'s words – between Allan and Prinsep resulted in Allan scoring. Edmonds restored his side's three goal lead after the RMA had pulled a goal back.

Predictably, he was named among the pick of Portsmouth AFC's forwards along with Adams and Prinsep. Even a late goal from the RMA did not mar the convincing success on the Eastney ground of the Marines, with a troublesome stiff wind blowing.

Curiously, the coverage was missing from the

Portsmouth Evening News' Football Special. Readers had to be content instead with details of Portsmouth Post Office FC v Eclipse FC at Governor's Green, Portsmouth Teachers FC v Wickham at Southsea Common, and RMLI v US FC at the US Recreation Ground.

Normal service was resumed as perennial fall guys Petersfield were next for the original Pompey and lived down to their reputation once more. Portsmouth AFC left the Heath satisfied with a three goal win. The game was Conan Doyle's first of the season in a footballing career just a few weeks away from ending. He helped his defence keep the first of many clean sheets of the season.

The opening fifteen minutes were evenly balanced until the visitors gradually forced Petersfield back, with a piece of rapid passing ending with a shot by Adams which the home keeper was unable to clear in time.

Portsmouth AFC piled on the pressure and S Allan notched a brace of goals with help from Arthy and GF Seddon. His brother, FJ Seddon, was among a further contingent of four players from the club chosen for the Hampshire FA match with Surrey at Winchester later in November to reflect the original Pompey's good start.

He was joined in the squad by fellow half-back W E Grant, centre forward GL Pares and Lieutenant Loring on the left-wing. In contrast, none from St. Mary's was selected.

Chichester were the next victims to be swept aside as Portsmouth AFC played on their fourth ground in four games. On the same afternoon, Portsmouth Rugby Club celebrated the opening of their new home with a visit from the mighty Saracens, which the home side won by a try to nil. The US Men's Ground was Portsmouth AFC's venue for another four goal walkover. The win was as easy as the scoreline suggested.

It took twenty minutes for the first goal to arrive, thanks to an Edmonds shot, which was quickly followed by another successful shot from GF Seddon. Arthy made it three before half time arrived. He hit another goal even though Chichester rallied after the break to generally keep the ball in midfield.

Conan Doyle was absent from the win but he was to be found four days later officiating in Portsmouth Post Office's 6–2 success in the Hampshire FA Minor Cup second round against Albion AC in a midweek game at Governor's Green, in front of a sizeable contingent of spectators. They witnessed the only known occasion when the increasingly successful author turned referee.

Portsmouth AFC were involved in a cup tie next as they battled to get past the first round of the

Portsmouth Senior Cup for the first time in two seasons. Twelve clubs had entered for the 1889/90 competition, just two more than in the previous season.

As well as Portsmouth and the holders Geneva Cross, they were the King's Own Yorkshire Infantry with two teams, Portsmouth Grammar School, Royal Marines Light Infantry, Havant, Emsworth, Royal Marines Artillery, Freemantle, Cowes and the Oxford Light Infantry (Parkhurst).

The first round draw pitched Portsmouth AFC against one of the King's Own teams. The game turned on a mistake by Private Walker in the soldiers' goal. The moment arrived in the second half. As the *Hampshire Post* saw things:

Eventually, Allen made a shot at goal, and although Walker stopped the leather he was unable to prevent it rolling between the posts, and the first point for the civilians was hailed with much applause.

The *Portsmouth Evening News* reporter considered that Private Walker had become flurried and could only fist out the shot for Allen to tuck away the rebound.

A record four clean sheets in a row were kept by GA Garrington in 1889/90.

A good number of spectators lined the pitch to watch Portsmouth AFC battle their way to the single goal win. The contest had been previewed by the *Portsmouth Evening News* as an interesting match between two teams with a good reputation. They lived up to that expectation with some early excellent combination and sharp play. Half-time was reached, however, with the sides locked at 0–0.

The second half was equally even as the original Pompey's keeper, Garrington, had to keep out a series of attacks by the light infantrymen in response to his side's efforts. His saves ensured the town club went through.

But the pleasure at their success was small compared to the interest at the sporting fixtures on the other side of Burnaby Road. The US Officers' Ground was the venue for the US clash with Portsmouth Rugby Club in which the visitors suffered their first defeat of the season by a try to nil:

These two matches were the most important played locally by far. The greatest attendance was at the Officer's Ground where feelings ran high, partisans lustily cheering on their favourites...

...wrote the *Portsmouth Evening News*.

The crowd was estimated by the *Evening Mail* to be more than a thousand strong. Portsmouth AFC's smaller band of several hundred fans were back at the Men's Ground four days later, on November 20th 1889 for another single goal win. Stubbington House School were the victims, this time to a shot in the dying minutes of the game.

Arthy was the scorer for his third goal in three appearances. He struck after FJ Seddon laid off the ball following a magnificent run which had been prompted by a clever pass from Allen. Garrington kept his fourth clean sheet in a row to create a record for an original Pompey keeper. He was helped by Conan Doyle's second appearance of the season at full-back. The doctor-turned-author played in the next two games as his side's defence held solid for 180 minutes more.

While the backs did their work competently, as Fareham were crushed 5–0, Arthy continued his run of good form with yet another goal. He set Portsmouth AFC on their way with their first of the game as his team mates poured forward from the kick off.

Jeffkins added the next two goals from excellent centres by GF Seddon and Allen rounded off the scoring with two more in an incident-packed first half. All this, and conditions were unfavourable. Rain, mist and mud counted against good play. The original Pompey overcame the obstacles to earn praise from the *Portsmouth Evening News*:

Portsmouth AFC obtained the goals from excellent passing and shooting among all of the forwards. All played a good game.

The second half was understandably a more muted affair. The heavy ground, drizzle and the rapid onset of darkness – it was November 23rd – combined to leave both sets of players struggling. Conan Doyle and his colleagues at the back with Durrell in goal – according to the match report line ups – repelled the attacks which Fareham staged in the closing moments of the game.

Alongside the match report was news of a merger between two of the football clubs in Portsmouth anxious to challenge the supremacy of the town team. The YMCA, who the original Pompey had beaten five weeks earlier to open their season, announced they were to join with Portsmouth North End. The amalgamation made the new outfit: 'One of the strongest playing under association rules in the county', according to the *Portsmouth Evening News*:

The members must number fifty and there are two teams of nearly equal strength and in fixture cards, which are in the course of preparation, there will be found forty-seven matches.

Portsmouth AFC showed they were undaunted by any challengers. November ended in the best possible way for the club to respond to their strong new rival. They put six goals past Portsmouth Grammar School without reply. Allen and GL Pares both netted twice, while GF Seddon and Loring completed the scoring at the school's Hilsea grounds. Garrington was back in goal for the town club and with Conan Doyle just in front, the keeper's safe hands ensured November ended as it had begun with the opposition kept at bay. As a playing record, that of the original Pompey was as good as it could get: P8 W8 D0 L0 F28 A3.

CHAPTER THIRTY-FIVE

The players had a week off to luxuriate in their achievements. It was no wonder other clubs around the town were fearful of taking them on. One side which decided to step into the fray was the US club. They left the pitch knowing better, the victims of a 5–0 mauling. Portsmouth AFC had the best of the game throughout against a scratch side and their excellent form rolled on.

But dark clouds eventually appear in the sunniest of skies. December 21st proved the point for Portsmouth AFC. The occasion was the Portsmouth Senior Cup second round. The opponents waited across the Solent in the form of Cowes, whose continuation in the competition had been a matter of debate earlier in the month.

The sight of FJ Seddon among the mainland half-backs was all the incentive Cowes needed to ensure their visitors were sent well and truly packing back over the water. The Portsmouth AFC regular had set the scene two weeks previously for the high octane clash. He had chaired the Portsmouth FA committee which censured Cowes for the furore which surrounded their first round tie with Portsmouth Grammar School.

Rowdy scenes dominated the game to the extent that a referee's report was sought by the committee. His version of the events prompted three resolutions which ordered Cowes to behave:

1. Portsmouth FA regard the behaviour of F Mouncher necessitated the referee ordering him from the field.

2. Portsmouth FA also requests the committee of Cowes FC to inform their members that referees' decisions must be abided by implicitly by players and any behaviour to the contrary will be severely dealt with by the association.

3. Portsmouth FA further wished to convey to Cowes FC, and to all other clubs belonging to the association, that in cup ties the home club will be held responsible for the proper roping off and proper preparation of the ground and proper behaviour of the spectators.

Moreover, the committee was only stopped from expelling the island side from the competition by the casting vote of FJ Seddon.

What Seddon's feelings were when he lined up against Cowes are unknown. But he put in an enterprising display in Portsmouth AFC's defence. So too did McDonald and Garrington. The keeper, though, was unable to maintain one of his regular clean sheets.

He was handicapped by the weakened team in front of him. Yet, even then, he kept the home side at bay until just before half-time after Cowes had forced the play into the visitors' half.

Garrington was also absolved of blame for Cowes' opener. A mistake by one of his backs gave a home forward a chance which was eagerly snapped up. That remained the only difference between the teams until well into the closing stages of the tie.

Two more goals then put the cup-tie, and the cup, beyond the reach of the original Pompey for a further year. The odds had been stacked against them from the kick off, with seven regulars missing from those who lined up alongside Seddon.

The absentees were the injured Grant and Arthy, Pares, Loring and E Seddon, who were out of town, Pugh missing because of business commitments and the India-bound Prinsep.

'Under these circumstances, the result was a fairly good conclusion,' concluded the *Evening Mail.*

But the lengthy list of the missing showed the hazards of being truly amateur club in an increasingly organised world of football. Portsmouth AFC were the undisputed champions of Portsea Island and its hinterland but they struggled beyond that limited area.

CHAPTER THIRTY-SIX

Their next game proved the point. They travelled in the opposite direction the following week to Aldershot. They faced the Hampshire Senior Cup holders Royal Engineers in the competition's second round. Again, when the going got tough, Portsmouth AFC's players got going away from the football pitch.

Full-backs Drew and Pugh were unable to leave work in time to travel the long distance to the north of the county. The original Pompey were forced to play their umpire, which may have accounted for the re-appearance of Conan Doyle in their ranks, and yet still lined up one player short.

The engineers quickly took advantage and were a goal in front within a minute. How much worse could the remaining eighty-nine minutes get for the visitors? Salvation appeared in the shape of Allen to give his side a full complement and begin the fightback. The rest of the match was a classic encounter – two sides battling each other with commitment and skill.

FJ Seddon led Portsmouth AFC's backs in some capital defensive play and all of the forwards contributed good work. It was rewarded in the twenty-fifth minute when McDonald equalised. Even better was to follow for the civilians.

GF Seddon put them 2–1 up to complete a four man move. It had begun with a good piece of passing between Loring, GL Pares and E Seddon. His cross saw the soldiers' keeper rushing out only for GF Seddon to put the ball past him.

RE were not to be denied the chance to hold on to the trophy for a while longer. They staged an attack along the right-wing which put them level. The lead changed hands for the last time when the home team snatched their third goal in the final seconds after both sets of players had given everything to win the game. Praise poured from the *Evening Mail's* man at the match:

There was little to choose between the teams, the result being entirely due to the superior combination of the home XI. All of the visiting team played well and vigorously. Had they had their full strength, the game might have resulted differently.

That last sentence was the most telling. Even for the most prestigious competition in which they played, Portsmouth AFC could not guarantee the appearance of all their players. No ground, no commitment – no wonder 1889/90 fell away so quickly after the new year began.

The successes of two months earlier counted for nothing as 1890 got underway. Only one player from that epic tussle at Aldershot remained for the club's

PORTSMOUTH AFC CUP TIES 1889/90				
Portsmouth Senior Cup				
R1	King's Own Yorkshire Light Infantry	USMG	W1-0	16.11.89
R2	Cowes	a	L0-3	21.12.89
Hampshire Senior Cup				
R2	Winchester	a		
(No record of game taking place before December 31 deadline. It seems Winchester did not turn up. The following game was played instead)				
R2	Royal Engineers (Aldershot)	a	L2-3	28.12.89

first game of the year. GF Seddon was the sole survivor who faced the US team on January 18th at the US Men's Ground. Five weeks previously, the clash of the clubs had seen the borough club romp to a five-goal win. This time, the sides' contrasting fortunes were reflected in a 2–4 defeat for the visitors.

The team of civilian strangers initially adapted well to each others' company to go two up by half-time. Whitmarsh scored both goals from the left-wing. The second half was a different story. Backed by the wind, US reeled in all the goals. The final two arrived in the last fifteen minutes.

A moment of relief for the original Pompey arrived in the gloom with a first win in four games, courtesy of the club's only hat-trick of the season scored against the Royal Marines Artillery on February 8th. The high-scoring victories in that earlier unequalled winning run had been achieved with four players sharing the goal-scoring honours.

Short, in his fourth and last appearance in the blue shirt, made it a memorable farewell with a hat trick. The match earned little coverage in the local papers, possibly because of Portsmouth AFC's rapidly fading campaign.

The *Evening Mail* reckoned that in spite of that the game was noticeable:

Both sides played a capital game, their passing and combination being exceptionally good.

The sides were level 2–2 at half-time before the borough team established their superiority with two further goals in the second period of play. The same scoreline had resulted when the teams met in the original Pompey's second match of the season. The return was their second to last.

The final game was also remarkable for being the only draw of the season for Portsmouth AFC. They faced the Royal Marines Light Infantry for the only time in 1889/90. The Marines scored first in the belated fixture in about the thirtieth minute of a well-contested opening period in which both sides had to defend. Armstrong pulled Portsmouth AFC level twenty minutes later. The match descended into monotony for the final minutes as the teams settled for a draw.

The *Evening Mail* mentioned future games against St Mary's (Southampton) and Fareham in the second

Portsmouth AFC - proud winners of the Portsmouth Senior Cup in 1890/91 after their epic games with the Oxford Light Infantry.

half of March. But the fixtures failed to produce any match reports that have survived the intervening century-plus gap, if indeed they took place at all.

The major interest of Portsmouth AFC's followers that month was the publication of Conan Doyle's new volume of short stories, *The Captain of the Pole Star*. Four days later, on March 15th 1890, the author was to be found as the guest of honour at the Portsmouth Senior Cup final between the holders, Geneva Cross, and Freemantle, who won 1–0.

He commented, as one of the pioneers of the cup competition for teams from the Portsmouth area, upon the fact that both sides in the 1889/90 contest were based around Southampton. Portsmouth AFC, in which he had such an important role in its formative years, were becoming more famous for his off-the-pitch activities than for his team-mates' on it.

CHAPTER THIRTY-SEVEN

Undaunted, the club reassembled for 1890/91 after an exceptionally long close season, with Conan Doyle presiding at its annual meeting on September 17th. Those present at the Albany Hotel decided to enter for the forthcoming Hampshire and Portsmouth Senior cups. They also elected AH Wood as their captain in succession to FJ Seddon, whose loss, the *Portsmouth Evening News* remarked, 'will be severely felt this season'.

Several new members were proposed and elected as well. They joined a club in reasonable financial, if not playing, health with a balance of almost £4. The report ended with the usual appeal for potential opponents to contact the club's secretary, WE Grant, at 3 Buckingham Villas, Villiers Road, Southsea.

On the same day as details appeared in the local press of the meeting, the club's players and officials would have been well served reading a comment article in the *Evening Mail*. It warned about the impact of professionalism upon football and the need to organise a competition for amateur clubs in the south to stop them joining the paid-for ranks. Its columnist, Augur, wrote in its 'Sports and Pastimes' section that football organisers around Portsmouth were at a watershed for the game during September 1890:

The advent of the football season warns us that we must soon face a serious difficulty. During the past three years, professionalism has increased to such an extent in the North of England that it is practically impossible for the amateur teams of the South to play any of the crack clubs of Lancashire and Warwickshire with any chance of success.

The wretched display made by the few southern clubs who reached the competition proper for the challenge cup last year proves this conclusively.

And it is a matter of common sense that a man in constant training must play better than a man who can only give one, or at most, two afternoons a week to the game.

The fact that the Corinthians were successful proves nothing, for not only are they the pick one might almost say of the UK, but the majority of them were university men and as such of course could give nearly as much time to the game as the professionals.

But with the majority of southern clubs, it's far different, and only two alternatives seem open to them – to engage professionals themselves or to organise competitions for amateur teams only.

Hardly anywhere except perhaps in London would the gates be large enough to warrant or to support professional players, and the latter seems the most sensible suggestion of the two.

To continue the present system of fighting against opponents immeasurably superior is ridiculous. The 'players', home bred and Scotch imported, are too good, and southern teams, brilliant and clever though they may be, must recognise that fact and submit to it.

CHAPTER THIRTY-EIGHT

That prediction proved to be at least partly correct. April 18th 1891, was the day football arrived in Portsmouth as a major sport. The date was exceptional and the crowd was exceptional. It was the first time the Association game had been played in the town so late in the spring, challenging cricket's traditional hold on April. It was also the first time that the size of the attendance of a football match in the area had been accurately reported. And for good reason.

About 4000 spectators, an unheard-of number locally, went along to see if Portsmouth AFC and The Oxford Light Infantry could finally be separated in their titanic struggle for the Portsmouth Senior Cup. On three previous occasions in the final over seven weeks they had competed against each other in a series of stalemates.

The possibility that the fourth clash might be different enticed the record-breaking crowd to the US Officers' Ground. Previous attendances had usually been dismissed in a few passing words, if at all, in match reports.

But the interest generated by the trio of cup finals and the standard of play, created the terrific turnout. Those thousands of onlookers had to wait until the fifty-fifth minute of an absorbing contest – and the

This patch of grass is the burial place of one of the most influential men in football's formative years in Portsmouth.

The unmarked area covers the grave of Major Alred Herbert Wood at the Highland Road cemetery in Eastney. Maj. Wood died suddenly on April 19th 1941. A half century earlier, and he was helping to lead the way in the development of football in the borough. He was the first president of the Portsmouth FA upon its inception in 1890. The official birth year of the association was just over a season after officials from the Portsmouth area had helped to set up the Hampshire FA to underline their dominant role in the sport's growth along the south coast.

Maj. Wood remained the president for the Portsmouth body for 14 important years. They included the rise of football as an organised sport with, first Portsmouth AFC, then Royal Artillery and, finally, the current Portsmouth FC leading the way.

In addition, the five consecutive and popular six-a-side tournaments put football firmly on the sporting calendar each year. The Portsmouth Senior Cup was launched in November 1886. The junior version followed seven years later. This was formed into a junior league after two seasons, expanded to two divisions in 1898 and increased by a further division three years later.

New clubs were being formed all the time and football gained a boost by the opening of the Stamshaw Recreation Ground in 1892, which grew in time to become Alexandra Park and then the Mountbatten Centre.

Over all this initial activity, Maj. Wood presided. Yet, like Sir Arthur Conan Doyle, his obituary in the *Portsmouth Evening News* passed over his contribution to football in the city.

Wartime newsprint restrictions meant space in the newspaper was tight but Maj. Wood's life was summed up in all too few paragraphs. The article categorised his death as the loss of 'a prominent freemason, sportsman and keen supporter of charitable work.'

He was 75 when he died in the Royal Pier Hotel, in Sussex Terrace, Southsea, and a bachelor. The tribute article said Wood, 'a member of the old Portsmouth FC' in a concession to his footballing links, had been educated at Portsmouth Grammar School.

His final year at the school saw him enjoy the unusual experience of being the honorary secretary of the Church Congress which met at Portsmouth.

Maj. Wood won an open scholarship to Brasenose College, Oxford, where he received an MA degree. He returned to Portsmouth as a master at the grammar school. 'He was a close friend of the late Sir Arthur Conan Doyle, then practising as an occulist at Southsea,' the paper inaccurately stated, 'and was for many years the famous novelist's private secretary and business manager.'

Maj. Wood had played for Hampshire Cricket club and was a member of the MCC. He had also been the Portsmouth FA president as well, the paper grudgingly conceded. He was initiated as a freemason. His other interests included the Royal Albert Yacht Club, of which he had been its honorary secretary during the latter years of his involvement.

His funeral service was held at St James's Church on April 23, 1941, and was followed by his interment at Highland Road Cemetery.

325th minute of the games between the sides – for the deciding goal.

McDonald, then Wood, then Grant were involved in the build-up. The half-back was also the club's secretary. He laid off the ball to Cook on the left-wing who shot home beyond Ashdown in the Infantry goal, 'to the loudly expressed satisfaction of the Portsmouth AFC partisans,' as the *Portsmouth Evening News* described the tumultuous scene, in the language of the era.

The *Hampshire Post* used less prosaic text to describe what happened next:

This put the Oxonians on their mettle and they played with renewed energy only, however, to find the defence of the town men impenetrable.

Over to the *Portsmouth Evening News*:

Oxford Light Infantry had two chances to equalise but on both occasions they were too anxious to score and missed.

Had the coolness of the Infantry keeper been matched by his team mates then Oxford would have won the cup. Portsmouth AFC and the Infantry had chances towards the end.

Back to the *Hampshire Post*:

Give and take remained the order until Portsmouth AFC claimed the trophy. At the end of the match, the players and spectators assembled in front of the pavilion, and General Harward, on behalf of the committee, presented the trophy to AH Wood, the captain of Portsmouth AFC.

The *Portsmouth Evening News* added that the General stated that the third and final of the replays was the most gallant match he had seen. He was highly complimentary about the efforts of both teams. Portsmouth AFC had lined up with three changes from the side which had contested the original final. But the back division remained the same, crucially, after solid displays in the initial clashes. The history books awaited for the players:

Portsmouth AFC: A Garrington, goal; H McDonald and D Lever, backs; AH Wood (c), WE Grant and Basil Pares, half-backs; AW Cook and J Flannery, left-wing; GL Pares, centre; SR Pike and Bernard Pares, right-wing.

Oxford Light Infantry: Ashdown, goal; Walters and Winspur, backs; Vernal, Barlow and Crook, half-backs; Heath and Lawrence, right-wing; Staite (c), centre; Kavanagh and Manion, left-wing.

The referee was Winchester resident A Tebbutt, while HF Hasting and Captain Love RMLI were the touch judges.

The soldiers had just about the best of the opening stages. They pressed for the first five minutes before the town club got the ball away from Lever to Wood and down the right-wing to the Infantry goal. The civilians won two corners, neither of which resulted in any advantage. Next to threaten were the Oxonians. Manion, Staite and Lawrence put in threatening shots before Flannery replied with an effort which just flew past the soldiers' goal.

Bernard Pares upped the pressure for the town club with a corner which had the fans holding their breath. The ball, in the words of the *Portsmouth Evening News*:

...almost seemed to cling to the right post, bounce along the crossbar and topple behind the line.

For all the thrills, though, half-time arrived with the contest goalless. Ten minutes later Cook changed that – and the course of football history in Portsmouth. The enthusiasm his goal generated led three years later to the formation of Portsmouth's first 'professional' club, in the guise of Royal Artillery. Seven years on from that, and the current Portsmouth FC were formed.

The 1890/91 Portsmouth Senior Cup finals were the games which convinced Victorian Portmuthians of the merits of soccer. The finalists were the best possible pairing that the sport's enthusiasts could have chosen, given the chance.

They had clashed as the year started in a six-a-side tournament when the second round tie was convincingly claimed by four points to one by the soldiers, who went on to win the event, at the Drill Hall in Alfred Road, Landport. Matters were much closer when the teams ran out in the Portsmouth Senior Cup final's first game on March 7th 1891. A large number of spectators were present for the contest, throughout which light rain fell.

In an exact pattern of the deciding game the following month, the first half lacked only goals, and it took an effort by Cook to open up play. He struck on the hour after a pass from Smith, who had set up the attack with a run along the right-wing. The Oxonians equalised within two minutes. Lawrence, Barlow and then Winspur combined for Staite to score out of a crush of players in front of the original Pompey's goal.

The military onlookers cheered very heartily the good fortune of their comrades and caps were waved by the score in the air...

...commented the *Portsmouth Evening News*.

More heated moments were to follow as emotions were strongly expressed, even for the usually repressed Victorians. The seventieth minute brought the Infantry the lead, or so the team and their supporters thought, until the goal was ruled 'out' by Southampton referee J Hendin after an appeal by the civilians. The *Portsmouth Evening News* again:

There was a great deal of booing when the goal was disallowed but the officials are to be commended for the firm and competent way in which they acted.

McDonald, Wood and Grant were Portsmouth AFC's most effective players and Crook, Walters and Vernal earned the accolades for the light infantrymen.

So, the final ended all square, and a conference was hurriedly held by the cup committee to decide what to do next. The outcome was a replay the next Saturday rather than thirty minutes of extra time. No extra time would have seemed necessary at the start of the final.

Its first chance fell to the military side as Heath and Kavanagh went on the attack without any joy. Garrington fisted a corner from the original Pompey goal to clear another moment of threat from the soldiers. GL Pares staged the civilians' opening attack with a shot. Another chance fell to the stalwart

H McDonald played a pivotal role in the 1890/91 Portsmouth Senior Cup triumph.

player but he was hampered by a bad knee and unable to make the most of his opportunities.

Back came Oxford Light Infantry with Manion and Staite combining to force Garrington to punch away at exactly the right moment to avert the danger.

Portsmouth AFC tried to reply as Cook and Seddon sent the ball to Pares, whose injury restricted his ability to respond to the pass. The action continued as half time arrived goalless. That changed in a two-minute spell to set up the first replay the following week.

Full time in the first replay arrived without any goals again. A very large number of spectators – put at 1200 by the *Hampshire Post* – were tempted along for the March 14th 1891 fixture to see who at the second attempt would succeed Freemantle as cup holders.

They had a long wait. The 120 minutes passed and still the teams could not be separated.

GL Pares was again the culprit as far as Portsmouth AFC were concerned. He was the team's weakest link. His lameness once more reduced his side's ability to make an impact.

The first half belonged to the Oxford Light Infantry. They went close on as many as twelve occasions. Four of those were good shots which they made, a further two went just past the posts of Garrington's goal, another couple were well stopped by the keeper, while two corners went begging.

Portsmouth AFC were no more successful on their rare forays forward. They gained a pair of corners, which were wasted, along with a free-kick given for hands. The teams were more evenly matched after the interval and neither could score the decisive goal.

The outcome was the same after extra time. Apart from GL Pares with his unfortunate injury, the original Pompey were well served by their wing men – including his brother Basil Pares and Smith, Cook and Pike. For their opponents, Staite, Manion, Barlow, Lawrence and Kavanagh earned the accolades.

The stalemate left the *Hampshire Post* perplexed:

Oxford Light Infantry men are decidedly seen to better advantage on dry ground but on Saturday their chief fault was the erratic manner in which their shots at goal were lodged.

Back the teams returned to the Men's Recreation Ground two weeks later along with an increased attendance from the first replay. Portsmouth AFC were without GL Pares, finally resting, while the Infantry kept faith with the same XI from the previous replay.

The game fell on Easter Saturday and the cup

Left-back D Lever scored a crucial goal in the 1890/91 Portsmouth Senior Cup success.

committee were starting to seek divine inspiration to reach a conclusion in a titanic struggle which had never before been seen in Portsmouth or, probably, all Hampshire.

Portsmouth AFC's Lever seemed to have provided the answer to their prayers after an hour. The attack had begun with a surge forward by the town side which ended with the ball resting on the soldiers' crossbar. A corner followed and the Infantrymen kicked it to what their defenders assumed was safety only for the left-back to return it with a long kick following a sharp bounce over the head of Ashdown in the Infantry goal. At last a goal had been scored, only for the equaliser to arrive within the next fifteen minutes. Staite was again the scorer.

His goal arrived from a scrum in front of the posts following a corner. The ground was alive with celebrating supporters, as the *Hampshire Post* noted after Lever's opener, though its reporter took a different view from the *Portsmouth Evening News* of the scorer for the military team:

...a performance greeted with ringing cheers, which were renewed when a few minutes afterwards, Kavanagh scored.

Not for the first time, the papers disagreed about the details, although conditions at the ground must have been crowded and difficult for the reporters.

Both sides tried to edge ahead as time ran out and extra time was played again in an effort to find a winner. But, still, the finalists remained evenly matched. The teams were puzzled about how to take matters to a conclusion. They were in uncharted territory as far as the organisation of the sport was concerned, as the *Portsmouth Evening News* reported:

At a subsequent meeting of the teams in the pavilion, opinion was divided as to what should be done in the face of very even play.

The suggestion on one side was that the tie should be played to a result.

On the other side, it was for both teams being presented with medals and holding the cup for six months each.

A special meeting of the Portsmouth FA was called for the Tuesday night, April 1st 1891, to make the final decision. The result was another game and another boost for the sport in the town, plus a triumph for its leading club.

The additional interest in the final and its staging also provided a welcome financial bonus for the Portsmouth FA. Their annual meeting five months later showed the extra income from the admission fees at the four matches was enough to wipe out the deficit from the previous season.

The association received half the gate money from paying spectators at the US grounds. These receipts from six matches, including the finals, amounted to £32.4s. They were added to the £2.15s of cup entrance fees paid by nine clubs to provide a total of £34.19s. This wiped out the 14s.3d deficit, which had been carried over into the £21.18s expenditure to leave a healthy £13.11d in the account.

CHAPTER THIRTY-NINE

Portsmouth AFC's cup run which led to the bonanza began at Hilsea five months before the contest was finally decided. The Netley Hospital side of Geneva Cross provided the opposition on November 8th. The *Evening Mail* provided a pre-match warning to the fans of the original Pompey not to get their hopes too high about a side from which many former favourites were missing:

Portsmouth AFC have suffered in losing their good men this season and will not be as strong as in former years but their team will doubtless give their opponents a strong run.

The paper predicted an interesting match. And it was. Pike scored the deciding goal for Portsmouth AFC eight minutes from the end. He struck from just three yards out from the Geneva Cross goal to give the keeper no chance.

He had also provided the blue shirts' opener. The right-winger had already put in two or three splendid centres from the touchline without any result before he centred the ball perfectly. It was sent back out by the hospital team's defence, only for Pike to return the ball for Smith to score. The teams turned round divided by the goal.

The situation changed in just a few minutes. Turner equalised with a soft goal from a cross by Hill on the left. Portsmouth AFC pressed forward as they sought to make progress in a competition which had brought them little joy for the past three years. GL Pares went close a couple of times when goals seemed certain but the treacherous nature of the ground saved the visitors.

The Portsmouth Evening News' *report on March 11, 1890, of the publication of* The Captain of the Polestar *collection of short stories by Dr Arthur Conan Doyle.*

Matters became frantic after Portsmouth AFC regained the lead as Geneva Cross went on constant attacks. They forced Garrington to fist out twice in the Portsmouth AFC goal and just manage a save on a third occasion, desperately kicking the ball upfield to preserve his side's lead.

Portsmouth AFC had a much easier time when their second round tie against Portsmouth North End finally got underway. January 10th was the day the teams eventually took to the pitch on a ground still hard from ice and frost during an exceptionally cold winter.

The game had been postponed on several occasions since its scheduled date of December 20th as the weather took its toll on conditions. North End must have wished they had never bothered to brave the freezing temperature. Supposedly strengthened by a merger just over a year earlier, they were played off the pitch, solid with cold as it was.

The 9–0 scoreline – Portsmouth AFC's highest cup score and biggest overall for two years – fully reflected the unbalanced nature of the play. There was only one side in it from start to finish, with the tackling and passing of the original Pompey far superior.

The whole team played well throughout the ninety minutes to leave the *Portsmouth Evening News* reluctant to pick out individual players for praise. It felt that would have been seen as unfair considered against such a combined effort. GL Pares, however, did lead the way for the borough's premier club with their first hat-trick in eleven months. Cook and JH Smith netted two each and Bernard Pares and Baker rounded off the scoring.

On to the semi-finals, and the rather stiffer opposition of a revived Woolston Works side awaited at the end of January 1891. The two teams clashed the previous week in the Hampshire Senior Cup to recall memories of their past regular fixtures. The side based on the banks of the River Hamble proved the victors in the country competition. Portsmouth AFC had the ideal chance just seven days later to put right that loss.

Only three hundred fans turned up at the Officers' Ground to watch them put the record straight in a tie packed with incident. They must have been disheartened, and fearing a repeat defeat, when Woolston stormed into the lead within five minutes.

Aitken was the scorer before an effort from Black was disallowed, which would have doubled the lead. The original Pompey retaliated with a goal of their own. Their forward Simpson followed up one good shot with another more successful one. It was Woolston's turn to protest after the original Pompey's dispute over Black's effort. Simpson went on to the score sheet after the referee, HF Hastings, had over-ruled 'some loud talk', to use the *Portsmouth Evening News'* description of the dispute.

Both sides had further changes before GL Pares sent in a strong shot which Meckleham was equal to in the Woolston goal. The half closed with an incredible three goals by Woolston left-winger Langlands all of which were disallowed.

The constant disputes saw tempers rising as Portsmouth AFC surged into a second-half lead. Goals from Wood and GL Pares put them on their way to their first Portsmouth Senior Cup final appearance in three years. The Southampton visitors could only pull one back, from Black, to be grudg-

---

Just how much Dr Arthur Conan Doyle came to mean to Portsmouth can be seen by the eulogy paid to him by the *Portsmouth Times* when he left the borough. The weekly newspaper devoted 99 lines of densely-packed words to the doctor and increasingly sought after author and his farewell dinner on Friday, December 12th 1890.

The occasion took place at Southsea's Grosvenor Hotel and was organised by Dr Doyle's friends in the Portsmouth Literary and Scientific Society of which he had become a stalwart and was one of its honorary secretaries.

The society also contributed much else to his life. Its president, a Dr Watson, is widely credited with providing him with the name for Sherlock Holmes's companion, though the great detective was absent from the tribute report.

But football's place in the early professional life of Dr Doyle was acknowledged, for once, along with his enthusiasm for cricket: 'His love of outdoor recreation is well known and he will be greatly missed by the Portsmouth Cricket and Association Football Clubs, in whose welfare he has taken interest,' the paper reported. Those pastimes were just part of the contribution which Dr Doyle had made to the life of Portsmouth in the eight years he had lived in Elm Grove. As the *Portsmouth Times* further commented:

The announcement that Dr Arthur Conan Doyle is about to leave Southsea for Vienna, where he will continue his special study of the eye prior to commencing practice as an occulist in London, has caused deep regret.

Portmuthians would have preferred to retain the skilled physician, the gifted literatur, and the genial, kind-hearted townsman. Dr Conan Doyle is essentially an 'all round man'.

During his eight years residence here, he has steadily made his way in his profession; he has found time to devote to literature, in which he has achieved a national reputation as a writer of sterling and stirring fiction; and, withal, he has gained renown as a cricketer and footballer.

Our readers will unite with us in wishing him Godspeed and success in his future career, both in the *medical and the literary professions.*

The *Portsmouth Times* gave a resume of Dr Doyle's writing successes to date, while omitting Sherlock Holmes. Dr Doyle, 31 or 32 at the time, according to the report, had showed his literary talent at the age of 18.

Several of the short stories which he contributed then to the *Cornhill* and *Temple Bar* magazines had been recently published in *The Captain of the Polestar* book. But *Micah Clarke* was given the accolade by the paper of being the best of Dr Doyle's early creative output. 'A work in which very many of our readers have doubtless found much to interest them,' according to the report.

It must have cost the author an immense amount of labour, for there is not a slipshod passage in it, and the minor details obviously received the same careful attention as the plot and characterisation.

The great demand for the book is in itself strong evidence of its popularity; it has now gone through five editions. Since then, the more sensationally. The Firm of Gridlestone, with its remarkably good character studies, had been published.

The White Company *was next off Dr Doyle's production line, with its appearance as a serial in* Cornhill *magazine the following year.*

That month, December 1890, an article by Dr Doyle on Dr Koch – the Berlin physician whose alleged cure for tuberculosis he had exposed as a fraud – was appearing in the *Review of Reviews*. Already, the literary aspect of Dr Doyle's life was overshadowing every other aspect, though he left Southsea for Vienna to study the eye with the intention of returning to London as a specialist in vision and keeping his writing as a potentially large source of extra income.

He arrived in London in March 1891 and set up a practice in Devonshire Place among the fashionable medical practitioners. But the venture failed to succeed and Dr Doyle decided to give up medicine and devote himself to writing.

ingly sent out of the competition by 3–2.

The Pares brothers, Smith, Grant, Wood and Simpson received accolades for their displays in the blue shirts. Mr. Hastings earned only scorn from the Woolston team. He reported the issue to the Portsmouth FA who were forced to convene a special meeting on February 25th to consider his report. Portsmouth AFC were in the dock as well for their part in a match which brought shame on the sport for its rowdy behaviour.

It was the first time in the cup's five-year history that both sides in a match had been charged with similar offences. The Portsmouth FA were concerned that the teams' conduct in the semi-final was at risk of ruining the reputation of football as a gentlemanly sport. So anxious were the committee members they thought only the severest penalty could be imposed on Woolston. In a unanimous vote, they decided:

That this meeting of the Portsmouth FA emphatically endorses the opinion of the referee in the semi-final tie for the Portsmouth and District Challenge Cup and hereby suspends Southampton Woolston Works FC individually and as a team from taking part in the competition for one year from this date, February 25th, 1891.

This effectively meant Woolston would have to wait until the autumn of 1892 before they could compete again for the cup. No mention was made in the *Portsmouth Evening News* of any penalty for Portsmouth AFC.

Almost two weeks earlier, the town club had lost their own protest against the naval works team after they had lodged a complaint against three of the side's players. A special committee set up by the Hampshire FA executive voted 5–4 in favour of the Southampton-based side.

The inquiry had centred around the presence of Aitken, Boyle and Black in the team in the previous Hampshire Senior Cup tie. Portsmouth AFC had alleged the trio had only arrived at the boatbuilders in April and so failed the cup's residency rules.

However, the special committee had found, after considerable trouble, evidence to prove the men had been in Woolston since the previous June or July. This meant they were qualified to play in the semi-final. The verdict left the original Pompey free to concentrate on taking on Oxford Light Infantry in the Portsmouth cup's final three weeks later. It was closer to May before the competition was decided in another headache for the cup committee but one at least in which the borough team provided a happy ending.

The third of the trio of roads in the North End area of Portsmouth with a link to Dr Arthur Conan Doyle.

CHAPTER FORTY

The rest of 1890/91 couldn't live up to the drama provided by the Portsmouth Senior Cup. It didn't even bother to try. The most significant other occasion occurred off the pitch with the departure of the club's loyal servant, Conan Doyle. He had failed to appear for the club that season. This made his game against the Royal Engineers in the Hampshire Senior Cup second round twelve months earlier the last time he had turned out in a navy blue shirt. The *Portsmouth Times* wrote of his leaving Portsmouth in its edition of December 19th 1890:

The announcement that Dr A Conan Doyle is about to leave Southsea for Vienna, where he will continue his special study of the eye prior to commencing practice as an oculist in London, has caused deep regret.

Portmuthians would have preferred to retain the skilled physician, the gifted literateur, and the genial, kind-hearted townsman.

Dr Doyle having, however, after mature considera-tion, decided to seek a wider sphere of usefulness, the good wishes expressed for his future welfare at the parting dinner at which he was entertained last night at the Grosvenor Hotel, Southsea, under the auspices of the Portsmouth Literary and Scientific Society, will be heartily endorsed by the inhabitants generally.

Dr Conan Doyle is essentially an 'all-round man'. During his eight years' residence here he has steadily made his way in his profession; he has found time to devote to literature, in which he has achieved a national reputation as a writer of sterling and stirring fiction; and, withal, he has gained renown as a crick-eter and footballist.

His love of outdoor recreation is well known, and he will be greatly missed by the Portsmouth Cricket and Association Football Clubs, in whose welfare he has taken a practical interest.

The paper, which put Conan Doyle's age at thirty-one or thirty-two, wrote of his success as an author. His first popular work, *Micah Clarke*, had gone through five editions, it reported. *The Firm of Girdlestone* and *The White Company*, which was about to be published, were also destined for greatness, in its opinion.

CHAPTER FORTY-ONE

Conan Doyle's former team-mates opened 1890/91 against the RN College at the US Officers' Ground on October 14th. A goal by right-winger Pike brought them victory, with Conan Doyle's place between the posts taken by the debut-making Eckersley. Along with his opposite number, he was called into action several times in the first half of the game, surprisingly held on a Tuesday, which doubtless limited the attendance.

Pike's goal arrived after half-time from a well-directed shot on the left of the pitch following a pass from GL Pares. Both players – along with Arbuckle – were among their team's most prominent members, along with the Seddon brothers, Grant and Whitmarsh.

Pares was next in action in Hampshire FA's win over Sussex four days later. He added the second goal in the 2-1 victory at Southampton. The result was seen by the *Portsmouth Times* as evidence of the increasing stature of Hampshire FA in the sport:

The victory......marks a distinct upward movement in the world of association football for our county, for Sussex has always been regarded as one of the most powerful teams in the south.

Years ago, it beat Hampshire FA by no less a degree than 9–0 and 4–1.

But things have changed since then and the play of Hampshire FA on Saturday earned the commendation of NL Jackson, than whom there is no greater authority on Hampshire FA football.

So has the management of the executive, for Mr. Jackson writes in his paper 'Pastimes:'

"The 'crack' players of Sussex do not support their county as they ought, and would do well to take an example from Hampshire FA who avoid frightening their players by making too many matches but also invariably get their best team."

Further proof of the strength of football in Hampshire was provided a month later when the Hampshire FA issued their handbook. It listed nine senior, thirteen junior and twenty-eight minor clubs. Ten belonged to Portsmouth, including RMLI at Forton, while Southampton had five more clubs, 'the cheerful reading of the handbook is that association football is flourishing in Portsmouth,' reported the *Portsmouth Times*.

Unfortunately, for Portsmouth AFC that good form was not carried over into their next fixture on October 25th 1890. They succumbed to a 0–3 defeat

How the Portsmouth Evening News *reported the death of Dr Arthur Conan Doyle – without mentioning Portsmoth AFC.*

PORTSMOUTH AFC CUP TIES
1890/91

Portsmouth Senior Cup

R1	Geneva Cross (Netley Hospital)	Hilsea	W2-1	08.11.90
R2	Portsmouth North End	Hilsea	W9-0	10.01.91
S-f	Naval Works Woolston	USOG	W3-2	31.01.91
F	Oxford Light Infantry	USMG	D1-1	07.03.91
Fr	Oxford Light Infantry (after 40 min aet 0-0 90 min)	USMG	D0-0	14.03.91
Fr2	Oxford Light Infantry (after aet 0-0 90 min)	USMG	D1-1	28.03.91
Fr3	Oxford Light Infantry	USMG	W1-0	18.04.91

Cup Winners

Hampshire Senior Cup

R2	Southampton Naval Works	Woolston	L2-3	24.01.91

against the Yorkshire Regiment, though their display earned some praise from the *Portsmouth Evening News*. Their old foes at Portsmouth Grammar School were the next opponents of the original Pompey, in a game whose facts have been lost, before the town club embarked on the first stage of their Portsmouth Senior Club marathon with Geneva Cross.

The first cup tie meant the cancellation of Portsmouth AFC's scheduled fixture with the Post Office to leave the mailmen's secretary, C Payne, appealing for other clubs to contact him at 7 Manners Road to arrange an alternative fixture.

No such worries for Portsmouth AFC. They next turned out against and turned over Stubbington. GL Pares, again, was the dominant player, with four goals from his side's six goal tally as he and his team mates built on a 2–0 half-time lead. A brother, Basil, added another goal and the score sheet was completed by Collins.

But the original Pompey slipped to their second defeat of the season with a 0–2 setback in their next game against United Services, in a fixture marred by foul play. The most alarming incident arose when a Portsmouth AFC player was seized roughly by the throat by an opposition player in the second half. Both the *Portsmouth Evening News* and the *Evening Mail* were united in their condemnation of the military team's tactics: 'It was a somewhat rough and unpleasant game,' stated the former, while the latter commented: 'The referee further had to caution some of the players for their unfortunate tactics.'

The papers were also agreed that the Services team, when they concentrated on playing football rather than strangling the opposition, were worthy of the win, with the combination of their forwards exceptionally strong.

But even their opening goal was surrounded by controversy. The twelfth-minute effort was allowed by the referee in spite of an appeal by the civilians for hands. The second goal didn't arrive until midway through the second half and was described in the match reports as 'somewhat lucky'.

The same day saw details of Portsmouth AFC's second round Portsmouth Senior Cup game with Portsmouth NE made public after the cup draw by the Portsmouth FA. The borough club was among those represented at the association's meeting along with Royal Marines Artillery, Royal Inniskilling Fusiliers, Fareham Rovers, Freemantle and Oxford Light Infantry. The Infantry were the next opponents for Portsmouth AFC as November gave way to December.

The result is unknown, but the original Pompey's following match on December 6th 1890 deepened the gloom which had begun to develop around their season. Winchester inflicted a further defeat, 1–2, in a game notable for being best forgotten. An obviously bored *Evening Mail* correspondent noted:

Winchester scored after a quarter of an hour. Nothing of consequence happened until the change of ends when Pares equalised.

This compelled Winchester to press forward harder, so Portsmouth AFC had to go on the defensive. A few minutes before the end and Winchester secured their win.

The *Portsmouth Evening News* reporter was similarly fed up with the fare offered by the players. He described the second half display as 'monotonous'. The original Pompey had gone in just two matches from a violent clash to one which induced sleep.

A similar mood-swing happened in the next game when Portsmouth NE were overrun 9–0 in the Portsmouth Senior Club second round. The fixture was delayed several times because of the severe cold, to leave the town team without a game for a month. They rapidly fulfilled their return friendly against Oxford Light Infantry in case the extreme frost set in again after the cup tie.

The military men were dispatched 3–1 in a match which, unknown at the time to the players, was a forerunner for that historic Portsmouth Senior Cup final. GL Pares, who went on to play in three out of those four final ties, was the man of the friendly. His selection was inevitable once more for he scored all of his side's goals to follow his three-goal haul in the clash with North End.

His prolific spell took his tally for the season to eleven in just seven known appearances. Predictably, he was named as one of Portsmouth AFC's best players in the win, along with his brother Bernard, Wood and Baker.

The winter weather held off long enough for the original Pompey to notch up another victory over a service team, the Yorkshire Regiment being defeated 4–2 on January 22nd to gain revenge for the early season defeat. The good form seemed the perfect build-up to the original Pompey's first appearance of 1890/91 in the Hampshire Senior Cup.

They travelled to the Naval Works Ground at Woolston next for what was their first match out of eleven to be played away from Portsmouth that season. GL Pares' golden touch continued on the road with both of Portsmouth AFC's goals in their 2–3 defeat.

Every goal in the game was scored in an action-packed first half. The match was another whose staging was delayed by the continual frost. Conditions may have been warmer when it was eventually played but they were hardly better as blinding rain fell in the second half.

The downpour gave the visitors an advantage, with the home team having to suffer the rain in their faces. But the borough side were unable to obtain the goal which would bring them level again.

The teams lined up against each other once more a week later when the score was reversed in their Portsmouth Senior Cup semi-final. It was a game which, incidentally, merited just a single line report in the *Portsmouth Times*.

CHAPTER FORTY-TWO

But that seven days had included a unique football event – an indoor six-a-side tournament held under gaslight. Somehow, it was just inevitable that GL Pares would be involved – and he was, in the biggest way possible. News of the innovative occasion was revealed in the *Hampshire Post* of January 16th. It reported that the brother of the famous footballing family had in hand an initiative which he hoped would benefit the Portsmouth Hospital Fund. He was on to a winner, according to the paper:

Should Colonel Mumby grant permission for the use of the hall, the novelty of the scheme should ensure plenty of patronage.

All the clubs in the immediate district having been invited to play, the response has been most favourably received and there's every prospect of a successful result. The competition will be on the principles recognised in county challenge cup ties and will be played in rounds.

Just six players would be on each side and each game would last fifteen minutes. The winners were in line for silver medals. The competition would take place after the Naval and Military tournament at the Drill Hall.

A few days later, the *Portsmouth Evening News* announced the 'novel football entertainment' had attracted twenty-nine entries.

Portsmouth AFC A- and B-sides were among them. The senior team were drawn against Havant, with the B-team facing Buckland Congregational. Perhaps as a result of the interest, the matches were shortened. Those in the preliminary rounds would last seven minutes. The semi-finals and final would be ten minutes long.

A week later, and the paper was reporting that a 'good crowd of spectators' had enjoyed the first night's action on Monday , January 26th, 1891. They were entertained by the band of the Portsea Island Workhouse, which performed every night under its conductor, Squire Graham.

Portsmouth AFC's A-team played first of the club's two sides. They needed five minutes of extra time to defeat Havant 23 points to 13, with four points being awarded for a goal and one for a corner. The success was exceeded by the B-team's convincing 28 points to four walkover against Buckland Congregational Church on the second night in front of 'a very large attendance', according to the *Portsmouth Evening News*.

The outstanding form continued into the second round when both original Pompey sides were pitted against each other. The A-team emerged 12–4 winners in accordance with their seniority. But the winning stopped in round three when Oxford Light Infantry romped home 4–1, and deservedly so in the view of the *Hampshire Post*. The Light Infantry went on the win the tournament 17–9 against Portsmouth Rugby Club in the final on Wednesday January 28th. The medals were presented gracefully and pleasantly by Mrs Norman Pares – who else? – at 10 pm after a total of five hours' play on the last of the three nights.

The *Hampshire Post* was lavish in its praise of the imaginative event:

The success of the tournament should lead the committee to consider the advisability of making it an annual one, for we doubt not that the game of football will have been considerably popularised by the exhibition.

Less complimentary was its verdict on the competition's winners. Portsmouth AFC and Portsmouth Grammar School were the best combinations, it considered, and the most powerful, while the Light Infantry's display in the final was 'not so good, but good enough'.

The *Portsmouth Evening News* was less impressed with the arrangement. The space inside the Drill Hall was a bit limited with the ball being repeatedly kicked among the spectators, it commented:

Hard knocks were sustained at times by some of them, being taken very good-temperedly.

Once, the ball became lodged in the hall's iron rafters and had to be knocked down by an enthusiastic spectator with a head for heights. The paper did praise the original Pompey's role in making the arrangements for the event, notably through the brothers Pares and a committee of Portsmouth AFC captain Wood, honorary secretary Grant and player GL Pares.

The *Portsmouth Times* welcomed the large sum which was on its way to the Royal Portsmouth and Gosport Hospital from the tournament's proceedings:

The matches were all contested with the greatest energy and the success which attended their initial efforts should encourage the committee to organise further tournaments.

Grant had the pleasant task of handing £20.7s.6d to the hospital in early March 1891 as a result of the tournament. The money was again hailed with glee

by the *Portsmouth Times*, which repeated its pleas for the six-a-side games to become an annual event in the football season in Portsmouth.

CHAPTER FORTY-THREE

But for the moment, it was a case of back to the outdoor pitches for Portsmouth AFC. Some matters stayed the same, though. The name Pares was still on the score sheet. On the latest occasion, on February 7th, it was Bernard's turn to lead Portsmouth AFC to victory. He notched both the side's goals in the 2–1 win with which the *Portsmouth Evening News* credited the side in their game at Fareham. The *Hampshire Post* was convinced the score was 1–0 in favour of the home side. Both papers agreed that the borough club were weakly represented. Only ten players turned out for them, after just seven arrived for the kick-off. Three unnamed substitutes took their places, two on the right-wing and one on the opposite side of the pitch.

Nevertheless, the original Pompey took the lead on fifteen minutes through the combined play of Shutte and Bernard Pares, a former scholar at Harrow. The second goal arrived before half-time from the feet of Pares, in the *Portsmouth Evening News*' version.

Fareham were determined to take advantage of their weak opponents and record a rare win but the

Private Flannery only played one game for Portsmouth AFC - and what a game! It was the 1891 Portsmouth Senior Cup win against the Oxford Light Infantry.

visitors' defence held firm until the last few minutes. The home side then pulled a goal back. It was too little to get them back into the match. The performance of Portsmouth AFC's backs and the clever runs of Bernard Pares were credited by the *Portsmouth Evening News* with the win.

In the *Hampshire Post*'s account of the match, Portsmouth AFC played a fine game in spite of their numerical disadvantage and did well to lose by only a single goal.

No dispute existed about the next win for the blue shirts as they moved towards the Portsmouth Senior Cup final. Portsmouth Grammar School were the victims as a single goal half-time deficit was overturned by two strikes, one from a Pares brother and the other by Grant, direct from a corner kick.

Portsmouth AFC had enjoyed the best of the opening forty-five minutes but both sides were weakened. Two of the Pares brothers, Garrington, Wood and Lever were all away for the borough outfit, making the club's continual problem of absentees only too plainly evident.

Several unfamiliar names were on the team sheet the next week as the same situation carried on. But the likes of S Payne, R Blurton, ES Cooper and Rollands were still too strong for Havant. FG Jenkins kicked two of the goals for the original Pompey on his debut. The other goal came from G Pead. All was looking good, in spite of the missing players, for the season's big match in the final a fortnight away when Portsmouth AFC took on Oxford Light Infantry to reclaim 'their' cup for the first time since 1888.

CHAPTER FORTY-FOUR

Matters were less positive off the field. As the final's first replay got underway, the *Hampshire Telegraph* reported growing anxiety among the sportsmen of Portsmouth about the completion of the long-awaited recreation ground at Stamshaw. With the football season ending, and cricket about to start, there was increasing alarm about the continual absence of any news about the project's likely opening date:

Work on levelling, fencing and other works preparing the ground has dragged slowly along and although we are now rapidly approaching the season of sports and pastimes, nothing has been heard as to when the final opening will take place.

We hear some hitch has occurred in the building of the pavilion which is likely to delay the opening until the commencement of the football season in the autumn.

But we're quite sure that if all representations were made in the proper quarters all difficulties of this site will be removed and the ground opened in time for cricket and all the summer pastimes.

August arrived and the paper was bitter about the continued absence of the ground from Portsmouth's amenities. Still no firm news could be obtained from the council about the site's eventual opening. A grant for the scheme had been given by the government years before and there should have been a time span of just months between its receipt and the ground being in use, the paper angrily reported:

There was a hitch, we are told by the members of the Parks and Open Spaces Committee, but we do not know what the hitch is. The excuse that the pavilion will cost too much is not good enough. A byelaw regulating the use of the ground was also put in place long ago. We doubt if the football season will see the ground in use. The cricket season is flying by.

Season 1891/92 dawned and the paper's prediction proved sadly true. The original Pompey were back at the US grounds where they had turned out for fourteen of their nineteen matches during the previous campaign. But the delay over the new ground and the death of one of the club's founders cast a shadow over the new campaign and wiped out any euphoria generated by the Portsmouth Senior Cup triumph just four months previously.

Amazingly, the club appeared to have made no attempt to defend the hard-won trophy. An honour which had been so stubbornly fought over on the pitch and in the committee room suddenly seemed to be meaningless as Portsmouth AFC went into hibernation.

The team played almost as many matches in the second of the six-a-side tournaments as they did during the rest of the season. The indoor event took place – again at the Drill Hall in Alfred Road – just before Christmas rather than the slightly later staging of the inaugural competition.

The *Portsmouth Times* was sure the change of date would make no difference to the continued success of the tournament:

The success which attended the tournament promoted by the Portsmouth AFC in The Drill Hall last year has encouraged the originators to repeat it.

And on the first three days of next week 'football by gaslight' will be all the rage.

No less than twenty-nine teams have entered, the most noticeable absentees being Oxford Light Infantry, last year's winners.

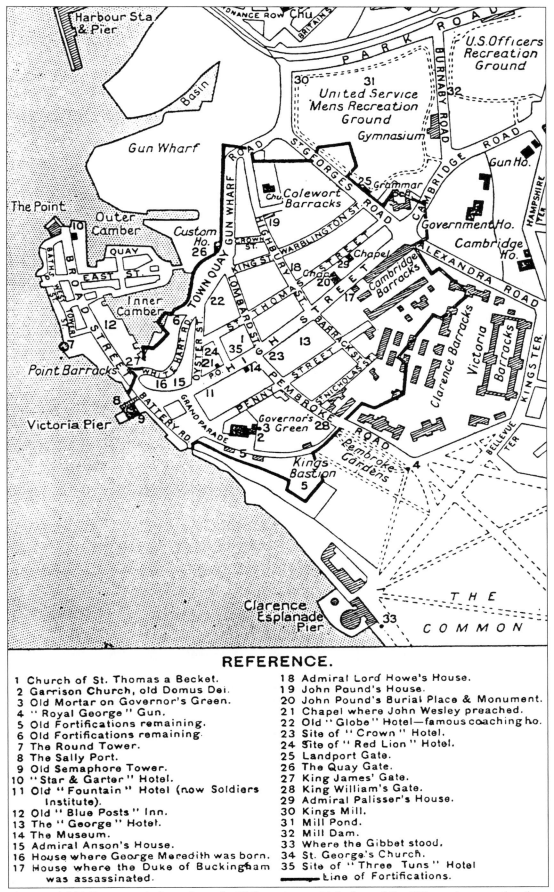

REFERENCE.

1 Church of St. Thomas a Becket.
2 Garrison Church, old Domus Dei.
3 Old Mortar on Governor's Green.
4 "Royal George" Gun.
5 Old Fortifications remaining.
6 Old Fortifications remaining.
7 The Round Tower.
8 The Sally Port.
9 Old Semaphore Tower.
10 "Star & Garter" Hotel.
11 Old "Fountain" Hotel (now Soldiers Institute).
12 Old "Blue Posts" Inn.
13 The "George" Hotel.
14 The Museum.
15 Admiral Anson's House.
16 House where George Meredith was born.
17 House where the Duke of Buckingham was assassinated.
18 Admiral Lord Howe's House.
19 John Pound's House.
20 John Pound's Burial Place & Monument.
21 Chapel where John Wesley preached.
22 Old "Globe" Hotel—famous coaching ho.
23 Site of "Crown" Hotel.
24 Site of "Red Lion" Hotel.
25 Landport Gate.
26 The Quay Gate.
27 King James' Gate.
28 King William's Gate.
29 Admiral Palisser's House.
30 Kings Mill.
31 Mill Pond.
32 Mill Dam.
33 Where the Gibbet stood.
34 St. George's Church.
35 Site of "Three Tuns" Hotel
———— Line of Fortifications.

A map of Old Portsmouth from the early 20th century which showed the US sports grounds where Portsmouth AFC played many important fixtures.

Senior, minor and junior clubs mingle together in the competition and I cannot but think that the executive might offer a special prize to the minor/junior club getting nearest to the final...

...wrote the paper's columnist, Augur.

The original Pompey made it through to the final, in spite of their lack of other action, only to come up against a services club. Unlike the Oxford Light Infantry in the Portsmouth Senior Cup, the 15th Company Royal Artillery were less accommodating. They brushed aside the borough team 13 points – three goals and one corner – to five points – one goal and one corner – with the scoring system remaining the same at four points for a goal and one point for a corner. The game was very fast and seemingly a fitting final for another successful event.

Officials at the Royal Portsmouth and Gosport Hospital could look forward to receiving another substantial cheque. Portsmouth AFC were represented by two sides for the second year running. The A-team faced Buckland Congregational in the first round as the B-side took on Portsmouth NE.

Other matches in the opening round included Portsmouth Red Star v Portsmouth Grammar School and the Royal Inniskilling Fusiliers v Royal Marine Artillery. Among the remaining entries were Havant, Fareham, St John's of Forton, Albion and St Simon's Institute. Music was provided by the Volunteer Band.

The tournament was overseen by the organising committee of Wood, Captain Cooper RA and Grant, Wood and Grant having organised the inaugural event. Only eight matches were played on the opening night of December 21st. The original Pompey's A-team breezed through their opening tie against the clearly over-run church team, accumulating 17 points from four goals and a corner to Buckland Congregational's single goal for four points.

They had a harder time in the second round when they came up against Portsmouth NE who had conquered the B-team by 20 points – five goals – to eight points – two goals. The borough club's senior side made sure North End did not achieve a double by winning 12 points to eight, or three goals to two.

It was a case of same again as Portsmouth AFC found themselves facing North End's B-team in round three. They outclassed their rivals with four goals and two corners – 18 points to nil. Just Fareham stood in the way of a second cup final appearance for the town club in eight months. Portsmouth AFC ran up an embarrassingly large score of 32 points – seven goals, four corners – to just 6 points – one goal, two corners – for the opposition.

CHAPTER FORTY-FIVE

A sign of how poor Portsmouth AFC's season was otherwise can be shown by the fact that this was their only meeting of the campaign with Fareham. Games outside of the five played in the Drill Hall were few and far between for the original Pompey in 1891/92. Their first fixture of just seven in all didn't take place until late November. The lead-in to the traditional start of the season in early September had been marred, anyway, by the news of the death of Robert Hemingsley.

He made thirty-eight recorded appearances for the club, frequently among the backs, in the four years from their formation in 1884. The details of his death were reported by the *Portsmouth Times* on September 5th:

An ardent cricketer and footballist, he acquired the friendship of lovers of those games, including Arthur Conan Doyle, who recently visited him in Birmingham.

He worked for the Portsmouth Times and Evening Mail before he went to Birmingham and then to West Hartlepool, where he was unable to take up his last job because he fell so ill. He died in Wolverhampton where he was born.

His age was not given. Hemingsley would easily have recognised the limited ambitions of the club he had left behind and of Grant in his role as the honorary secretary, if not of the new captain, ES Cooper RA. Portsmouth AFC's parochial fixture list for 1891/92 was criticised in the *Portsmouth Times*, unusually for the generally supportive press.

The match card, such as it was, didn't appear until late October. It contained, in the paper's words:

...no fewer than twenty-eight matches, all the clubs engaged being local.

One would almost think that this powerful committee might occasionally soar beyond local matches and try conclusions with a good Metropolitan club.

Whatever happened to that busy fixture list was not reported, but tellingly, the first appearances of the season for Grant at half-back and GL Pares on the left-wing came in Hampshire FA's 4–2 win over Sussex at Chichester on October 17th 1891.

Pares showed that the apparent inactivity for the borough outfit had done him no harm by notching Hampshire's second and fourth goals in front of several hundred spectators. He didn't have the chance to repeat the feat for the original Pompey the next Saturday.

The following Monday's edition of the *Portsmouth Evening News* again revealed the absence from the pitch of the town's supposedly superior team.

Match reports appeared for Albion Athletic Association v Portsmouth Wanderers, St Simon's Institute v Southsea Rovers, Portsmouth Grammar School v Brogians and Portsmouth NE v Oasis of Gosport as well as a variety of cup ties.

Such sparse news of Portsmouth AFC as emerged showed that they had been given a bye in the first round of the Portsmouth Senior Cup. Three other teams of the twelve who had entered were awarded similar treatment. No more details were reported about the blue shirts' involvement in the competition. Their most recent final opponents of Oxford Light Infantry were in action in the first round.

However, they were mired in controversy from the start. *Portsmouth Evening News* reader James Williams from Southsea complained of the Infantrymen's tie against Freemantle. He alleged that the service team's first goal was only awarded because the referee had been influenced by the shouts of the team's supporters. The ball did not go within a foot of their opponents' goal, he complained:

To prevent the possibility of another disputed goal of this character occurring, might I suggest the use of some network extending rearward from the goalposts?

Goalnets were indeed being introduced nationally. They were initially used in the January of 1891 in a north v south match and were approved by the FA the month after, but the legislators held back from recommending their immediate use until the price to be charged to the clubs by the inventor was worked out.

No such problems were likely for Portsmouth AFC. They had too few games to worry about goalnets. Their opener to the season finally arrived on November 28th. They lost to a single goal scored before half time by Whitman, the centre forward of their opponents, HMS *Excellent*.

The game took place in a downpour, which made the Men's Recreation Ground pitch heavy and play difficult. Old favourite Garrington returned to the civilians' goal for his only known appearance of the season in their next game – a month later. He was, however, unable to prevent a further loss by 0–3. That time, the opposition was provided by the defeated cup finalists, Oxford Light Infantry. The contrast between that hard-fought occasion and the repeat fixture between the rivals was as great as possible.

Less than nine months separated the matches but the only thing they had in common was the general venue, though the Men's Recreation Ground was used as opposed to the Officers' Ground on the opposite side of Burnaby Road.

Another burst of torrential rain dominated the latest game on December 30th 1891. Oxonian centre forward Staite was the only player to delight in the squelchy conditions. He scored a hat-trick for all his side's goals, against a club he was soon to play for.

CHAPTER FORTY-SIX

Portsmouth AFC's prospects were as gloomy as the weather. January fixtures with Winchester (away), RMA (home) and Chichester (away), were listed in the local papers only to disappear when the match reports for the corresponding Saturdays were printed. The next match for the borough team of which there is a record was a draw with town rivals, Portsmouth NE. How recently had the original Pompey swatted the upstarts away. How they struggled in the latest contest between them.

The conditions, again, were against a decent game of football. Portsmouth AFC were back at their initial home of Alderman Kent's meadows next to his Stubbington Lodge in North End a further month later. The still rural area had not staged a football match for more than five years. It showed. The *Portsmouth Evening News'* verdict for the derby clash was that the 'ground was in a very bad condition'.

For the *Hampshire Post*, the fixture took place 'under somewhat unfavourable conditions'. Why Portsmouth AFC played there again went unexplained. It can be no coincidence, however, that the club's keeper was Kent!! He conceded a single goal scored by Pead in the second half to equalise Allen's strike in the opening forty-five minutes as the game ended 1–1.

Portsmouth NE had warmed up with a game against the Hampshire Regiment. Other matches that previous Saturday saw the likes of Portsmouth Post Office take on Portsmouth Wanderers, HMS *Excellent* play Portsmouth Red Star, Southsea Juniors play each other and even Portsmouth Wanderers 2nd XI and Portsmouth Red Star B team stage a match.

But no Portsmouth AFC. And so the season continued. They were due to play the Post Office on February 6th until more poor weather caused the fixture to be abandoned. The constant rain led to all that day's fixtures being washed out. At last Petersfield came up on the original Pompey's sparse fixture list. They performed their usual role in the life of the borough club – as willing victims.

The 4–2 win allowed Portsmouth AFC to claim their first victory of the season on February 13th in just their fourth apparent match. Even then, the town club had to do things the hard way to be able to claim that modest joy. The home side easily went ahead through a first-half goal on the pitch at Petersfield Heath. The visitors were handicapped by arriving two players short. They had missed the train to the game. A pair of short substitutes filled in for them, according to the match reports.

Portsmouth AFC took control in the second half. Goals by Collins and the Allen brothers saw them home in spite of a late goal for Petersfield.

Captain Cooper enjoyed a fine game in goal for the original Pompey along with one of his backs, Miller. The Allens were also congratulated for their fine combination.

Portsmouth AFC made it two wins in a row in their next game, which followed yet a further month later on March 12th 1892, after advertised games with Havant and Oxford Light Infantry never made it into print afterwards. Plenty was known about the original Pompey's next opponents. Portsmouth Grammar School had reached the Portsmouth Senior Cup final with a last four win over the Hampshire Regiment by 3–0 before several hundred spectators. This cast Portsmouth AFC in the unfamiliar role of warm-up merchants. They proceeded to ruin the school's preparations for their big game.

In their best display of the season, although there was a distinct lack of choice, the town players battled their way to a 2–0 success. Pead and Williams scored the goals, one in each half, in the match at Hilsea.

To put the match into perspective, the same day saw the rapidly strengthening Southampton St Mary's add to their reputation with a comprehensive 5–0 thrashing of the Medical Staff Corps at Aldershot to clinch the Hampshire Senior Cup. Some 4000 fans watched that victory which enabled the Saints to boast of a hat-trick of triumphs in the county's leading football competition. They went three goals up before half-time and kept their grip on the game throughout.

Seven days later and it was the turn of Portsmouth Grammar School and Freemantle to contest Portsmouth's cup. The trophy followed the Hampshire version in making the journey in the direction of Southampton. Freemantle won 2–0. Portsmouth AFC could only watch from the side-lines.

It was preferable for them to being on the pitch. They took on the 2nd Battalion South Staffordshire Regiment on March 22nd, and lost 0–3 in their equal worst display of the season, such as it was.

The 'campaign' concluded with a one-all draw with HMS *Excellent*. The first-half was a goalless but entertaining affair, somewhat against the odds, and R Allen rounded off the original Pompey's truncated fixture list with an equaliser to right-winger Macready's opener for the sailors. The game took place on what was virtually the last match day of 1891/92, March 26th, with the previous year's cup final extensions a distant memory.

Portsmouth AFC's absence went unremarked in the summary of the football season by the *Portsmouth Evening News*:

During the winter, the growth of this particular sport has kept pace with that of the last few years and the contests since last November have been at least as to numbers eminently sufficient.

Frost and snow has interfered but little with Portsmouth this season and the average number of matches each Saturday in the district have been about twelve.

That was more than the borough club appeared to have played all season.

The club's dismal hopes of a bright future were transformed within a month.

CHAPTER FORTY-SEVEN

No sooner had cricket gained the upper hand on the sports pages than came the news every sportsman in Portsmouth wanted to read. The North End Recreation Ground was about to be opened at last. The long-awaited boost to leisure pursuits in the area was revealed in the *Portsmouth Evening News* of April 13th 1892. The facility was to come into use on Whit Monday, June 6th.

The preparation of the site had been overseen by one of those committees so favoured by local authorities of any period. Those who belonged to this particular body revealed the scope of the new ground – a representative of each athletic club in Portsea was included, along with the eighteen members of the corporation's Parks and Open Spaces Committee. That amounted to eleven cricket clubs, four cycling,

> PORTSMOUTH AFC
> CUP TIES
> 1891/92
>
> No cup ties played by Portsmouth AFC

two football, two athletics and one each from gymnastics and bowling. The final weeks soon passed in the build-up to the opening.

The Portsmouth FA's centenary handbook of 1990 set the scene for the occasion:

There was plenty of space for selecting the site of a new recreation ground, since the fourteen wards comprising Portsmouth and Southsea extended little farther north than Winstanley Road, Southsea, save for isolated farms and large villas. And there was little development east of London Road, and virtually none to the east of what is now Copnor Road. The area chosen was to the north of Stamshaw brickworks, and became known as the New Stamshaw Recreation Ground, and by 1893 was sufficiently developed to acommodate four pitches.

Tempering the enthusiasm, though, was the delay in seeing the plans for the scheme become a reality. The initial attempts to set out the ground had been made two years earlier under the control of a popular groundsman, Mr A Edmonds.

But June 1892 arrived and the papers were full of details of the overdue initiative. The *Portsmouth Evening News* of June 3rd commented that the new ground comprised twenty-four acres. About ten of them were reclaimed mudland bought by Portsmouth Corporation from the government's Board of Trade for £25 an acre.

The rest is corporation land that, until recently, was partly arable and partly let out in allotments at small rents...

...it stated.

Another £4500 had been spent by the corporation laying out the new ground, according to the paper. A pavilion, which would not be completed until the winter, would cost a further £1500.

The following day's *Portsmouth Times* added Winchester College to the details of the area's previous owners.

Cricket pitches, a cinder cycling track, a running track and lawn tennis courts were all ready for use, to make the ground 'one of the finest recreation grounds in the south or anywhere in England,' the paper boasted.

A similar accolade was bestowed by the *Hampshire Telegraph* in its coverage of the opening ceremony, though the paper could not resist recalling its campaign of a year earlier against the constant delays in the completion of the ground.

Its comment column talked of a wasted two to three years to bring the project to fruition. That,

however, was history. In what was:

...once the merest wilderness in a really pastoral area, under the able hand of the borough engineer, Mr Boulnois, now constitutes a recreation ground which bears all-round comparison with any in the kingdom.

Mr Boulnois had been succeeded by Mr Murch, who had carried on his good work, in the paper's opinion. Alderman T Foster Scott, Portsmouth's mayor, performed the opening ceremony. He told the watching crowd of his pride that the new ground added to the array of public leisure facilities which had been provided by the corporation in the past fourteen years.

At that time, Portsmouth only had government-controlled Southsea Common as an open space. Those days had been replaced by Victoria Park being opened as well as Canoe Lake, Kingston Recreation Ground and others besides them.

A series of competitions was held to launch the new ground to show the breadth of sports which could be enjoyed there. D Perkins, of Portsmouth Gymnastics Club, won the long jump in 17ft 7^1/$_2$ ins, the 440 yards hurdles was clinched by JH Ward in 59.35 seconds and Portsmouth Harriers' EG Cobden took first place in the mile flat handicap with a time of 4min 53.15sec. A one-mile cycle race, an elementary schools' team race and a bicycle handicap over a mile for boys aged fourteen and under also took place.

Alderman Scott Foster laid the foundation stone for the pavilion on October 21st. Construction was expected to take two months and would produce a building with a large room, two dressing rooms and terraces on its north and south sides.

CHAPTER FORTY-EIGHT

By then, Portsmouth AFC's players and supporters had surprisingly decided to shun the new site although they had played a major role in campaigning for its provision. They accepted the offer of the use of Governor's Green, instead, for their regular games. It was a new-look club which adopted the seafront site as its home. For the club's annual meeting, on September 26th 1892, had been a joint affair with Portsmouth NE. Members of both outfits voted to amalgamate. The decision delighted the *Evening Mail* which regarded the move as signalling a bright future for football in Portsmouth:

After some discussion by the members of both clubs, it was decided to amalgamate them for their mutual benefit to more thoroughly represent the association footballers of the town and to promote the interest of the game to a greater extent than formerly. The Portsmouth club should now occupy a more prominent position among clubs in the county. It is hoped successes may be more assured.

Lieutenant H Dawson RA was unanimously elected as the captain of the new club and a representative committee was formed. Several new members were also elected at the meeting. Another vote saw the combined club entered into the Portsmouth Senior Cup.

Players who wanted the chance to be involved were asked to write to the honorary secretary, WE Grant, no change there, who had earlier reported a healthy balance sheet to the meeting, at his usual address of 3 Buckingham Villas, Villiers Road, Southsea.

The meeting was held a month after Mr Grant had told a similar story to the Portsmouth FA's annual meeting held at the same venue of Landport's Albany Hotel. He told the members of the association they had more than £13 in hand in their account. They gave him a hearty vote of thanks for his hard work. The closing date for the cup competitions was set as October 1st. Each entry would cost 5 shillings, to be sent to Mr Grant.

Fourteen clubs came forward for the 1892/93 Portsmouth Senior Cup and the original Pompey were drawn against the RMLI in the first round. But it was the Hampshire Senior Cup which provided the town club's best and worst moments of the season.

The first occurred at the Stamshaw Recreation Ground, which had obviously been earmarked for special occasions. As ground debuts go, an 8–0 victory take some topping. That was the size of the beating which Portsmouth AFC handed out to their south coast rivals Bournemouth in the competition's opening round.

A goodly gathering of spectators lined the ropes for the November 26th tie. They witnessed a rout. The *Portsmouth Evening News* stated in its preview:

This should be an interesting and exciting match. Portsmouth AFC for the first time in many years have the luck to play at home. Bournemouth are well-known cup fighters.

They left their reputation at home in a game which was dominated by its wet and slippery ground made even wetter and more slippery by the rain which began to fall soon after the 2.50pm kick-off. The *Portsmouth Times* likened conditions underfoot to a swamp. The original Pompey's left-winger, B Williams, revelled in the conditions. He

Basil Pares scored twice as Bournemouth were beaten 8-0 on the debut of the original Pompey at the Stamshaw Recreation Ground.

contributed a hat trick towards his side's victory.

He opened the scoring towards the end of the first-half. He finished off a good bout of combined play by his team mates. Five minutes into the second-half, Williams struck again and rounded off his contribution with one of a group of three goals for the home side which sealed a 'deserved and brilliant victory', in the words of the *Portsmouth Evening News*.

Portsmouth AFC's other goals were shared between Basil Pares and GL Pares, with two each, and Pead with one. Seven of the goals came in the second half.

Basil Pares scored his side's third a few minutes after Williams had opened up a 2–0 lead following a dribbling rush and excellent passing among the borough club's forwards. The visitors, who had started the game by putting the home team on the defensive:

...were thoroughly demoralised and goal after goal was obtained in quick succession by the Portsmouth AFC forwards. The visitors made desperate rallies at Portsmouth AFC's goal. Two or three dangerous rushes were stopped by the excellent play of Portsmouth AFC's backs...

...as the *Portsmouth Evening News* reported.

The paper added that Bournemouth had suffered from the loss of their county right-winger, Stroud, who had severely strained the tendons of his right foot. He had to be content with watching his team suffer as he ran the line. Portsmouth AFC member John French was the home linesman, with Mr Felgate making a return visit as the referee.

The strength of that seven goal second-half onslaught lived up to the prediction of a stronger, combined Portsmouth AFC ready to take the town forward in the footballing world. The momentum continued to gather when the team returned to the recreation ground eight days before Christmas 1892, for the second round tie with the Medical Staff Corps who had travelled from Aldershot.

More spectators than usual were attracted for the ground's undoubted record attendance. Among them was the MP, Alderman Baker, whose son was making his third recorded appearance of the season for the home team's defence. He and the rest of the crowd went away happy, having seen the original Pompey clinch a 3–0 win over the previous season's beaten finalists.

On the pitch, Portsmouth AFC, not for the first time, had the Pares family to thank for their success. Basil scored two of the goals and his brother, GL, scored the other to continue their scoring record from the previous round.

The first goal arrived in the dying minutes of the first half thanks to Basil. He neatly shot home after a good run from the halfway line, good passing and combined play in which he had featured with his brother alongside Williams and Pead.

The Medical Staff Corps were one man short for an unspecified reason but made the home side, in white shirts for the occasion, battle for their victory. It took Portsmouth AFC until the eighty-fifth minute before they could open up a two-goal lead. The decisive strike came from GL Pares who managed to kick the ball between the posts after a goalmouth scramble. Lunney, the visitors' keeper, saved and put the ball on to his bar, only to see it rebound off the underside into the goal.

Shortly afterwards, it was Basil's turn to seal the success with a splendid run rounded off with a good shot. Just as importantly as the shooting skills of the Pares siblings, Portsmouth AFC were able to ride their luck, as evidenced by their second goal.

The *Portsmouth Evening News* summed up the situation:

The good fortune which had attended the club in cup ties did not desert it.

Lady Luck's goodwill was seen most clearly when the Medical side were twice awarded hands against the home team. The first occasion came around the twenty-fifth minute. The kick was taken from right in front of the civilians' goal but the visiting player failed to take account of the wind and wasted the chance.

Basil Pares (who else?) saved the day by kicking the

Historical Portmuthian to be remembered in new pub name

by Michael Short
The News

NATIONAL pub chain Wetherspoons will be celebrating an influential man from Portsmouth's past when it opens up a new outlet in the city.

The group is spending more than £1.5m developing a new pub on the site of an empty Lloyds TSB bank in London Road.

Some 30 new full and part-time jobs will be created at the pub, which will be called the Sir John Baker.

It is named after a former MP and JP who owned several shops near to the site of the pub. He was also a former owner of North End Manor House, which stood on the corner of Stubbington Avenue.

J D Wetherspoon has already been granted a licence for the new pub by Portsmouth magistrates. Planning permission has been given as well.

The company already operates pubs in Portsmouth, Cosham and Havant and building work on the Sir John Baker will start in September, with the opening planned for February.

The pub will be music free, have no pool tables and one third of it will be a no smoking area.

There will also be a disabled access and customised toilets for the disabled.

Wetherspoon chairman Tim Martin said: 'We have enjoyed great success in Portsmouth and believe this pub will prove just as popular.

'We're certain that people in the area will be pleased to see the empty building restored and back in use once again.'

Alderman Sir John Baker is recalled in July 2000 for the name of a new pub close to the site of his North End Manor House, which stood on a corner of Stubbington Avenue.

ball away from his keeper and to safety. Ten minutes into the second half, and Portsmouth AFC gained another reprieve as the Corps missed a good opportunity to draw level.

They had previously watched in despair as one of their forwards, J Lunney, ruined a good shot by sending it too high. Portsmouth AFC also had their share of chances. The prospect of taking the lead in the twentieth minute went begging as a kick for hands was sent over the bar by an unnamed forward.

Basil Pares made the same mistake with a couple of chances in the second half after he had given his side the lead. Williams and Pead then combined in a charge towards the Aldershot side's goal, but Lunney was equal to Pead's shot. The keeper also played a large part, with his defenders, in preventing runs by Wood, Grant and Cook from succeeding with some excellent play. The home backs also came to their side's rescue, especially when a swift movement between Stothard, Griffin and two other forwards threatened the home goal. The *Portsmouth Evening News* had built up the match by saying:

There is a greater interest in Portsmouth AFC after they acquitted themselves so well against Bournemouth.

The result of today's match is being looked forward to with great interest to see if the local club at least maintains its form.

CHAPTER FORTY-NINE

The Medical Staff Corps, however, were unhappy with their defeat. They lodged a protest with the Hampshire FA which met the following Thursday at the Adelaide Restaurant in Southampton to consider the matter. The complaint centred around Portsmouth AFC's strip on match day.

Sergeant Lunney, from the Corps, told the meeting that the home team's choice of white shirts, instead of their usual blue tops, had caused confusion because it meant all the players turned out in the same colour.

The original Pompey's secretary, Grant, called the objection frivolous, saying no rules had been broken. He had checked in the rule book before the kick-off to ensure that was the case. The referee of the match had also written in to condemn the protest.

His view was upheld by the committee of the association, which allowed Portsmouth AFC to take their place in the semi-finals. Freemantle representative, FO Clarke, suggested a rule change to the rest of the committee to avoid the same situation happening again. But his colleagues decided to wait until their annual meeting to tackle the matter.

They immediately set about making the semi-final draw. It pitched the original Pompey against St Mary's and Freemantle against Cowes. Both ties were to take place at Southampton's County Ground on consecutive Saturdays.

The intensity of feelings in the already fierce rivalry between the original Pompey and their Solent rivals was increased by ninety minutes of hostile play when the tie finally occurred in early February 1893. The pitch became a battleground rather than a sporting venue.

The Saints won 2–0 on goals and by several dozen fouls if the match reports are to be believed. Over to the *Evening Mail*:

The Portsmouth AFC men were favourably impressed by the manner in which Saints made use of their hands, arms and elbows.

The correspondent who covered the bout for the paper commented that two rules in particular were frequently broken:

One – The thrower facing the field of play should throw the ball over his head with both hands.

Two – No player shall use his hands to hold or push an adversary.

If this last rule is not rigidly enforced, the game is spoiled. There is no more objectionable way of keeping a man off the ball than by the use of hands or elbows, and it ruins the game and tempers of the best players.

Referees should be, and in this district generally are, very firm on the point.

To judiciously, or even injudiciously, use one's weight can't be grumbled at but to re-inforce the feet with a liberal use of the hands is most objectionable.

The match details were obscured in the anger at the tactics employed by the Saints to secure their place in the final and deny Portsmouth AFC the chance of becoming finalists for the second time in four years.

Portsmouth AFC prepared for the semi-final by hoping their good form of the previous two rounds would be repeated. The *Evening Mail* was confident they would uphold the honour of the naval port:

The combination is sure to give a good account of themselves, even if they do not beat the Saints outright.

The 'plan of company' which has proved so successful in previous rounds will be carried out and Bombadier Williams (left-wing) comes from Shoeburyness to preserve the combination.

Further evidence of the town club's good chance of playing well was provided when GL Pares, on the opposite wing, scored the winning goal for the Old Etonians in a London Senior Cup match the previous Saturday.

A reduced fare was on offer from the London and South West Railway Company to encourage Portsmouth AFC's fans to cheer on their side in Southampton for what the *Portsmouth Times* dubbed 'is sure to be a splendid struggle'.

The paper was less enthusiastic about the cut-price travel:

It's a pity the time of departure is limited to the 11.30 am train. Why not the 12.25 pm?

All the high hopes of success disappeared under a flurry of flailing red-and-white shirted hands and elbows. The *Evening Mail* reflected the mood among Portsmouth AFC's players and followers. 'Everyone was ultimately disappointed,' it wrote:

Portsmouth AFC had shown such admirable form in previous rounds that their chance of securing the cup was thought to be a great one.

To be defeated by the Saints by 2–0 was certainly no disgrace and it must be remembered that the Portsmouth AFC XI, though composed of first-rate players, had not had many chances of playing together.

CHAPTER FIFTY

The contrast between the cup ties reflected what was very much a season of two halves in 1892/93. The first eleven of the nineteen fixtures represented the original Pompey's longest unbeaten run. Buoyed by the merger with Portsmouth North End, the initial results proved the wisdom of the amalgamation. The start of 1893 saw a change of form. The final batch of eight matches yielded just four wins.

A magnificent seven goals welcomed in the new season on October 8th. Portsmouth Post Office were the visitors to the original Pompey's newly adopted home of Governor's Green. If only all their opponents were so easily brushed aside. The early minutes showed no sign of the one-sided affair which the curtain raiser would become.

The even play soon gave way to domination by Portsmouth AFC. They had got the measure of the postmen's defence by half-time with a three goal lead and swept them aside with a further four goals after the interval.

EH Humby had just one shot of any difficulty to save in the Portsmouth AFC goal. 'The left-wing (of Pead and Williams) shone conspicuously for Portsmouth AFC and the sound defence of the half-backs and backs completely spoilt the Post Office attack,' in the *Portsmouth Evening News*' view.

A week later, and the original Pompey were given a rougher ride by the RMA on their way to a 4–2 win. The town club began with just ten men but were soon two goals up. One of them came from Pead. He added to it by giving his side a 3–0 lead before the Marines pulled back a goal from a free kick.

Half-time was reached with the score at 3–1. The second forty-five minutes were more even as the original Pompey's short defence were at a disadvantage against 'the heavy and unscientific charges of the Marines', according to the *Evening Mail*.

Their 'hustling and charging' style of play brought them a second goal. But the *Evening Mail* was clear as to whose fault it was. The culprit was the official:

...the mistake of the referee who thought the ball had gone just under instead of just over the bar.

Goalnets had obviously still failed to find their way into the barracks. But the civilians had scored a

PORTSMOUTH AFC CUP TIES 1892/93				
Portsmouth Senior Cup				
R1	Royal Marines Light infantry	a	W4-0	5.11.92
R2	North Staffordshire Regiment	USMG	L0-6	14.1.93
Hampshire Senior Cup				
R1	Bournemouth	Stamshaw	W8-0	26.11.92
R2	Medical Staff Corps Aldershot	Stamshaw	W3-0	17.12.92
S-f	Southampton St Mary's	County Grd	L0-2	4.2.93

fourth goal a few minutes earlier to put the result beyond doubt.

Poor shooting lost the blue shirts the opportunity to make it a hat-trick of wins when they took on Havant at Governor's Green on October 22nd, a day after work on the pavilion at the new Stamshaw Recreation Ground had started. A goalless draw seemed a fair result from a match which was even from start to finish.

Portsmouth AFC put out a weak team, with six changes from their last game. They were saved on three occasions by Humby, who had kept his place in goal, with a trio of skilful stops.

But the Portsmouth AFC forwards lost many excellent chances of scoring, particularly in the second half, by poor shooting...

...stated the *Portsmouth Evening News*, 'Agate defended his goal in fine form', his display allowing Havant to gain a rare draw with their larger neighbours. October was brought to a close with a ten-man Portsmouth FA team, which seemed to be Portsmouth AFC in disguise, clawing back a two goal deficit to scrape a 3–3 draw with their first service opponents of the season, the 1st Company Southern District Royal Artillery. An own goal gave the civilian side hope by reducing the arrears, Matson netted a second and H Pead got the equaliser by rushing the ball home from a scrum.

CHAPTER FIFTY-ONE

Cup action provided a welcome change for the original Pompey as the side set off in search of reclaiming the Portsmouth Senior Cup for the first time in two years. The RMLI's Forton Barracks was the destination for the first round tie on November 5th 1892 and a 4–0 win the outcome.

Tensions ran high as the match came close to being abandoned. The flashpoint was the second goal for Earp and the visitors in the second half. His shot appeared to go in but its validity was questioned by some of the large number of spectators present. The *Evening Mail* reported drama around the dispute:

One of RMLI's players left the ground and the game was suspended for some minutes.

The goal still stood in spite of the protests. The missing man returned – and Portsmouth AFC proceeded to wipe away the last remnants of opposition from the Marines. Two more goals were scored in quick succession by the civilians. They achieved

the victory against a general background of rowdy behaviour:

A great deal of unsportsmanlike behaviour was shown on the ground with respect to refereeing decisions. There was considerable hooting and groaning mingled with cheers...

...continued the *Evening Mail*.

Portsmouth AFC had gone straight on the attack from the kick off and into the lead with a well-directed shot by Earp. They came close to adding another when a player's shot hit the bar and rebounded. The second half's opening followed the same pattern. Fast play and smart passing by the town outfit kept the home side constantly on the defensive.

Portsmouth AFC's sparkling early season form for 1892/93 made little impact on the selectors at the Hampshire FA. Counting against the players was the club's failure to keep pace with the fast-developing nature of football. Predictably, Southampton had the biggest contingent in the county side against Surrey.

Their four players compared with a brace for Bournemouth, and one each from Banister Court, Royal Engineers, Winchester and Freemantle. They won 5–1.

The next scheduled opponents for Portsmouth AFC were the North Staffordshire Regiment and Petersfield, though no match reports have survived in spite of both games being included in the fixture lists of the previous day's papers.

The next game in which Portsmouth AFC were definitely in action was the 3–0 midweek success over the Cameronians in mid-November. The result proved the perfect tonic for their Hampshire Senior Cup opener against Bournemouth which stretched the naval port's side's unbeaten run to eight games.

News of the Portsmouth Senior Cup followed within a couple of days of the latest success.

The original Pompey were drawn at home against the North Staffordshire Regiment for the second round. The military team had earned their place by defeating Geneva Cross 3–1 in a first round replay after a one-all draw.

Pride of place in the opening round went to the fast-emerging 15th Company RA for a 7–0 victory over Fort Monckton Athletic Club. Cup holders Freemantle had scraped through by a single goal against the Hampshire Regiment. The other winners were Portsmouth Grammar School, 4–2 over Havant, and the RMA, with a 3–1 win over St Simon's Institute, following a 2–2 draw. It was also decided at the Portsmouth FA meeting, where the draw was made for the second round, to hold the 1892/93 six-a-side tournament on January 28th. The venue was switched to the Stamshaw Recreation Ground to create the biggest sporting event in its short history.

The choice of location was revealed in the *Portsmouth Times* in an eve of season preview. It welcomed the move from indoors at the Drill Hall to the western shore of the upper reaches of Portsmouth Harbour: 'The new park promises to be as good for football as it was for cricket,' was its verdict.

The Chichester game, destined to take place next, was another which has disappeared from the archives, but the goalless draw against an HMS *Excellent* side lacking a player at the US Men's Recreation Ground on December 10th 1892 is one result which has made it through the centuries. Next came the contentious Hampshire Senior Cup win over the Medical Staff Corps.

At the same time as the Hampshire FA meeting which determined the outcome of that cup match, Portsmouth AFC's players were at the US Men's Ground again to take on another military side in the shape of the Hampshire Regiment.

Right-winger Williams gave the civilians an ideal start with a goal just six minutes into the game, which became their record-breaking eleventh undefeated match.

The civilians tried to build on the lead, with some neat attacks, especially in the second half, only to find the Regiment's keeper Burton in energetic form. His left-winger, Inggs, put the soldiers level just after the break and that was how the score stayed. The result was an accurate reflection of the fair play shown by both teams. The best work for Portsmouth AFC was displayed by Wood, Matson, Williams, Cook and Earp.

An apparent Christmas Eve fixture away to Freemantle and a Boxing Day derby with Portsmouth Red Star at the Stamshaw Recreation Ground, one of four games on the day, were followed by a journey to Winchester on December 29th. The trip ensured the players of the original Pompey were busy during the festive period. None of the results has survived.

CHAPTER FIFTY-TWO

1893 began with another cup tie. Its result in the second round of the Portsmouth Senior Cup was less pleasant for the original Pompey than others so far that season. A large crowd gathered at the US Men's Ground on January 14th to see if they could build on their initial Portsmouth Senior Cup success over Forton and the recent Hampshire win against the Medical Staff Corps. A 6–0 rout at the feet of the North Staffordshire Regiment provided a compre-

hensive riposte to their optimism.

There were mitigating circumstances. Four members of the successful original Pompey team which faced the Corps were absent against the latest military opposition. On top of the high number of expected absentees, the civilians started the tie two men short.

They were further handicapped by a keeper, Humby, who insisted on kicking the ball instead of catching or punching it through the game. Snow also began to fall during the first half to add to the softness of the ground and worsen conditions. The soldiers, meanwhile, were at virtually full strength and determined to take advantage of their superiority of numbers.

The original Pompey's absentees were missing through a combination of business commitments and illness. The brothers Pares, Williams, Wood, Rundle and Lever were all unable to appear. Gough and Shepherd also failed to take their places in the starting line-up. Shepherd eventually arrived fifteen minutes late to slot into his side's right-wing. Gough never did show up. W Pead agreed to make up the numbers for the blue shirts after going along to watch the match.

The setbacks made little difference initially to the original Pompey but the Staffs gradually got on top

The absence of AW Cook hindered Portsmouth AFC's progress in the 1892/93 Portsmouth Senior Cup.

of the game in spite of the sound defensive work by Dawson, Grant and R Baker. Two goals in quick succession put the military men in the lead by half time. By then, a blinding snowstorm dominated the game.

It took more than that to deter the Victorian footballers and on they played. Except for Pead. His kind offer to help out the civilians came to a virtual end when he ricked his knee and was forced to do no more than become a limping passenger to his team mates. The Staffs attacked from the start of the second half and happily accepted a gift third goal. Humby totally missed one of his kicks out to leave the soldiers' right-winger, Fillingham, an easy task to score.

Portsmouth AFC tried unsuccessfully to get back into the game through Dawson and Grant but the only goals to follow were a further trio for the Staffs. In the words of the *Portsmouth Evening News*:

The North Staffs Regiment completely wiped out Portsmouth AFC in the second half.

The *Evening Mail* said:

The North Staffs Regiment forwards were tricky and pressed very cleverly. Their defence was not severely tested...

But the paper did praise Humby, though his unorthodox tactics played their part in the downfall of the original Pompey, as it wrote off the game as a meaningless display with its cup status counting for nothing:

The very easy defeat of the Portsmouth association club by the North Staffs Regiment will afford little satisfaction to either side. The game, which was in the second round of the Portsmouth Cup, was played in a fearful snowstorm and the fact that Portsmouth AFC were not only short of practice but had six absent from their regular team detracted from the interest of the game.

With their full team, the town club would have run the soldiers very close, even if they had not beaten them.

The original Pompey soon had the chance to find out the truth of that statement. Attention switched to the annual six-a-side tournament and the North Staffs stood in the way of the town club's progress to the quarter-finals. They inflicted a second defeat in a fortnight on their way to winning the popular event.

As many as forty teams had entered the tournament on January 28th 1893 and the *Hampshire Post*

reported that conditions for its first staging at the Stamshaw site were ideal. The ground was in excellent condition and the wind favourable when the sides lined up for the noon kick-off.

They must have represented a superb sight for those committed to seeing football continue to grow in Portsmouth. Four pitches – each 75 yards by 45 yards – were laid out side by side.

The organising committee of Wood, French, EA Gould, W Hookey and Grant, in his usual role of secretary, had decreed that offside would apply, with the second defender counting against the attacker instead of the third as usual, and that the games would last ten minutes each way, with five minutes of extra time. Goals would count for four points and corners for a point.

Two teams were entered by Portsmouth AFC. The B-side with Earp in goal, Grant and Burke at the back and the forwards of Pead, Whittington and Matson, fared best. They overcame their opening opponents, the C Company of the North Staffs Regiment, by four points – four corners – to nil.

The second round saw them pitched against the regiment's H Company and emerge the winners by six points – a goal by Grant in the first minute and two corners – to nil. The same score, with a goal by Matson, saw them through round three, when they faced the Regiment's D Company. But their defence was finally breached in the fourth round. They were beaten by 4 points – one goal – to 15 points, achieved by three goals and a corner, by the regiment's second team. (This score given in the local papers is wrong. It should be 13 points.)

The North Staffs first team made it to the final, which was an all-military affair – a sign of the immediate future for football in Portsmouth – against a team from the 15th Company RA. The regiment won by six points to nil. They notched up a goal and two corners. Sergeant Hughes played for the winners in the final with a broken collarbone.

His opposite number, Llewellyn, had an eye injury to even the situation in casualties. It would have been difficult for the 1500 spectators to see the keepers. The tournament's five hours of action ended in semi-darkness:

The attendance of spectators was at first rather thin, but the numbers gradually increased as time wore on until at last there was a very good attendance and the ground presented a most gay and animated appearance...

...wrote the *Portsmouth Evening News*.

The *Evening Mail* was also convinced of the popularity of the tournament:

SHERLOCK HOLMES WAS A POMPEY KEEPER

The tournament at North End was a tremendous success and it is satisfying to learn there will be a balance of a few shillings on the right side.

The play was interesting throughout and the two finalists were possibly the best teams on the day.

No one will grudge the Staffords their victory, for the fact that no less than ten teams entered from the regiment speaks volumes for their sporting spirit and enthusiasm.

The 15th Company could spare their rivals the win, added the paper, with a season's record beyond compare so far, of W17 D1, with 85 goals scored and 13 conceded.

Meanwhile, Portsmouth AFC's A side at the tournament could have done with some of that success. They failed to make progress at all. Their only game, in the second round, after a bye in the opening fixtures, was unfortunately against a strong Geneva

Ways to commemorate the centenary of Dr Arthur Conan Doyle's arrival in Southsea in 1882 were being considered by Portsmouth City Council as the anniversary of the date approached.

The most likely way to mark the important occasion was also one of the most obvious. City Council leader John Marshall told the *Portsmouth Evening News* in August 1982 – a month before the centenary – that a plaque was probably to be installed at the site of Bush House, upon which had been built flats following the wartime blitz which had flattened Sir Arthur's former home and medical practice.

Mr Marshall said: 'We have Doyle Avenue and Conan Road at Hilsea but I think a plaque would add a bit of interest.' However, the plaque idea seemed distinctly dull compared to the imaginative suggestion to remember Sir Arthur put forward by a journalist on the paper in its By The Way column of October 10, 1967. He envisaged the great detective staring through a magnifying glass at the onlookers below. The reporter was convinced the proposal would be a winner.

'I am prepared to bet that pilgrims in their thousands would be attracted to the site,' he wrote. 'Most of them would be visitors from the USA. For the Americans go nuts over everything to do with Sherlock Holmes. When will Portsmouth realise that Sherlock Holmes runs Dickens a close second when it comes to local literary associations?'

Never – to judge by an article which had appeared in the newspaper just four days previously. The short report concerned the presence of one of its reporters as the only person to respond to a bid by Southsea resident Winston Caldecott to set up a Sherlock Holmes Society in Southsea. But there was such a society in London and its members were in favour of the plaque being installed. They paid £50 in September 1982 towards its cost. The backing effectively enabled the idea to go forward and the plaque was accordingly unveiled on November 17, 1982.

The Sherlock Holmes Society's secretary,

Captain William Mitchell RN, who was born in Portsmouth, adopted for the occasion the traditional deerstalker and pipe so beloved of the detective.

He spoke of Dr Doyle's struggles during his early days in Southsea. He combined his daytime work as a doctor with his night-time role as a master of fictional mystery.

Cpt Mitchell said: 'For the first year, *A Study in Scarlet* failed dismally and Sir Arthur eventually had to sell it and the copyright for just £25. It finally appeared as a supplement to a *Mrs Beeton Christmas Annual* in 1887.'

A living link to Dr Doyle's time at Bush Villas was revealed in the *Portsmouth Evening News* the following June. A Mary Burdett from Gosport wrote to the paper to say that her late mother had known one of the owners of the property – Mrs Mullins – after him.

The genial doctor turned author once arrived on the doorstep of Bush Villas with his second wife. He asked Mrs Mullins, the then owner, if he could show Lady Doyle where he used to cook his frugal meals.

Mrs Mullins readily agreed and Dr Doyle stepped over the threshold of Bush Villas once more. She was a widow who lived in Waterlooville, north of Portsmouth, when she became friendly with Mrs Burdett's mother, who had died in 1961 aged 90.

Despite her advancing years, Mrs Mullins could remember a lot of details about Bush Villa. She described it as a roomy property which she and her businessman husband had converted to suit their wishes. The ground floor consisted of a shop which two flats above. The name of the shop was Madame Lee and Mrs Burdett believed that Mrs Mullins once managed the premises.

The goods which it sold were made at the corset factory, one of many in the Portsmouth area, owned by Mrs Mullins. The eve of the centenary of Dr Doyle's birth was marked on May 20, 1959, by special screenings of *The Hound of the Baskervilles* at a Southsea cinema.

Cross and ended in a single point defeat for Humby, Gough, Gibbons, Lieutenant Kirwan, Collins and Sheppard.

Cup football in a different competition occupied their minds. They agreed to scratch an impending fixture against Portsmouth Grammar School to allow the school to fulfil its Portsmouth Senior Cup tie second round game with the Post Office at Hilsea.

The *Portsmouth Times* was confident of success for the school, with its good passing and first class player and sometime-original Pompey man, Wood. Rare news of a former Portsmouth AFC player was given in the same edition. The previous season's captain, Captain Cooper RA, had become stationed on Gibraltar. Word had got back that he was training the Artillery team for the Gibraltar Challenge Cup.

Portsmouth AFC, for their part, were up against the greatly stiffer opposition of Southampton St Mary's in the Hampshire Senior Cup semi-final. A second cup disappointment in three weeks was the result, to continue their poor form in early 1893.

Insult was added to wounded pride straight afterwards when Freemantle pulled out of their fixture with the town club in order to play their February 18th semi-final in the Portsmouth Senior Cup against the 15th Company Royal Deport Artillery.

Petersfield volunteered to fill the gap in the borough club's 1892/93 fixture list on February 18th. The north Hampshire club must have thought they could reverse their long-running series of defeats in the games when they took a 2–0 half-time lead against the wind.

Portsmouth AFC were weakened by the absence of Wood and Bernard Pares, playing for Portsmouth Grammar School, and Grant, who was turning out for his college in London. But their loss failed to stop their club hitting back to secure a convincing win with five second-half goals.

Portsmouth AFC made it two wins in a row at Havant the following week. This time, it was their turn to score goals before half-time. F Waddington was the player behind the opener, from an awkward position, and H Pead struck home a splendid shot from Grant's pass.

Pead wasted several chances to put the original Pompey further ahead late on in the game through poor shooting. The visitors dominated the initial forty-five minutes and spent the last fifteen minutes camped around Havant's goal. The home keeper, Agate, was in excellent form early on, while the good defence of R Burke and the Portsmouth AFC half-backs at the other end ensured that few Havant attacks made any progress.

The win took Portsmouth AFC's playing record by the end of February, as reported in the local papers,

to: P15 W9 D3 L3 F43 A18.

Respectable enough, even if the bare statistics hid the fact that two of the losses had been in the most significant games of the season.

CHAPTER FIFTY-THREE

The *Portsmouth Times* was not fooled by the apparent success. The particular cause of its dissatisfaction was the long-standing lack of a ground for what was still Portsmouth's leading football club. The forced continual ground-hopping existence as 1893 wore on was lamented by the newspaper on February 18th:

What a grand day it will be for the Portsmouth FA when 'socker' catches on in this district and spectators line up in their thousands and large gates are the order of the day. Then will the Portsmouth FA run a ground of its own and provide enthusiastic supporters with a surfeit of good things.

Honorary secretary WE Grant has been obliged to reject overtures from Marlow, Windsor and Eton and several London clubs owing to the lack of a ground.

'No gate, no game' is the order with teams on tour. It was highly probable Bolton Wanderers would come south at the end of April. If so they would have met Arsenal at Plumstead on the Saturday, where they will be rewarded with a good gate.

Then it was hoped a small guarantee from the Portsmouth FA, St Mary's and Bournemouth would lead to their entertaining Hampshire.

With the help of the Staffords, 15th Company RA, Portsmouth and District, a team would soon have been forthcoming but the ground, as usual, proved the obstacle.

The service grounds will then be closed to football, though every facility would have been given by those quarters if either had been available. Hence, Portsmouth had to decline the offer.

William Pickford, the Hampshire FA's secretary, was left with the task of keeping the Lancashire giants happy by talking to their secretary, an old friend, to leave a glimmer of hope they could still visit the county one day.

The paper's dismay at the state of football in Portsmouth was increased soon after with the news that Portsmouth AFC's Hampshire Senior Cup semi-final against Southampton St Mary's resulted in a gate of £55. The *Evening Mail* took up the theme:

But the club gets nothing because the money goes to the Hampshire FA. St Mary's and Freemantle also get good crowds but they have the advantage of closed grounds.

The *Portsmouth Times*, again, reported that the semi-final in the Portsmouth Senior Cup, for which Freemantle had spurned Portsmouth AFC to take on 15th Company Royal Depot Artillery, attracted three hundred and ninety-one spectators at 6d entrance for each.

The subject of a ground just would not go away. Portsmouth AFC's secretary, Grant, was forced to reject Crouch End Rovers, from London:

Once more, it's a case of 'no gate, no game...'

...moaned the *Portsmouth Times*.

A welcome piece of good news for the followers of the original Pompey came with the announcement that Hospital Challenge Cup contenders, St Mary's Hospital from London, had agreed to visit them on March 4th. Before that came Portsmouth AFC's turn to cancel a match – with the Post Office – to make room for the prestigious fixture.

The town club seemed to be involved with more games that never came about than with actual fixtures as 1892/93 drew to a close. That didn't stop the Hampshire FA selectors from choosing Grant and Basil Pares for their game against Dorset at Southampton on March 18th. Grant was selected as the team's captain and Pares as their centre-forward.

Basil Pares's hopes of warming up with a run out against St Mary's Hospital were denied when the London side scratched their fixture at the last minute, because they were unable to raise a team. Their abandonment, however, came with the promise of a match at a later date.

The forward had been expecting to take on his own medicos as they faced up to tackling Bart's for the London Hospitals' Challenge Cup. He was nowhere to be seen when Portsmouth took on North Staffordshire Regiment in a hastily arranged fixture at the same venue as the intended St Mary's fixture of Governor's Green. He was wise to keep away.

Portsmouth AFC fared no better than in their previous clashes with the regiment. The latest of those bruising encounters to their ego resulted in a 1–7 debacle. The match confirmed that the town club suffered from a lack of players as much as the lack of a ground.

They were again forced to line up two men short. Earp and Wood were the absentees. A Royal Artillery man, Cook, offered to fill one of the gaps and Gibbons the other place among the half-backs ten minutes after the start.

The civilians defended the Garrison Church end but all the initial action was at the other goalmouth as they made light of being a man short by forcing Lieutenant Milburn in the Stafford's goal into a couple of smart saves. The soldiers broke away to score, only for Matson to miss a ridiculously easy chance to equalise for the blue shirts.

From then on, the soldiers had matters all their own way. Two more goals arrived in the first forty-five minutes. Portsmouth AFC tried to get back into the game with a tactical swap between Waddington and Grant in the back and forward lines.

It had no effect. The side went six goals down before H Pead kicked a consolation effort in the middle of the second half. The regiment merely added another goal to their large tally to restore the goal difference.

Meanwhile, the *Portsmouth Times* was back on its soapbox about the lack of a permanent football ground in Portsmouth. The first XI of the London Polytechnic had offered to play Portsmouth AFC during the forthcoming Easter week. Their enquiry contained the phrase 'You have a gate, I presume?'

'It's wrong to presume in this case,' opined the paper.

Cowes AFC were another team to decline to travel once it became apparent Portsmouth AFC were merely lodgers. The Portsmouth Red Stars, however, were so keen to overcome the handicap of the absence of any available space they were reported in the paper to be prepared to travel to a ground outside Portsea Island to fulfil the fixture with Crouch End Rovers, which Portsmouth AFC had been forced to forgo, if their original choice of Governor's Green was unavailable.

The status of football in Portsmouth in 1893 was aptly summed up by the cancellation of the original Pompey's home fixture with Winchester on March 11th. The *Portsmouth Times* reported that Winchester were unable to raise a team because several of their players preferred to watch

St Mary's take on Freemantle in the Hampshire Senior Cup final than to play against the blue shirts.

Several of Portsmouth AFC's team felt the same way, apparently. The club, though, managed to fix a game against the Depot RA, on cup final day. The town club won 3–1 with goals from Earp, Matson and an own goal. Portsmouth AFC's replacements gelled well to ensure that the team's combination was superior to the determined efforts of the soldiers.

Those at the US Men's Ground were witnessing the shape of football in Portsmouth – and it wasn't in the blue shirts of the town club. Their opponents included Reilly, Harms, Patterson, Maxwell, Hanna and Simpson. All of them would go on to play for Royal Artillery (Portsmouth) FC when the Glory

Gunners were formed the next year.

In Southampton, Freemantle ended Southampton St Mary's run of three wins in the Hampshire Senior Cup with a victory in front of 5000–6000 spectators.

Taking on the Royal Marines Artillery at Governor's Green, as Portsmouth AFC did in their next game, seven days later on March 18th, must have seemed insignificant. Goals by Buckwright, Lieutenant Dawson and Waddington – Buckwright's only goal for the club in his second appearance – earned the civilians a 3–1 win in a lacklustre match played in a strong wind. In the *Evening Mail*'s words:

The game was poor and neither side showed the slightest combination.

Southampton St Mary's rounded off Portsmouth AFC's season on March 22nd with a 0–3 away defeat to take out their frustration at relinquishing the Hampshire Senior Cup. They would have triumphed by a bigger margin in the midweek fixture, with only G Pead's fine form in the Portsmouth AFC goal standing in their way of more goals.

The game was arranged at the Saint's request to aid charities in the city. It was timed for 5pm on a Wednesday – in March without floodlights – to give as many fans as possible the chance to watch.

One further game had been lined up for the original Pompey but the 15th Company RA called off the fixture. While the town club were sitting idly that day, March 25th, Freemantle were securing a cup double with a single goal triumph against Portsmouth AFC's frequent conquerors, North Staffs Regiment, before a crowd of 3000 in the Portsmouth Senior Cup Final at the US grounds.

The win was the third time in a row Freemantle had clinched the trophy. It was their fourth success overall to put them one ahead of the total number of triumphs of Portsmouth AFC. Only Geneva Cross, in 1889, had interrupted the initial dominance of the two clubs in the competition.

CHAPTER FIFTY-FOUR

The *Portsmouth Times* could only look at the final with envy. One of the most exciting games in Portsmouth, the decider had yielded the most takings the town had yet achieved, at £26, though the sum was less than half the receipts from the final of the Hampshire Senior Cup a few weeks earlier.

There was no doubt in the paper's view of the reason for the gap in the admission proceeds:

…this is nothing like representing the full number present, as at least one thousand soldiers and sailors came in free.

Those who had to pay found half their admission fee going to the US ground authorities and half to the Portsmouth FA. Such a restrictive condition on the takings limited the association's ability ever to raise enough money to gain a ground of their own as yet another in a fixture list of clubs had to be turned away from playing in Portsmouth.

The mighty Clapton FC, semi-finalists in the London Senior Cup, were the latest side to make overtures about visiting the naval town. They had in mind a fixture during Easter week. They also had in mind a closed ground on which to play and a guaranteed sum for taking part. Neither of the latter two conditions was forthcoming from the would-be hosts.

'To find the first is a big enough task, but to find the second as well is too great an undertaking for the Portsmouth Club,' the *Portsmouth Times* informed its readers, who had read of little else in its sporting news for the past month.

But the journalist was convinced brighter times were in prospect:

We hope there's some truth in the rumour that the Portsmouth Club intends to come up with a ground of its own next season.

Then we shall not chronicle with such frequency the fact that because there's no ground or no 'gate' there will be no game.

More than 900 years of history links the pioneering footballers of Portsmouth AFC and their modern counterparts. The common bond is the proud emblem of the city which they represent on the football pitch.

The star and crescent moon badge has been a constant feature of Portsmouth's footballers apart from a brief period in the 1970s and 1980s.

The crest dates from the granting of Portsmouth's first charter dated May 2, 1194, when it was decided to adopt the crescent moon and eight-pointed star as the borough arms.

The motif formed part of the seal of the Chancellor, William de Longchamp, bishop of Ely, and the King at the time was Richard I, the Lionheart. The charter was an important document. It gave several important privileges tot he citizens of what was then a town.

Of these, the right to hold an annual fair and a weekly market brought trade and wealth into Portsea Island.

For the moment, there was no ground as 1892/93 ended just as there had been no ground at the start of 1884/85. Nine seasons of action had taken the club to a host of venues but no further forward as an outfit. At least Portsmouth Red Star showed some enterprise. They finally played their fixture with the visiting Crouch End Rovers.

Red Star hired the Portsmouth Rugby Club ground in North End for the occasion – and promptly ran up a rugby score of a result in the Good Friday game. They won by eight goals to nil to overrun a team described by the *Evening Mail* and the *Portsmouth Times* as 'a bit of a fraud'.

Crouch End were missing four regulars and proved no match for the Red Stars. The gate was 'fairly satisfactory', in the *Portsmouth Times'* words, but the fixture hardly lived up to expectations. The game was a fitting climax to Red Star's season record of: P19 W13 D2 L4 F64 A21.

And the final words on the season should come from the *Portsmouth Times* of the following week in April in its report of the Hampshire FA's campaign – which included a 4–0 win over Dorset with the help of Grant at half-back and Basil Pares at centre – to maintain an unbeaten record which stretched back to November 1890.

Again, Portsmouth was missing out on the best football on offer: 'It's a pity we can't have a county match in Portsmouth but with no gate it's difficult and we can hardly expect secretary Pickford to look here,' the paper commented.

CHAPTER FIFTY-FIVE

What a difference six months can make. The 1893/94 season was heralded in the same newspaper with enthusiasm. The fresh optimism could be summed up by the presence of the Stamshaw Recreation Ground at which Portsmouth AFC would be playing more regularly. But the ground was to become a graveyard for the hopes of the town club, with the newly-formed Royal Artillery (Portsmouth) FC hovering like a spectre determined to feast on the remains of the civilian footballers.

Just one day ended the new-found hopes that Portsmouth AFC could at last succeed in the increasingly professionally organised world which football was becoming. November 18th was the date, Southampton St Mary's were the opponents. To make matters worse, the occasion was the Portsmouth Senior Cup's first round. The fixture was the biggest opportunity that the original Pompey had been given to break out of the ranks of the also-rans.

The build-up to the game had begun an unprecedented five weeks earlier. The cup draw was made at a Portsmouth FA committee meeting on October 4th 1893 at Portsmouth's Albany Hotel. Fourteen teams featured in the cup. They were given a deadline of December 2nd to play their ties. The local papers wasted no time in speculating about the impact of the most important derby gate to date and the chances of its being used to show off the still new Stamshaw Recreation Ground's potential for staging big occasions.

First to comment about the possibilities was the *Portsmouth Times* on October 7. It accompanied news of the draw with the plea:

It's hoped Portsmouth AFC may get the use of the Stamshaw Ground for the cup tie as the corporation have stipulated one or two days on which the ground may be closed this year.

Otherwise, the club may possibly play at Southampton as it's understood St Mary's have offered them the gate to do so.

This, of course, would be a great temptation as the funds of Portsmouth AFC are not so flourishing as they should be.

The following week's edition added to the pressure on the corporation to turn the public ground private for the cup match. To refuse that would disappoint the many football followers in the naval port, stated the paper.

The group of councillors with whom the decision rested was, once again, the Parks and Open Spaces Committee. They should consider the wider interests of the borough, the paper commented:

...for a match which will prove to be of the greatest interest to a very large section of the town. It's a thoroughly amateur sporting club and one would think that the concession might readily be made, especially as the ground has only been closed once for football this year.

The fact is that the Portsmouth club has never received the support to which it's entitled as the 'town' club and while St Mary's has over 750 subscribing members, the finances of the Portsmouth club are not so satisfactory as they deserve to be.

The news that the paper wanted arrived on October 25th when the *Evening Mail* reported that the committee had given the original Pompey permission to charge admission to the recreation ground. A couple of days later, it added:

It is a matter of great satisfaction that the Parks and

Open Spaces Committee have met Portsmouth AFC in a liberal spirit and granted the use of the Stamshaw Recreation Ground.

Local footballers will have the chance of seeing a really good match, certainly one of the most interesting of the season. And the town club will not have to face the disadvantage of meeting Saints on their native heath.

It was a contest for which St Mary's would have to be at their best and make every attack count, the paper reckoned, to stand a chance of winning:

Even then, they may be second to Dawson and the other ten good and true men of Portsmouth AFC.

November began with the *Evening Mail*'s parochial anticipation of the cup tie – original Pompey's second with Saints in two seasons – growing. The clash 'would be one of the best things of the season'. With seven days left, the paper was sure the importance of the match to the town, and the club, would have fans flocking to watch:

Portsmouth AFC may rest assured there will be plenty up at Stamshaw to cheer them on when they play the redoubtable Saints.

It was unsure, though, if their enthusiasm would be matched by a win for their favourite players, in contrast to the optimism of just a few weeks earlier:

Portsmouth AFC men may make a great show but the general anticipation hardly points to them as winners.

Some consolation was to be found in the words of the esteemed Mr Pickford, the honorary secretary of the Hampshire FA and widely recognised as the father of football in the county. The *Portsmouth Times* wrote that Mr Pickford had commented 'stake not your coppers on comparative form' – and his words had a ring of truth about them:

For instance, Portsmouth AFC beat the Hants Regiment 2–1, the regiment only lost to Cowes by 1–0 and Cowes drew with Southampton St Mary's. Therefore, Portsmouth AFC ought to be able to beat the 'Saints' when they meet them at Stamshaw.

This is rather a large order, and though the Portsmouth AFC men may make a good show, general anticipation will hardly point to them as winners.

Still, we can never tell...

The *Evening Mail* reported why realism was setting in:

Southampton St Mary's last Saturday got through to the second round of the English Cup preliminary competition and have a very good chance of reaching the Cup's first round proper.

CHAPTER FIFTY-SIX

Portsmouth AFC could only dream of even entering the only national competition of the time. The Cup had reached its twentieth anniversary the previous season and the original Pompey were as far away as ever from being able to take part in it. November 18th 1893 showed why. The match didn't even last the full ninety minutes because it was so one-sided in favour of the visitors. Saints were winning 8–0 with ten minutes left when the game was abandoned. An occasion which the *Evening Mail* had so enthusiastically anticipated as having the ability to raise a good attendance and football's profile in the town became a miserable fiasco instead.

The chief culprit, besides Portsmouth AFC's outclassed players, was the British weather. A severe storm of driving rain and strong winds lashed the exposed Stamshaw site. The anticipated record crowd was reduced to a hardy three hundred who decided to brave a drenching. How distinctly preferable their warm homes must have seemed by the time the first forty-five minutes were over with the home team losing by six goals.

The *Evening Mail* began its match-day coverage with the ominous words:

St Mary's have a reputation for being one of the best, if not the best, teams in Hampshire. Until 1890, they were a junior club and won the Hampshire Junior Cup in 1888, 1889 and 1890.

On promotion to the senior ranks, they have continued to carry all before them and won the Hampshire Senior Cup in 1891/92.

About the match with Portsmouth AFC, the reporter continued:

Ruffell did not have a shot to save in the St Mary's goal, Portsmouth AFC's' forwards being very poor indeed.

The captains agreed to end the game after eighty minutes because of the torrential rain which had been falling since half-time, after heavy rain during the first-half.

St Mary's were unaffected by the atrocious conditions and went ahead after just five minutes. That

PORTSMOUTH AFC CUP TIES
1893/94

Portsmouth Senior Cup

R1	Southampton St Mary's	Stamshaw	LO-8	18.11.93

Hampshire Senior Cup

R1	bye			
R2	Bournemouth	North End Rec Grd	D1-1	9.12.93
R2r	Bournemouth	a	W1-0	16.12.93
R2r2	Bournemouth	County Ground	W1-0	13.1.94
S-f	Royal Engineers	County Ground	LO-2	10.2.94

was just the start of a busy afternoon for G Pead in the original Pompey's goal as his team were outclassed throughout.

Worryingly, the *Portsmouth Evening News* of November 20th stated that the home team of G Pead, A Earp, P Burke, AH Wood, WE Grant, Lt Dawson (c), Matson, WH Wild, BC Lear, C Williams and H Pead was the town club's full-strength line-up.

The Pares brothers were, amazingly, absent, unavoidably so in the paper's word, and this must have had some effect on the home side's defence and attack. But the players who represented Portsmouth on that notable day were simply not good enough.

A beautiful shot from visiting right-winger Angus opened the scoring. Soon after, some fine work by the heads and feet of the Saints players led to their second goal. Grant provided some relief to his already hard-pressed defence by going on the attack for the blue shirts but the visitors' defenders deftly took play back to the home end where Pead failed to stop centre-forward Offer scoring goal number three.

Portsmouth AFC's wingers tried to get the side back in the tie only to fail to find a way through the Southampton rearguard. Pead was called into action twice to save his side but it was beyond him to do so on the third occasion when he was beaten by a Saints goal from half-back Marshall.

Goal number five arrived a few minutes later. A well-directed shot from Angus, who played well throughout, beat the keeper for his second goal of the game.

A free-kick brought the first half scoring to a close as Nicholls, a left-winger, made it count. Angus notched up his hat-trick, and the seventh for the Saints from the penalty spot soon after the restart.

Play became more even for a while, it could hardly have been more one-sided, as both sets of players began to adjust to the bitter wind and rain. Saints

proved the better at that. The home side were back on the defensive before long. A neat piece of play near to their goal ended with a pass by Kiddle to Dorkin who shot. Pead fisted out well only for Dorkin to put the rebound away. The *Portsmouth Evening News* rounded off its comments:

Soon after, Portsmouth AFC deeming it futile to continue, threw in the sponge and Saints left the game winners by 8–0.

The rout gave St Mary's a season's record of: P10 W7 D2 L1 F41 A9.

Generosity in defeat sums up the *Portsmouth Times'* response to the debacle. Saints won deservedly:

Every credit for its success and being a first rate team. It must be mentioned the team is strengthened by importations.

Offer had played for Arsenal in their last amateur season of 1890, hat-trick man Angus, whose long shots were a feature of the game, was connected to Ardwick, who preceded Manchester City, and Taylor, one of Saints' halves had links with Everton, it detailed:

On the day, and possibly any day, St Mary's were immeasurably the better team. By the first goal, they were the only one in it and the Saints forwards carried all before them.

Kiddle, a well-known sprinter, and the lightweight Nineham had combined with the other three attackers to create a clever, fast and tricky unit, in the opinion of the paper.

In contrast, Portsmouth AFC's forwards were so poor 'it's kindest to refrain from comments'. They were far removed from the strikers who had put on a display to torture Havant the previous week. Of the rest of the players, the home side's halves did some fair work, with Grant playing the best.

Earp defended well, while G Pead was occasionally brilliant in goal, though was also often at fault. But the paper qualified its criticism with the comment:

It must be admitted that the high wind which was blowing rendered shots very difficult to judge.

The rain drenched the miserable knot of spectators well before the first-half had ended. 'It was shocking bad luck for Portsmouth AFC that the weather was so bad and gate receipts must have been virtually nothing,' the paper added.

If the sun had shone, the club might have looked forward to a nice little sum to help its not very flourishing financial condition but now, after the printing bill has been paid, there will probably be a deficit.

Portsmouth AFC's cash flow was dealt a further blow by the news in the *Portsmouth Times* on the same day of November 25th 1893. An article in the paper's Hotspur column illustrated just how the odds were stacked against the club. Portsmouth Corporation's Parks and Open Spaces Committee, again, cut the charge for athletics meetings to be held at the Stamshaw site. The previous one-third take by the corporation of ticket sales proved too steep for the clubs after they had paid for their printing and advertising.

The corporation's share was reduced to a fixed sum of seven guineas. For the original Pompey, though, the one-third of the takings rule still applied.

CHAPTER FIFTY-SEVEN

The club enjoyed far better luck in a more bitter off-the-field struggle which they staged to keep their fast-fading season alive just two weeks later.

The saga echoed the club's fight with Hilsea Ramblers in the Portsmouth Senior Cup six years previously.

Step forward as the latest villains, Bournemouth, in the Hampshire Senior Cup. The dispute centred around the presence of one of the original Pompey's backs, W Caldecott, in the cup tie between the clubs.

Caldecott was a master at Basingstoke Grammar School. Bournemouth protested that the distance between Basingstoke and Portsmouth made him ineligible for the competition. It took three games,

several meetings and a mass of paperwork to resolve the dispute in favour of the naval port club.

December 9th saw the first instalment of the skirmish. The home match at Portsmouth Rugby Club, failed to ignite the interest of the public, perhaps because of the outcome of the previous cup tie with Saints a few weeks earlier. As the *Evening Mail* noted:

A very limited company was present in spite of it being an important match.

Those who stayed away were spared the sight of a match which was poor, in spite of the off-the-field heat it was about to generate. The *Portsmouth Times* was unflinching in its criticisms of the conditions:

It was not a good game. In the first place, the North End Recreation Ground is quite unfit for association football. The turf is all lumps and the ball jumped about in a most eccentric style.

Then Portsmouth AFC had nothing like their full team. Wood was laid up with flu and the Pares brothers could not play and, for one reason or another, a very scratch combination represented the town club.

The secretary received no less than seven refusals out of the eleven men originally selected.

That sentence summed up everything about the unsuitability of Portsmouth AFC to survive in football. A big game, and most of the club's first choice players wanted away. Those that could be bothered to turn out did their best to make up for the lack of interest of the absentees.

Portsmouth AFC's backs were praised by the *Portsmouth Times* for keeping the town club in the cup. The centre of attention, Caldecott, defended finely and Burke, in spite of a tendency to miskick, came through the game well enough. G Pead added to the strength of the backs by keeping goal well. That said, a soft own goal, as the ball bounced off his head from a Bournemouth attack two minutes into the second half put the visitors ahead.

Doyle equalised with a shot which completely beat the Hampshire FA keeper Stokes in the Bournemouth goal fifteen minutes later. The quick reply was in keeping with a game which had begun with a spell of give-and-take play before the home side gained the upper hand. They had the ball between the Bournemouth posts three times, only for two of the efforts to be ruled out because of offside and the other disallowed through handball.

'After this,' reported the *Portsmouth Evening News* succinctly, 'the game was somewhat monotonous and nothing was scored. Just before the end, it rained heavily and it was decided not to play extra time.'

The decision paved the way for a replay the next Saturday at Bournemouth's Dean Park ground. In the meantime, the Hampshire FA had drawn the winners against the Royal Engineers in a semi-final scheduled to take place at the County Ground in Southampton on February 10th 1894.

The gap of two months was needed to settle the argument caused by the original Pompey's single goal win in the second round replay on December 16th. The decider, when it arrived, was unremarkable. The ball dropped into the home team's goalmouth from a corner and was bundled home by an unidentified original Pompey player in the fifty-fifth minute. The row it sparked was certainly more noteworthy.

Caldecott, the cause of the dispute, was prominent in Portsmouth AFC's defence and C Williams and D Poat put in some good shots at the other end. Bournemouth were unlucky with some shots and forced several corners but failed to score. The goal gave the visitors encouragement and they continued to attack as Basil Pares put in two hot shots. Bournemouth were still dangerous and G Pead nearly allowed them to equalise when he fumbled a shot. P Read and Grant worked well in defence in front of him as the home side piled on the pressure in a late, late effort to stay in the cup. Their centre-forward, Hartley, was just inches wide with a shot after a run through the Portsmouth AFC defence. But the final whistle was only the beginning of a committee room row.

The *Evening Mail* was certain Bournemouth's protest about the appearances of Caldecott for the original Pompey was a severe case of sour grapes. The Greenshirts, as Bournemouth were then known, had been smarting since their eight-goal drubbing by the town club the previous season, the paper reckoned:

> *Bournemouth do not accept defeat graciously. Last year's 8–0 defeat was a terrible infliction and they accordingly protested against Portsmouth AFC on the grounds of a 'late start'.*
>
> *This year's 1–0 defeat was still too many for them and so a protest has been entered against Caldecott, the very neat back who has been doing splendid service for Portsmouth AFC this season, who hails from Basingstoke.*

Not satisfied with this rebuke, the paper accused Bournemouth of being the victims of their own complacency. They were so sure of success playing on their ground, and with a stronger team than in the original tie, that they rested one of their prominent players. They wanted to be sure he would be fit for the semi-final game which they were convinced was theirs for the taking. 'At any rate, he may now take a much longer rest from cup tie troubles,' gloated the journalist.

He then turned his attention to the rule-makers in Hampshire football. The row centred around Rule V of the Hampshire FA's handbook, he helpfully informed his readers. This stated:

> *In the case of players, who were not residing within six miles of any club belonging to the association, they shall be allowed to play for the nearest club that entered for the competition not being a military team.*

But what happened if the nearest alternative clubs – which were the Southampton outfits of Banister Court, St Mary's and Freemantle – did not require him? All three of them had written to Portsmouth AFC before the cup replay to state that fact:

> *Bournemouth protests of his playing for Portsmouth AFC, of which he has been a member all season, so either he had better give up senior football or the rule should be translated into plainer language.*

The *Portsmouth Times* took the same view of Caldecott's fate, even if it was expressed in gentler language:

> *Under these circumstances, he cast his lot in with Portsmouth AFC and it's difficult to see how the Hampshire executive can disqualify him unless they want to shut him out of senior football altogether.*

The paper also remembered the reason behind the protest:

> *Portsmouth AFC accomplished a very good feat in defeating Bournemouth in the Hampshire Senior Cup second round.*
>
> *Bournemouth are the oldest association club in Hampshire and the fact they were playing on their own ground rendered their defeat all the more unexpected.*

CHAPTER FIFTY-EIGHT

But they received a reprieve when the Hampshire FA executive committee gathered on December 29th 1893 at Scullard's Rest in Southampton. The first item on their agenda was the matter of Bournemouth's protests. They unanimously decided to wipe out Portsmouth AFC's victory. Bournermouth went for the most damage

Passions surrounding the Portsmouth Senior Cup run as high in the 21st century as they did in the 19th.

Dr Arthur Conan Doyle and his team-mates would be delighted to know that the competition which they founded remains keenly fought over on pitches around the city – and occasionally in Portsmouth FA committee meetings.

Just how important the trophy remains was shown in 2003. The episode of controversy had remarkable echoes with the infamous ties between Portsmouth AFC and Hilsea Ramblers in 1887–88, the cup's second year.

An ineligible player was at the heart of both disputes. The semi-finals were also at the centre of the rows, which were separated by centuries but united by the common cause of getting hold of the cup.

The more recent Portsmouth Senior Cup dispute hit the headlines in March 2003 as the 2002–03 competition failed to unfold. The semi-finalists' hopes of joining the winners of the past 116 years were suddenly shattered when the Portsmouth FA scrapped the contest.

It was the first time in 80 years that a season was to end without the trophy being awarded, war years excepted. A difference of opinion about the rules of the competition caused the abandonment to deny a club the chance to be crowned the champions of Portsmouth soccer.

The row focused on the condition that a player in the cup should not have played in a more than five senior cup matches in the same season. News about the dispute emerged in mid-March in the week that cup holders Hayling United were due to meet Fleetlands in a semi-final replay. The other semi-final was Havant and Waterlooville Reserves taking on Horndean.

But neither of the matches was ever to take place. The reason? A complaint by Hampshire League club AFC Portchester after they lost their quarter-final 1–4 against H and W Reserves. They accused the winners of fielding Craig Leworthy when he should not have played.

The Portsmouth FA rejected the accusation. However, Portchester appealed to the Hampshire FA which overturned the original decision. Portsmouth FA life vice-president Bert Greenwood confirmed:

There has been a problem over the eligibility rule and we therefore felt it was appropriate not to carry on with

the cup this season. For many years, the spirit of the competition has been that it is open to all senior clubs in this area, but confusion has arisen over some of the wording in our rules.

Portchester secretary Colin Brands defended his club's actions. He stated that Leworthy had played twice in the FA Trophy that season, once in the Dr Martens League Cup and twice in the Hampshire Senior Cup. 'We didn't get anywhere with the Portsmouth FA, so appealed to the higher authority and won our case.' he said.

Kev Latham, the club's manager, put the blame for the problem on the Portsmouth FA:

It was the Portsmouth FA who made the error, telling Havant and Waterlooville their player was eligible to play when in our eyes he wasn't. According to their own rules, he clearly couldn't play. We do feel sorry for the likes of Hayling, Fleetlands and Horndean who, like us, have put a lot of time, effort and expense into the competition. I can assure people we have checked the rules meticulously and have played by them.

Havant and Waterlooville secretary Trevor Brock was adamant the West Leigh Park club were in the clear:

We have done nothing wrong. Before the game, we checked with the Portsmouth FA that our player was okay to play. They gave us permission to include him in our squad for the tie. We played this by the book.

Bemused bystanders Horndean and Hayling were left helpless by the abandonment of the cup. As holders, Hayling got to retain the trophy by default. But Graham Dollery, their manager, did not regard becoming cup holders for a second successive season in that way with any satisfaction. 'I feel sorry for the other teams in the same position as us who have been deprived of the chance of a big day out at a cup final.'

He bemoaned the actions of the Portsmouth FA for reflecting poorly on the exertions put in by the clubs in getting to the cup's semi-finals. Hayling filled in the gap left by the loss of their semi-final with a late rearranged home game against Colden Common. They won the home fixture 2–1 to help their bid to take the Hampshire League first division title.

For Horndean, a similar feeling of anger about the disappearance of the cup competition from their fixtures was expressed by Manager Paul Ryan.

they could inflict on their victors, to live down to their image as poor losers.

They said Caldecott's violation of the rules for being outside the six mile radius was compounded by the inclusion of Selly and Read in the original Pompey team, from within the six mile distance, because they were soldiers.

Committee vice-president Woolridge proposed that the protest which related to Caldecott should be carried. He was seconded by G Fellows. The other members agreed. The issues about Selly and Read were withdrawn by Bournemouth.

So, the Dean Park outfit had got their way. Wooldridge's further proposal that the second replay should take place at Southampton on or before January 27th was also backed. The *Portsmouth Times* slated the outcome of the meeting. Seizing its chance to protest, it said:

But surely the spirit of the law has been complied with? Here was a bona fide amateur willing to play for the nearest club that would have him and yet he is not to play for it because there are other clubs nearer who don't want him. The position is absurd and illogical.

The *Portsmouth Evening Times* listed the guilty men who had sentenced Portsmouth AFC to an unwarranted game. They were: Dr Bencraft (chairman) with vice-president JA Nethercote, EF Moberly, CS Wooldridge, CG Ellery and A Tebbutt. The delegates to the meeting were: C Miller, HB Johns, REAC Knight (Southampton); JWE Masterman, J Nutman (New Forest); WH Parker, Sergeant Delicarty (North Hampshire); J French (Portsmouth); G Fellowes (Isle of Wight); W Pickford, honorary secretary.

Mr Masterman, speaking for Bournemouth, opened a preliminary discussion with details of the club's case. He said Caldecott was disqualified because he lived outside the six mile radius. Read, as a soldier with the Cameron Regiment, had not been in the district during the necessary six months immediately before the cup tie. Selly also had no qualification on the same grounds. It was decided the cases should be taken seratim and Mr Wooldridge said the proof had to be with the protestors.

Mr French claimed Bournemouth had conveniently decided to protest because of their exit from the Hampshire Senior Cup. If Bournemouth had moaned about Caldecott after the first draw, the original Pompey could have selected another player to take his place, which the club had been prepared to do.

But the meeting's chairman, Dr. Bencraft, ruled that issue was outside the scope of the meeting. They were unaware if Bournemouth knew at the first match of their obligation to protest if they thought something was wrong.

With the central plank of the defence of Portsmouth AFC dismissed, the meeting had little difficulty in overturning the club's win. The committee members did, however, also unanimously state their belief that the matter had been caused by a misunderstanding of Rule V rather than by a deliberate flouting of the regulation.

That mercy failed to satisfy Mr Masterman. There was no let up in his persecution of Portsmouth AFC. He asked the committee to rule on the matter of the soldiers and their eligibility for the contested cup tie. French retorted that he could show both Read and Selly were perfectly qualified to play. This caused the committee to drop the issue after Mr Masterman eventually backed down.

Only Read of the trio was present on January 13th 1894, when the original Pompey and Bournemouth took each other on for the third time in the second round of the Hampshire Senior Cup. G Pead kept a clean sheet in the Portsmouth AFC goal in the County Ground fixture as the result of the first replay was repeated – a single goal win for his side.

Basil Pares scored the goal in the second half with a low cross shot. It arrived after a spell of Portsmouth AFC pressure and some fine crosses by Middlemass on his debut. Stokes had previously proved equal in the Bournemouth goal to the attacks.

Bournemouth tried hard to get back on level terms for the second match in a row. But they were kept at bay by the fine defence of Read, Grant and Hoose, who took Caldecott's place. Basil Pares broke away once and came close to extending Portsmouth AFC's lead, only to miss an easy chance.

Back came Bournemouth in search of an equaliser and Read doubtless took great pleasure in repelling their late attacks.

He was prominent with Hoose in the game's early stages as Bournemouth opened the strongest side with several rushes at the blue-shirted defence in an initial period described by the *Portsmouth Evening News* as 'rather slow and uninteresting' on a fairly slippery ground. It was then the turn of Stokes to save his side from an attack staged by the Pares brothers. Both teams gained corners and Bournemouth took a free-kick close to their opponents' goal without any joy as half-time arrived.

The *Portsmouth Times* began its post-match report with the words 'Hurray and Hooray' to sum up the mood in the town:

The result of the replayed match with Bournemouth was awaited with keen interest and the one topic of conversation on Saturday evening was Portsmouth

AFC's victory.

The general feeling was that they had been badly treated and the Hampshire FA decision which disqualified Caldecott – though possibly correct as a matter of law – was an anomaly as a matter of fact.

Bournemouth had availed themselves of a technicality to have another shot at the cup, and failed. Portsmouth AFC's victory was by only a single goal and in all three matches only four goals were scored, pretty good proof of the strength of both lots of backs.

According to the paper, the win was even more deserved because the original Pompey lacked Wood and Dawson at half-back but compensated for their absence with probably their best display of the season among the forwards. The three Pares brothers also added a great deal with their help to the attackers while Read impressed everyone with a sterling game at half-back.

No real grounds existed for him to be barred, the *Portsmouth Times* added. His county qualifications came from his residence at Aldershot and he was stationed at Portsmouth during cup ties.

All this backed the paper's view of the previous week that widespread agreement existed that the Hampshire FA had treated the original Pompey illogically and was especially cruel on Caldecott:

Their action has shut Caldecott out of senior football and Bournemouth have not to face the sturdy defence of that splendid little back. Possibly, they did not desire to do so. But, be that as it may, their protest does not commend itself to the uninitiated as sportsmanship.

CHAPTER FIFTY-NINE

They were history, though, as far as that season's *Portsmouth Times* was concerned and the paper was convinced that the Royal Engineers would follow them after they had been defeated by the town club in the semi-final which would arrive after all the arguments had finished. Portsmouth AFC's place in the final of the county cup on March 10th 1894 was assured, therefore.

Whoever optimistically wrote those words must have been unaware of the soldiers' record. When they ran out to face the civilians on February 10th, the military men had put together fourteen consecutive victories. They accomplished number fifteen with a 2-0 success as Portsmouth AFC returned to the County Ground in happier circumstances than their last enforced visit.

The *Portsmouth Times'* praise of their display in their previous cup game was quickly forgotten as the original Pompey's familiar failing of being a collection of amateur players rather than a cohesive team surfaced again in contrast to the settled pattern of their opponents' side.

Portsmouth AFC were weakened by the absence of the brothers Pares and, as usual, was a rather scratch combination,' it commented. The want of a regular team of players seriously affects the club's chances of anything like consecutive successes. One week the team is strong and the next week not. Until they get more playing members and a reserve team, they will not be strong enough to keep up the traditions of the club.

With its best team, Portsmouth AFC can play any amateur combination in Hampshire, but when one or two men cannot play, their places have to be filled by strangers and the combination is not...

...the comment ended as abruptly as the hopes of the original Pompey.

That criticism aside, one of the imported players who came in for such flak was nominated by the paper as Portsmouth AFC's man of the match, the previously controversial Read of the Cameronians. The defender slotted into an unfamiliar looking back line with Elliott and Hargreaves among its members as the teams ran out in front of a crowd of about a thousand spectators.

Hammett, in the Royal Engineers goal, averted an early civilian lead before the soldiers started to assert their superiority with their strong forward play. Elliott, Selly and Read had to produce some clever tackles to keep their side in the game. The soldiers' occasional shots at goal kept the play in the town club's half and Boardman opened the scoring to trigger a furious response from the blue shirts. G Williams and W Middlemass showed excellent form on the left-wing but their work was wasted because, in the words of the *Portsmouth Evening News*:

The front rank was very much as sea and, but for this fact, more than one good chance might have been successfully taken.

This failure to accept their chances in a generally poor game saw Portsmouth AFC pushed on to the defensive for much of the second half. A foul by Selly during one of the reargurard actions led to a penalty for the Royal Engineers. But Evans failed with his spot kick and the original Pompey could breathe again.

They showed little ability, though, to claw back even a one goal deficit. It was their opponents who got the ball in the net again, only for the effort to be ruled out because of hands. Back came the soldiers and G Pead missed a dipping shot in the Portsmouth AFC goal only to see the ball bounce back off the bar.

The second goal, which had been threatened for so long, finally arrived a little later to put the semi-final beyond the reach of the original Pompey. The Royal Engineers coasted into the final with the security of that two-goal buffer in the remaining minutes of the fixture.

CHAPTER SIXTY

A military team in the shape of the Hampshire Regiment provided Portsmouth AFC's first fixture of the 1893/94 season on the opening weekend in October. The weeks beforehand had seen evidence of how popular football was becoming in the naval port. The first indication came in the *Portsmouth Evening News* on the unusually early date for football of September 8th:

The rapid growth of football clubs is widespread in Portsmouth and has kept pace with other parts of the

---

Football was a brutal game in Victorian times. The primitive equipment and basic medical care meant players could be playing with their lives. The fate of Arthur William Richmond was proof of that.

A Royal Navy sub-lieutenant, he was killed on February 9th, 1894, during a match at the US Men's Ground in Portsmouth.

Richmond, aged 20, died from traumatic peritonitis caused by a ruptured bowel. He passed away at 1.10am on the day after the fateful game.

He was playing in goal for the Royal Naval College at the Dockyard in a routine fixture with the Cameronians. An inquest held by the Hampshire coroner, E Goble, at the Haslar Hospital on February 13th heard the full details of that fatal encounter.

A reporter from the *Hampshire Telegraph* was present. It appears that Richmond was winded when a Cameronian player charged forward after the ball in a perfectly fair challenge for the period. Richmond went back between the posts but was replaced a few minutes later.

Private William Rowe, aged 23, was the Cameronians' player involved in the collision. He told the inquest that both he and Richmond kicked at the ball and he believed that it must have caught the goalkeeper when they knocked into each other.

The injured goalie sat between the posts for ten minutes and then walked to the dressing rooms. Match referee, Sergeant CJ Rynott, of the Royal Engineers, said the collision was accidental. He did not give a foul and no claim was made by the college players for one to be awarded.

Another player, Sub Lt Martin Stapleton, said his teammate Richmond was taken by a cab from the team's dressing room to the college in much pain. Surgeon Frederick Burns, of the hospital, said Richmond's condition grew suddenly worse during the night to lead to his death.

His post mortem revealed the cause of death to be a perforated small intestine.

The inquest jury returned a verdict of accidental death and expressed sympathy to the dead player's father, Dr Sylvester Richmond, and his mother.

Mr Goble said the fatal accident was to be deplored. He urged footballers to be cautious when they played the game to avoid a repeat of the tragic situation.

The *Portsmouth Time*s of February 17th, 1894, called for the FA to learn from the death of Richmond and use the tragedy to frame new rules for the game. The goalkeeper's untimely demise overshadowed every other event in the local footballing world, the paper added.

The accident once more calls attention to the question of charging goalkeepers at all and there is no doubt that the FA, might with advantage, alter the rules on this point.

The goalkeeper is at a distinct disadvantage – he has to look after the ball and not the man who is charging him – and it is not too much to say that many of the serious accidents which occur at Association football can be traced to it.

This is certainly a matter which calls for the interference of the FA.

With regard to the great question as to whether a single fatal accident now and then is to be taken as proof that football on the whole is dangerous, it is unnecessary to say much.

Thousands of men and boys play football every Saturday and accidents must, in comparison, be insignificantly few compared to the myriad players.

Regrettable they are when they occur, but in proportion to the numbers who take part in the game, they are probably no more numerous than those that occur in other sports in which Englishmen delight.

country during recent years.

And by the arrangement of fixtures of several clubs which are already to hand there is no reason to doubt that from the end of the present month to the close of December there will be an abundance of matches in the district.

So many, in fact, that demand for the new Stamshaw Recreation Ground was too great for the available pitches. The *Evening Mail* this time:

The football season at the North End Recreation Ground will start on the first Saturday in October and last for six months.

The ground has been brought into good condition by Mr Edmonds and the pitches are so much in request that the Parks and Open Spaces Committee have had to refuse all applications by the second and third teams for Saturday matches. But on the understanding the ground is available on other days of the week.

Portsmouth AFC's curtain-raiser against the Hampshire Regiment headed the initial list of fixtures at the venue. A total of nine other games by the town club were lined up there into the middle of the following March.

Other outfits in the round-up of matches published on September 13th showed the continuing neighbourhood nature of football in Portsmouth - the clubs included North End Alpines, Portsmouth Red Star, Buckland Congregational, Portsmouth Eclipse and Gosport Victorias.

The *Portsmouth Times* joined in the enthusiasm for the forthcoming campaign in its September 25th edition:

Next week the football season will fairly commence in the Portsmouth district and it promises to be both a busy and interesting one.

The paper added that the growth in interest in the sport had prompted the launch of the Portsmouth Junior Cup for civilian clubs with the final to be held at the North End Recreation Ground to provide a competitive edge to their season.

The battles in prospect on the pitches were equalled in the newspaper offices with fierce rivalry of their football coverage between the *Portsmouth Evening News* and the *Evening Mail* and its sister paper, the *Portsmouth Times*. The *Evening Mail* fired the first shots in what promised to be a gruelling campaign in newsprint in its September 25th 1893 edition:

In view of the growing interest in football in

Portsmouth, and in the neighbourhood, football news dealing with the game locally and generally will be published in the Portsmouth Times *and* Evening Mail *each Saturday.*

We shall be glad to receive from secretaries their cards of fixtures and any information concerning their clubs and players.

One item of news which soon emerged – in the *Portsmouth Times* on September 30th – weakened one of the few links Portsmouth AFC maintained from their early days nine years previously. Grant retired from the role as the club's honorary secretary. His decision was described by the paper as a 'severe loss' to the club. He carried on turning out for the team and, indeed, he missed just one of the fifteen games which made up the original Pompey's 1893/94 season for which team line-ups have survived. But he also gave up his role as captain in favour of being the vice-captain. Lieutenant Dawson succeeded to his position on the field and French became the new secretary. The paper hoped the changes would have no impact on the club's quest for success:

The club has several new members of promise and should show up well in the senior competitions.

Grant was hardly heading into retirement even with his workload reduced for Portsmouth AFC. He was staying as the secretary of the Portsmouth FA and was helping to run the Portsmouth Senior Cup as well as the new Junior Cup and the annual six-a-side tournament. His address was given as 40 Chetwynd Road, Southsea, to where entries for the new cup had to he sent. The closing date for the competition, which had received the official go-ahead from the footballing authorities, was October 7th.

CHAPTER SIXTY-ONE

Grant spent that afternoon with Portsmouth AFC as they took to the North End Recreation Ground for their season opener. The match with the Hampshire Regiment turned into a brawl. Fighting erupted in the second half after H Pead had scored Portsmouth AFC's first goal of the season after twenty minutes. The *Evening Mail* of the day reported:

A great roughness was instilled in play after half-time which ultimately led to blows. One of the regimental team was seen to collide violently with one of his opponents, whether intentionally or not it's difficult to determine. Certain it was, however, that the Portsmouth AFC man was seen to retaliate by striking his opponent in a truly pugilistic fashion.

The game was brought to an abrupt standstill and a scene of indescribable confusion ensued which certainly outraged the laws of friendly rivalry and some minutes elapsed before the disputants were separated and pacified.

But the next Saturday, the paper took a more reflective view in its Football Notes of events:

A great deal has been made of what has been described as a 'free fight' at Stamshaw in the match between Portsmouth AFC and the Hampshire Regiment. That unpleasant contretemps did take place is undeniable. But reports of such things grow quickly and nothing like the pitched battle between the teams as the term 'free fight' suggests took place.

Two players came to blows and they will no doubt be dealt by the powers that be in due course. A more serious matter is the objectionable language which it's stated was freely used on the ground by certain sections of the community.

This is the kind of thing which in the north of England has developed into referee baiting as a popular Saturday afternoon game.

Partisanship is all very well in its own way but enthusiasm must not vent itself in language which would prevent ladies from being present on the football field.

The *Portsmouth Times* also sprang to the regiment's defence in answering a London journalist's slur that the soldiers generally played roughly when they were getting the worst of play:

The game in question may have been a rough one but the soldiers as a rule play fairly.

Amid the fighting, a football game took place in a match that was keenly contested and fast paced throughout. Pead's opener was followed after the interruption by an own goal which put the civilians two goals up. The Hampshire Regiment refused to give in and pulled back a goal to leave the final score at 2–1.

Portsmouth AFC were back at the recreation ground seven days later for a fixture against their longstanding rivals from Freemantle, the holders of the Portsmouth Senior Cup for the third season in a row. The match was as equally notable as the previous week's but for different reasons. Portsmouth AFC made their first attempt at getting on to a professional footing by levying a 3d admission charge for spectators who wanted to watch them take on one of the strongest sides in Hampshire. The trial

was wasted because of the meanness of the town club's followers. As the *Portsmouth Times* reported, the fans took advantage of the free entry for the other games on the site:

Funny it was to notice how many people when they reached the gate were interested in the other matches but when they got inside took a casual look (which lasted all afternoon) at Portsmouth AFC v Freemantle.

The result also went against the home side as they fell behind to a goal in each half. The first came against the run of play as Portsmouth AFC went on the attack in the opening period. It arrived after thirty minutes and the original Pompey's hopes of equalising were ruined when left-winger Matson handled an excellent chance. HJ Pead was ruled offside to see another effort wasted as half-time approached. It was the visitors' turn to waste chances in the second-half.

They were awarded a penalty for hands against the home full-back Earp only for G Pead to save Hawkins' shot from the twelve yard line – the penalty spot had yet to appear – with the rebounded ball cannoning off his body to the right.

The original Pompey keeper repeated the feat to send the ball over the goal when Freemantle gained another penalty for hands, this time against Wood.

In between, the Southampton-based side had managed to double their lead.

The 0–2 score was how the match ended with Freemantle showing better combination throughout against a home side whose passing was poor, though their backs helped to keep the score down.

The *Portsmouth Times* was sanguine in defeat and observed that a two-goal loss was reasonable:

It must be remembered that though the game was played in Portsmouth the home side had no advantage in knowing the ground. Alas, Portsmouth has no ground to know.

On the same theme, and a further sign of the professional nature of football, the £30 guarantee – equal today to £1700 – which Southampton St Mary's had made to tempt the mighty Bolton Wanderers to Hampshire at last was welcomed by the paper. It was convinced the cost would be easily recouped with a large crowd for the touring fixture on October 23rd. Bournemouth was to follow on the Lancashire club's visit to the south coast.

'No doubt the Wanderers might have been persuaded to extend their visit to Portsmouth could we but guarantee a £30 gate. Not much,' was the paper's verdict on the state of football in Portsmouth.

Action of an unusual nature on a football pitch was

reported in the *Evening Mail* on the following Monday with the failure in Portsmouth to prepare proper facilities for the popular sport in spite of the new recreation ground. According to the Aerial column in the paper:

Round the town I hear that at the Men's Recreation Ground on Saturday some of the teams changed their clothes in full view of the spectators.

If so, this was very improper and if there is insufficient dressing room accommodation, more ought to be provided.

Football is not a game to which the ladies of Portsmouth evince much devotion but for all that the spectacle of young fellows changing their garments in the middle of the field is far from an edifying one.

CHAPTER SIXTY-TWO

Swearing, fighting and now nudity, and it was only the second Saturday of 1893/94. None of the added features were evident when the original Pompey were back in action on October 21st with a 3–2 win over Portsmouth Grammar School at Hilsea. The town club set pulses racing with a two-goal lead in just ten minutes. H Pead notched the first in the fifth minute and Poate joined in five minutes later. Williams put them three up before half-time. The school retaliated with two goals after the break with the wind behind them but could not do enough to overturn the town's commanding lead, although Portsmouth AFC's limitations were again shown when the next military team appeared among their fixtures.

The civilians made the short journey to the increasingly unfamiliar surroundings of the US Men's Ground to take on Depot RA in their final fixture of October. The powerful soldiers inflicted a 0–4 defeat. Their team featured Reilly at back and Maxwell on the right-wing along with Samson and Hanna as the centre-forward in the nucleus of the RA (Portsmouth) side which would begin a remarkable rise through football's ranks in the south just under a year later. They were simply too strong for Portsmouth AFC.

The first forty-five minutes saw the Depot continuously on the attack as they built up a three goal lead to reverse the civilians' fortunes of the sides' previous game. The town club came more into the game after the break and staged some good attacks. None was successful and the military team rounded off their scoring twenty minutes from the end to reflect their superb combination. The result prompted the *Portsmouth Times* to return to one of its two favourite football themes:

Four goals to nil is a rather big majority and until Portsmouth AFC can command their best men regularly they cannot hope to do much better.

With their full team they are strong enough to meet the strongest clubs in Hampshire with a fair chance of success.

But on Saturday the combination of the forwards was very poor and, but for the strong defence of the backs, they would have got an even worse beating.

Portsmouth AFC were back on surer footballing ground at the start of November as well as on the Stamshaw Recreation Ground when they took on the Post Office for their next game. They romped to a 9–1 win for the sort of result which gave a false indication of how powerful they were away from their parochial civilian rivals.

The goals were shared between seven original Pompey players for the second greatest scoring spread in the history of the club. Grant, Lear, H Pead, Williams, Wild, W Pead and Matson were the scorers, with a further brace coming from the unfortunate Post Office backs.

The postmen kept their enthusiasm and managed to obtain a solitary consolation goal during the second period. The *Evening Mail* commented: 'Portsmouth AFC won with ridiculous ease.'

The game was described as 'a walkover' by the *Portsmouth Evening News*. An even higher score was achieved in the following fixture as the borough club overwhelmed Havant 11–0 for their best result of the season.

Havant had lost their previous game by seven goals and lined up fearing the worst. It happened. With impressive understatement, the *Portsmouth Evening News* called the outcome an 'easy win' for Portsmouth AFC, but the *Evening Mail* was more accurate in its description of a 'hollow victory'.

The blue shirts poured forward in attack from the kick-off but, remarkably, failed to make much headway initially because of their poor play. Williams eventually gave them the lead and added another, with an addition from Wild, to put Portsmouth AFC three up after the first forty-five minutes.

The second half, similarly, got off to a slow start until Portsmouth AFC gradually improved the accuracy and timing of their passing to prove too much for their opponents. Matson and Wild's improved combination enabled them to put the pressure on the Havant defence with ease. H Pead and Williams on the left recovered their shooting powers and, with B Lear feeding the wings, all of the forwards joined in the scoring spree. Havant's forward line played well in the opening period when they came up against the hardworking Poate and Earp only to fade away as the game progressed.

CHAPTER SIXTY-THREE

The town club's next opponents were of a different calibre entirely – Southampton St Mary's – who could claim to be the best team in Hampshire with three Hampshire Junior Cups in a row and one win in the Hampshire Senior Cup, all in five years. And too good for the original Pompey, that's for sure.

The *Portsmouth Times* had previewed the Portsmouth Senior Cup game in its matchday edition of November 18th 1893, hoping for a Portsmouth venue to stage the cup final after a few years elsewhere:

The Portsmouth District Cup promises to be one of the good things of the season. Bournemouth and the Royal Engineers are the only really important Hampshire clubs not entered into it and that's because they are not qualified to enter.

By the time the final is reached, the interest will be immense. The final could possibly be played at the Men's Recreation Ground because the Parks and OpenSpaces Committee has already given the

'There is no death,' was the theme of a visit by Dr Arthur Conan Doyle to Portsmouth to attend two packed public meetings. The famous novelist returned to the south coast where his road to fame and fortune had begun to fulfil his well-publicised engagements. The first was in June 1921 and Dr Doyle was quick to espouse about his favourite subject of spiritualism to hundreds of residents who had turned out to hear him speak.

He arrived in Portsmouth straight from a tour of Australia and New Zealand where he had also been spreading the word about the spiritual world. His first venue on June 6th was the Portland Hall in Southsea. This was followed by a gathering at the Town Hall. Dr Doyle was enthusiastically received by the large audiences.

He said it was always a pleasure to obey any call that came from Portsmouth. 'The dear old city,' as he put it, though it was not his mother city, had been a good foster mother to him. He never wished to be in a better place, he added. Some of the happiest recollections of his life dated from the days he spent in its streets.

His interest at that time concentrated on the mental and physical aspects of life. But he had come to realise as he grew older that something more important than that existed. That element was the spiritual side of being, but Dr Doyle freely admitted that spiritualism was a subject of great debate. Friends, and even relatives, sharply opposed him, so great was the divide of opinion on the matter.

Dr Doyle left the podium for the lecturer, unnamed in press reports, to address the crowd on the evening's topic – messages from the other side.

It was the creator of Sherlock Holmes, however, who was the undoubted attraction at the civic building. As well as Lady Doyle, a distinguished list of guests had turned up for the chance to glimpse the great author. Among those present was the mayor of Portsmouth, Councillor John Timpson RP, the Rev EJB Kirtland and the deputy inspector general CW Buchanan-Hamilton.

Just over five years later, and Dr Doyle was expounding his controversial views again in Portsmouth. His destination on October 20th 1926, was Kingsley Hall in Fawcett Road and the cause was one which was sure to gain his support – the building fund of the Portsmouth Temple of Spiritualism at 73 Victoria Road, Southsea.

Dr Doyle was probably the most distinguished opener of any bazaar in Portsmouth when he performed the function at the fundraising event in the hall.

He used his welcoming speech to talk of what he termed the religion of the future. He predicted that the decade to come would see places of worship established in the back parlours of peoples' houses. But halls would always be needed to allow the faithful to gather together, to compare experiences or learn from those with more experience.

Spiritualism was essentially a religion of knowledge and not of faith, he explained. A lot of progress had been made in the acceptance of spiritualism in the past five years.

Dr and Lady Doyle were introduced by Mr T E Howell to the crowd of onlookers and bargain hunters who packed the brightly-decorated hall of flags and bunting.

Mr Howell said a new church was necessary because the number of spiritualists in Portsmouth had outgrown the present building. It had been in use since 1908 and was entirely unsuitable for the faith's present needs.

Portsmouth FA two days next season at Stamshaw for the tournament and final of the Portsmouth Junior Cup.

Of course, half the gate is a good price to pay for the ground but then it is central and where can another be found in Portsmouth?

The comment proved academic long before the end of the original Pompey's tie with St Mary's. Any hopes the club had of a quick recovery from the debacle were wrecked a week later when the players did find themselves at the US Men's Ground.

They had the misfortune to come up against another of the well-organised military sides who were leading the way in football's development on Portsea Island.

Number One Company RA became the second successive team to put eight goals past the shell-shocked G Pead in Portsmouth AFC's goal. Even more worrying for his club, was the inability of the returning Pares brothers to avert the heavy defeat.

Half-time arrived with the original Pompey well adrift 1–6 as their defence was ripped to shreds.

Williams had scored their lone reply of the initial forty-five minutes. The civilians managed to claw their way back slightly after the break and they pulled four more goals back compared to the two further strikes by the RA as they defended their huge lead.

Williams scored one of Portsmouth AFC's second-half goals and Basil Pares marked his first appearance of the season with a hat-trick.

Williams was again on target in the next fixture as the original Pompey got back to winning ways, over Connaught Rangers, for the first time since that 11–0 victory three weeks earlier. The forward struck, and got December off to a successful start, when the Rangers' keeper, Hall, could only parry a shot from the opposing centre, Portch, to leave Williams with the easy job of following up the loose ball. That capped his brilliant display as well as putting his side 2–0 up, coming as his goal did shortly after Wild had given them the lead during the second half.

The goals prompted Connaught Rangers – who were a late replacement for Chichester – to renew their attacks. Poate, who had replaced the hapless Pead in goal, was called into action several times to keep a clean sheet. The *Portsmouth Times* was amazed by the performance of the town club:

Portsmouth AFC played with any amount of spirit and it was difficult to recognise them as the same team, or practically the same team, as made such a mild show against St Mary's.

There were, though, six changes in the town club's team. A sign of the times among them was apparent in the shape of Selly in the defence. The back had come from Shrewsbury where he had played for the Shropshire club on a trial. The newspapers were impressed with the potential recruit. In the words of the *Evening Mail*: 'Without being brilliant, he gave a sound display and should prove an acquisition.' The *Portsmouth Times* gave its opinion: 'Selly...gave a very good display at back. He is not a great kicker but is very safe and difficult to pass.'

The paper also hinted at the possible arrival of former New Brompton player, Manning, who worked in Portsmouth Dockyard. He failed to materialise, while Selly did play a further part in Portsmouth AFC's fortunes, starting with his fateful appearance with the eventually long-running Portsmouth Senior Cup saga with Bournemouth.

In the meantime, the Portsmouth FA's other trophy – the Portsmouth Junior Cup – was another competition getting into difficulty in only its first season. The October meeting of the association was dominated by protests from some of the cup's ten entries against the inclusion in the first round draw of Southsea Rovers alongside the likes of St Simon's B-team, St Simon's Reserves, Portsmouth Wanderers and Vickery's School.

It was felt that the Rovers were too strong. The association's committee, chaired by Wood, decided that the hearsay was not enough to ban Rovers. Professional sides were excluded from the cup and rules were adopted to stop 'superior clubs', as the *Hampshire Telegraph* dubbed them, sneaking into the contest in an underhand attempt to win a trophy.

The matter was resolved by the Rovers themselves, five weeks later. They informed the Portsmouth FA they no longer wanted to take part in the cup.

It was decided by the committee to return their entry fee. The October meeting also heard that the corporation's Parks and Open Spaces Committee had granted the use of the Stamshaw ground for the Portsmouth Junior Cup final on March 10th as well as for the yearly six-a-side tournament the previous month.

The Bournemouth episode filled half of the intervening weeks before then. The first game between the sides took in a rare display of co-operation between Portsmouth's rugby union and association football clubs. The rugby club agreed to scratch their home game to allow the soccer cup tie to go ahead. Five weeks later, and with the acrimonious matter finally settled in Portsmouth AFC's favour, the soccer club returned to the more usual friendly fare with yet another defeat against a well-drilled military side.

Coming seven days after the triumphant resolution

of the Bournemouth dispute, the 0–3 defeat against Depot RA was a grave setback in spite of a good display by Manning. The reason, quite firmly pinpointed by the *Portsmouth Times*, was the old, old story of a shifting set of players:

> *Portsmouth AFC suffers from the want of constant players. One week it's strong and another week it's not strong, was its latest lament on a familiar theme.*
>
> *Last Saturday was a not so strong week and Depot RA beat them pretty easily.*
>
> *The game was marred by a lot of offside and only the strong defence of the Portsmouth AFC backs prevented the town club getting more badly beaten. At the same time, when they met the Depot RA they had a good team to deal with while Portsmouth AFC really is two XIs of playing teams.*
>
> *The absolute first team of the club is a very good one. The two wins over Bournemouth proved it.*
>
> *But when the first team can't play the ranks have to be filled by men who are either strangers to other players or else not in playing form.*
>
> *The starting of the second XI after the commencement of the season was a step in the right direction and if only a full list of matches is arranged by the reserves for next season Portsmouth AFC may flourish again.*

CHAPTER SIXTY-FOUR

The reserves arrival was really too late to save the club from drifting further behind football's ever-burgeoning popularity. Just how far from the main stream of soccer Portsmouth had become was illustrated by a complaint from the *Evening Mail* about the new venue of Portsmouth AFC – the Men's Recreation Ground. The site was always held up as the top sports ground in Portsmouth and yet it lacked goalnets, three years after their use had been approved by the Football Association. The paper condemned the poor state of affairs:

> *By the way, is it not time some decent goal posts and nets are put up at the Men's Recreation Ground?*
>
> *There's only one decent set but on two of the other grounds the posts have no nets, merely a piece of loose rope or tape suspended from one post to the other. Proper crossbars ought to be put up at once.*

The goals, with or without nets, were not in too much use in the return clash with Connaught Rangers on January 27th 1894. The match saw the original Pompey fail to achieve what would have been its only double of the season in a one-all draw. Doyle – not Arthur Conan Doyle – scored the town club's effort.

Dr Arthur Conan Doyle's early love of football failed to trouble his obituary writer on the *Portsmouth Evening News*. The death of the famous author prompted the expected large obituary on the day he passed away – Monday, July 7th 1930.

The thousands of words detailed at length Dr Doyle's time in Southsea and his beginnings as a GP. Sherlock Holmes received less of a mention than might be expected. But of spiritualism there was plenty. Paragraph after paragraph after paragraph gave a lengthy insight into the enthusiasm of Dr Doyle for the subject and his resignation, eight months previously, from the Society of Psychical Research of which he had been a member for 36 years.

His earlier sporting interests of cricket and billiards among others received mentions in passing. His time as the honorary secretary of the Portsmouth Literary and Scientific Society also got a mention. But football – and Portsmouth AFC – in which he had played such a prominent role was omitted. Not one word was written about the sport and the 81 known games which he played for the club. His efforts in the navy blue shirt were wiped from the history book.

Yet the work of Dr Doyle and his team mates established the game in the city and helped to elevate it to its current leading prominence among south coast sports.

Twenty-five years later, and the omission was repeated when the *Portsmouth Evening News* gave only brief details of the reinternment of the bodies of Dr Doyle and Lady Doyle. The ceremony took place on the anniversary of the death of Dr Doyle. Lady Doyle had passed away nearly ten years later – on June 27th 1940.

Their remains were transferred from the East Sussex town of Crowborough, where the couple had lived for 22 years until Dr Doyle's death, to his family's burial site in the village churchyard of Minstead in the New Forest. The paper's edition of July 21, 1955 – belatedly – reported that Dr Doyle:

> *...formerly resided in Southsea, where he began his medical practice, as well as his career as a writer. He later lived at Bignell Wood, a house within Minstead parish and the New Forest provided the background for more than one of his early novels.*
>
> *His grave is at the extreme end of the churchyard, under an old oak tree with a fine 30 ft spread of bough, and dates back to the 13th century.*

They were weakened by the absence of Manning, in spite of the favourable impression he created the previous week, and Read. The half-back was a last minute withdrawal as he travelled with the US team to Bath.

The draw did little to dent the confidence of Portsmouth AFC that they would defeat the Royal Engineers in their next game to reach the Hampshire Senior Cup final for the first time. But the optimism proved to be misplaced and the side failed yet again to get past the last-four stage.

The defeat was the effective end of the 1893/94 season, on the premature date of February 10th. Portsmouth AFC were in action of sorts a few days later in a midweek exhibition match with Portsmouth Grammar School across the Solent in Newport. The town club won 3–2 in 'an interesting match', to quote the *Portsmouth Evening News*.

The next weekend Portsmouth AFC battled their way through wind and rain to achieve a draw with Chichester, though the true insignificance of the match can gauged by the news on the same day that Southampton St Mary's were turning professional. Their announcement came a month after the Southern League was launched. Several prominent London clubs had already signed up to the venture, along with Reading.

All the Portsmouth AFC could seek solace in was the 1893/94 staging of their six-a-side tournament. The popular event attracted a record entry for Hampshire of more than fifty-three clubs. They all came from within a ten-mile radius of Portsmouth. So many clubs were involved, different groups of entries had to be established in the initial stage.

The Stamshaw Ground was kindly set aside by the corporation for the big day of February 24th, leading the *Portsmouth Times* to welcome the continued choice of venue by revealing how broken windows and poor attendances at the Drill Hall in Alfred Road in 1891 had left the tournament's second year barely breaking even.

Tournament day duly arrived and the organising committee of Wood, French, Grant and W Morris could reflect on an event of all-round success. More than three hundred players took part in matches of twenty minutes each. Six pitches were marked out two-thirds of the usual size. Some 1500 spectators gathered around the many touchlines, some having climbed the perimeter fence to get in.

They watched as the Portsmouth AFC C team beat the club's B-side 20–4 points in the first round. The second round saw the A-team in action for the first time and they sent Fareham packing 9–4, but the town club's B-side exited the tournament by the same score because of the King's Royal Rifles B.

The home team's interest ended entirely in the third round when the A-team were sent crashing 13–4 by the 15th Company RA. It was the Artillerymen's B-side which went on to win the main tournament. The Junior winners were the Ryde B-team. One player who caught the eye of the *Portsmouth Times* reporter during the games was Manning, back in the team again. He was said to have played 'a rattling good game' for the town club in spite of his tendency 'to stick with the ball too long'.

But, as one player arrived, so another departed. Lieutenant Dawson RA, the side's captain, had been away since Christmas on extended leave and his absence was set to be made permanent with his company expecting orders to sail to India. But he was still around long enough to turn out in the Hampshire FA side which faced Corinthians at Bournemouth on March 31st. His appearance at centre failed to stop a 5–2 defeat.

By then, Portsmouth AFC's familiar failing of amateurism caused the club to scratch their fixture with the triumphant 15th Company RA.

Withdrawals had left the civilians with just six players on the eve of the game. There was also bad news concerning Wood. He was ruled out for what remained of the season because of the after effects of a chill he caught in the cup tie the previous November with St Mary's.

Even worse for the club, however, must have been the prospect of seeing the Southampton side generate so much interest for their appearance in Portsmouth for the Portsmouth Senior Cup final against Freemantle. The *Portsmouth Times* compared the enthusiasm for the March 17th clash with that for the epic finals between Portsmouth AFC and Oxford Light Infantry three years previously.

The visit of the two sides from Southampton was also acting as a spur for much-needed improvements off the pitch as well as adding insult to injury for the followers of the origininal Pompey. A record crowd was expected for the final at the Men's Recreation Ground, reported the newspaper as its autumn plea for Portsmouth to stage a major game was answered. 'Separate seats for which an extra charge could be made should be placed inside the ropes,' the paper suggested.

The idea, which is in vogue in many grounds, is a good one. It will bring in extra money and seated people inside the ropes will create a capital barrier to keep out those standing outside.

A ring of seats several feet deep did indeed line the ropes on match day. The final also saw a press stand in use for the first time in Portsmouth.

The Portsmouth FA were being charged 50 per cent of the proceeds by the service authorities for the use of the ground as well as having to allow free admission for any servicemen who wanted to watch.

In contrast, the North End Recreation Ground could have been the association's for a 33 per cent cut of the receipts by the corporation without the need to permit any free entries. The choice generated some debate in the press, but the service ground's central and convenient location, as well as its facilities, made it the ideal choice, even if it was 'the happy hunting ground of free passes,' to quote the *Portsmouth Times*.

Freemantle won 2–0 and collected £40 from the gate, considerably more than in the previous year, though the cup final attendance was never specified. The result made it an unhappy double for the Saints. They had been defeated in the Hampshire Senior Cup final the previous week by the Royal Engineers, the conquerors of Portsmouth AFC.

Both Freemantle and Saints went on to play Easter matches against touring sides like Ilford, the Civil Service and Clapton as well as the US and 15th Company RA.

The *Portsmouth Times*, meanwhile, took the opportunity to praise the work of its late employee, and Portsmouth AFC player Robert Hemingsley, for helping to develop the Portsmouth cup competition. It had grown from five clubs initially to fourteen.

The success had not been matched by that of the town club. As its Southampton rivals developed constantly, all the *Portsmouth Times* could report about the leading side in Portsmouth was:

It's understood that Portsmouth AFC are likely to have a private ground next season but the exact location is at present a secret.

CHAPTER SIXTY-FIVE

Near to Portsmouth AFC's original home in North End, Portsmouth RFC were showing the way forward in spite of being two years younger. They attracted some 3000 spectators to an Easter Monday game against the mighty Bradford side visiting for their first club match in Hampshire. Portsmouth were ahead until the last ten minutes when the northerners got in front. The Yorkshiremen eventually piled on the pressure to win by 8 points to 6 with one goal and one try to a penalty goal and a try for the home side.

At a dinner that evening, Alderman Fellows revealed how far ahead the visitors were in the organisation of sport. They had 2000 subscribers,

gate receipts between £100 and £400, a ground which could take a 10 000 crowd and were formed into a limited company.

He urged Portsmouth, as a progressive town, to follow Bradford's lead as regards to sport. Portsmouth's mayor replied that he wanted to see greater sporting facilities in the area. The next bank holiday, Whit Monday, showed his view of sport being an important part of the town was widely shared.

Between 10 000 and 15 000 spectators turned out for an athletics meeting at the North End Recreation Ground. The size of the crowd, eight to ten people deep around the cycle track, was a sign of the widespread public interest in the event.

But the 1894/95 season dawned much the same way for Portsmouth AFC, as the previous campaign had stuttered to a halt in spite of people's growing enthusiasm for sport. The club were homeless and without a committed band of players. At best, the original Pompey were at a standstill, at worst, they were going backwards when compared the RA side which was about to be formed with the advantages of the service facilities at the US Grounds and the use of a regular and fit group of players.

Portsmouth Rugby Football Club's Dave Thomas in 2003 with the club badge proudly showing the 1886 date of its formation and the Star and Crescent civic symbol.

Noticeably, as well, as the new club came into being the football season was stretching. Football news began to appear in The *Hampshire Telegraph* of August 4th with details of the Hampshire FA's annual meeting at the Adelaide Restaurant in Southampton the previous day. Alarmingly, the Portsmouth division had just five affiliated clubs against ten in North Hampshire and the nine in Southampton. The New Forest also only had five recognised outfits, while only the Isle of Wight had fewer with just four.

The lack of numbers did not prevent Portsmouth AFC's honorary secretary, John French, from being on his way to being appointed to the Hampshire FA council for the coming season. He also appealed in the *Portsmouth Evening News'* August 18th 1894 edition for clubs who who wanted a game with Portsmouth AFC reserves to contact him at 16 Somers Road, Southsea. The appeal would prove optimistic in its indication of the strength of the club.

September brought a growing sense that the next six months would determine the future of the club. It was make or break time, a decade on from their formation. The *Portsmouth Times* reported that scarlet stockings were to be the original Pompey's main hope of success during the season.

The September 22nd edition of the paper noted that the club's annual meeting three days previously had involved an intense debate about the kit for the important games ahead.

Blue shirts with white sleeves and distinguishing stockings were decided upon. These last are especially intended to assist the forwards to pass and it's a fact that the Portsmouth AFC forwards want assistance of some kind to encourage them in this branch of football.

More seriously, the paper noted the major impact that 1894/95 would have on the club's future:

A great effort is being made to revive the Portsmouth AFC this season and a special appeal has been launched with a view to obtaining public support for this, the prime civilian club of the town... but up to the present all efforts to obtain a private ground have failed.

The absence of this, of course, cripples the funds of the club, but let them start winning matches and a collection on the ground will meet with a liberal response. This has been tried on other free grounds with success.

The club's new impetus also involved asking the borough mayor, Alderman Leon Emmanuel, to be their president and arranging an ambitious programme of matches.

Lear was appointed captain at the club meeting on the suggestion of Grant who declined to stand after he was proposed. French was re-elected as the honorary secretary and treasurer. A group of energetic players filled the committee with its members being H Pead, Collins, W Paice and Matson. The captain, secretary and Pead were chosen as the emergency committee. Wood was again appointed as the club's auditor.

The *Hampshire Telegraph* added on the same day:

The secretary announced the club would open on Saturday next with a scratch match against Portsmouth Grammar School. It was established that expenses for the season would be £50 and the secretary advised members to help him raise that amount.

To help, it was decided to hold a smoking concert in a month's time.

The money was needed to pay for fixtures against Chichester, Havant, Connaught Rangers, Cowes, Royal Engineers (Aldershot), RMLI, St Mary's and other favourites from the past. The Hampshire Senior Cup had also been entered alongside the twenty-four friendly matches. More were in prospect, depending on replies for games from Poole, Freemantle, Royal Engineers (Chatham) and Vampires.

But even this comparitively lengthy list was overshadowed by the thirty-five games lined up by the 15th Company RA at Fort Fareham. In addition, the service side had entered the RA southern division cup, the Portsmouth Senior Cup, the Army Cup and the Hampshire Senior Cup.

The Portsmouth FA, which had met earlier in September, could only tinker with the rules of the Portsmouth Junior Cup, which was contested by Vickery's School and Southsea Rovers Reserves in its first final, to turn it into a league format for the following season.

That apart, it was a case of same again as far as personnel were concerned for the association. Grant was wholeheartedly re-elected as the honorary secretary in recognition of the way in which he had carried out his work in the previous year.

But the increasing amount of paperwork caused a new position of assistant honorary secretary to be created. B Hayden was chosen as its first incumbent. Wood, who had chaired the meeting, was re-elected as the association's auditor in a repeat of his role with the Hampshire association. He had overseen accounts in the previous year which had ended with a satisfactory balance of £35.14s.1d.

CHAPTER SIXTY-SIX

On the playing side of 1894/95, Portsmouth AFC's fortunes immediately went into deficit. The club's September 29th practice game with the grammar school at Hilsea ended in a 1–3 defeat after half-time had arrived with the teams level at a goal apiece. Paice scored the first goal of the season when he put the town club in front but they were unable to defend their lead.

The *Portsmouth Times* was cautious about the result's bearing on the rest of the season, considering that the match was not to be taken too seriously.

Portsmouth AFC still had the ability to be a strong side, the paper added. The best of the established players were available again along with plenty of newcomers. One player who had put on his boots for the last time was Wood. His illness had probably taken too big a toll for him to continue. Plenty of other players were eager to put on their kit.

The *Portsmouth Evening News* of September 27th reported:

The winter game at the North End Recreation Ground will this season be even more actively pursued than in past years. But, although five courses (pitches) have been prepared instead of four previously, fully one-third of applications have necessarily had to be rejected.

Senior clubs have been given nine days each and Junior clubs six or seven days each.

Those who used the site faced having to pay for the

privilege for the first time, the paper explained. It had been decided, undoubtedly by the Parks and Open Spaces Committee, that a deposit of a shilling (5p) had to be paid to the groundsman, still Mr Edmonds, by the team which had booked the pitch on the Wednesday before the Saturday of the match.

If such a deposit is not made, the ground will be let to the team next on the list of applicants. This course has been adopted in consequence of many clubs engaging the ground and then not turning up to play their matches. The shilling will not be returned.

But with the arrangements in place, and as the season proper got underway, the *Portsmouth Times* carried a report which signalled the beginning of the end for Portsmouth AFC. The days were numbered for its purely amateur existence:

Rumour is current that a Portsmouth club - name not mentioned – has designs on introducing a professional or two next year. This presumably would be the thin end of the wedge for a real live professional team in Portsmouth. The promoters will be well advised if they remember Punch's *advice to those about to marry – don't.*

A professional team would simply mean the sacrifice of legitimate sport to spectacular entertainment conducted by paid performers who hunt vagrant leather for a living.

The proper and legitimate object of football is to train and cultivate the young man's physical ability making him powerful, active and healthy. But the success of professional football, almost its sole aim, is in the 6d gate. Besides, will it pay?

It may be news to the speculative gentlemen who talk of professionals for Portsmouth to know that the majority of league clubs are encumbered by heavy liabilities which they have not much chance of paying off.

Such a damning view of the future of the game was entirely in keeping with the 'muscular Christianity' movement of the 19th Century. Manly sports, such as boxing, were promoted and the ideal of a Christian gentleman with a classical education, equipped mentally and physically for life, was espoused by Dr Thomas Arnold, the headmaster of Rugby School.

The generation of public school boys raised in his robust image sparked the sports surge of the Victorian era. The YMCA, which Portsmouth AFC occasionally played, epitomised the image. Physical joined spiritual, mental and social conditioning among its aims, as gyms and swimming pools mush-

'Don't' – the verdict in the October 20, 1894, edition of the Portsmouth Times *to those thinking about forming a professional football club in the town.*

roomed in its growing range of buildings.

But such idealism was at odds with the way football was developing. As Portsmouth AFC opened their season, clubs such as Arsenal (1891), Aston Villa (1885), Barnsley (l888), Blackburn Rovers (l880), Bolton Wanderers in the same year, Chesterfield (1891) and Leicester City (l888), among others, had long since become professional outfits. Portsmouth AFC, in contrast, had to take their turn in the queue to beg for a public pitch.

They used the first of their alloted days at the coveted Stamshaw site to open their season proper on October 6th. The occasion was a visit by Chichester and it proved a happy one for the home side. Yet the result left the visitors from the cathedral city wondering how they were on the wrong end of a 2–1 scoreline.

Portsmouth AFC found themselves two goals up in the first half, thanks to Wells and H Pead. Hislock pulled one back for Chichester after half-time with a shot but his team-mates' efforts to equalise came to nothing. As the *Portsmouth Evening News* reported:

The Portsmouth AFC defence proved too wide awake and King's defence of his goal too good for them.

For the *Portsmouth Times*, the victory was a hollow one against a team who had started the season well and were the better team on the day:

The combination of the home side was as weak as ever, a family bereavement kept Lear out of the team and yet they won.

It's one of those things no fellow can understand. Seriously, the design of the Portsmouth AFC team is an indifferent one and, unless they pull themselves together, their record at the end of the season will not be brilliant.

Regardless of the original Pompey's shortcomings, half-back P Read was selected as a reserve for the Hampshire team in the South East Counties championship clash with Sussex on October 17th at Southampton. The county team was dominated by players from the Southampton area, reflecting that team's entry into the Southern League.

St Mary's provided two members of the line up, Freemantle had the highest number with three and Banister Court supplied one. The rest of the side came from the Royal Engineers (two players), 15th Company Fareham (two) and one from Cowes. Alongside Read in the reserves were a further trio from Freemantle, and one each from Bournemouth, Eastleigh, St Mary's and Cowes.

But Read was missing when Portsmouth AFC returned to the North End Recreation Ground on October 13th 1894 for their next fixture. Havant were the opponents and the home side took the opportunity to try out a number of the new players the press had enthused about. Their debuts, though, failed to impress the watching *Portsmouth Times*:

'It was not a very brilliant effort. Portsmouth AFC, trying several new men, will no doubt improve as the season goes on.

'Moreover, Havant were re-inforced by several players from the King's Own without whom they would have made an exceedingly poor show.'

The strengthened visitors went a goal up through Wilcox before Lear led the way for the original Pompey by putting the side he captained level from a free-kick. Half-time arrived with the teams at a goal apiece. Wilcox scored again to put Havant back in front only for the home side to hit back with a penalty from Lear.

Borland put the blues ahead for the first time before that man Wilcox completed his hat-trick to make the score 3-3. Moore added his narne to the score sheet

PORTSMOUTH AFC CUP TIES 1894/95					
Portsmouth Senior Cup					
R1	Royal Marines Artillery		a	D2-2	17.11.94
R1r	Royal Marines Artillery		Stamshaw	L1-3	1.12.94
Hampshire Senior Cup					
R1	Cowes		a	2-5	10.11.94
	(abandoned h-t, heavy rain)				
R1r	Cowes		a	LO-2	24.11.94

as Havant went in front once more only for an unidentified Portsmouth AFC player to leave the sides level on four goals apiece.

CHAPTER SIXTY-SEVEN

Portsmouth AFC next took to the pitch when ten men tried to take on Connaught Rangers – and failed.

They put up enough of a fight to make the match on October 20th 1894 a close and interesting one which was decided by a lone goal against the blues.

The following week, the original Pompey's cup build-up took an even bigger turn for the worse, though they were not at fault. They turned up at the US Men's Ground only to find that their opponents had not. The town team's players were left with an idle afternoon and could only watch the other games at the venue. Annoyingly, the full cup team were available.

Their preparations were boosted by the news that Hampshire representative Read would be available for the rest of the season. Rumours that his regiment, the Cameronians, were going abroad proved unfounded. The *Portsmouth Times* welcomed his continued availability but it took the chance to add a further gloomy assessment of the borough club's prospects:

He is a rattling good man but it is doubtful whether Portsmouth AFC will ever take its place as a representative town club until it can play an exclusively town XI.

The large number of clubs in the town is against them in this matter and no doubt the committee are fully aware where their weakness lies.

They had already acted by fixing on a cup side which consisted of regular players, the paper noted approvingly. Another step in an apparent right direction was the departure of Manning. He returned to New Brompton. A clever forward but a bit selfish, sniffed the journalist.

Sea dogs, let alone forwards, were needed when Portsmouth AFC made the first of two successive journeys across the Solent to face Cowes on November 3rd. The short crossing proved a nightmare in an 1894/95 season which was fast collapsing around the club. The adventure turned out to be a disaster from its start to its finish.

The first hint that anything was wrong was the weather. Storms are far from being the ideal conditions to sail to the Isle of Wight especially when the regular methods of crossing have been ignored and the trippers have hired their own boat to save money on fares.

The vessel, loaned by boatbuilders Vosper, was tossed about by the wind and waves. The *Portsmouth Times* yet again added its downbeat voice to its account of events:

When the team reached Cowes, they were decidedly wet, not to mention showing signs of mal de mer. *No wonder they were badly beaten.*

The defeat consisted of seven goals conceded and none scored. The after effects of the crossing were apparent as the islanders cruised into a 0–6 half-time lead.

'Portsmouth AFC attacked first but the ball was kicked away and Cowes scored goal after goal. Portsmouth AFC played better in the secornd half and kept Cowes at bay apart from one extra goal,' wrote the *Portsmouth Evening News*.

As preparations go, that match had to be the worst. The town club had to brace themselves for the return journey the following week for their first competitive outing of the season in the Hampshire Senior Cup. The weather and the outcome were the same.

So bad were the conditions that the tie was abandoned at half-time with the home side 2–5 ahead. But impressions of a poor showing by the team from the mainland were wrong. The visitors had learnt the lesson of the previous week and made it to the island in good time and good shape.

They were, though, missing four regulars – Reed, Borland, Street and Paice. But the patched-up side played well considering they found themselves facing the strong wind and torrential rain during the game's only half. So well, that the *Portsmouth Times* threw off its pessimism of the past few weeks to proclaim:

When the game was stopped, Cowes led by 5–2 but so well had Portsmouth AFC been showing up against the wind it's not at all improbable that they would have won.

The match reporter backed his remarkable assessment with remarks that the town side's halves – Redshaw, Grant and Lear – had played well. However, full-backs Selley and Priest were rather slow. A fairly good crowd of spectators, to quote the papers, braved the atrocious conditions. Some of them returned a fortnight later to see the home side complete the job on the last Saturday of November.

Cowes were simply the better team all round in the replay. They were quicker on the ball and Portsmouth AFC were let down by a weak combination among their forwards. Cowes went in front after ten minutes of opening exchanges in which neither side gained an advantage.

G Pead, the visiting keeper, was temporarily disabled by a kick from a home forward as he tried to save the scoring header.

Five minutes later, and Pead was again unlucky as another attacker pounced on the rebound after he had saved a goalbound effort. The third goal followed a quarter of an hour later. It too was surrounded by controversy, being apparently offside and unsuccessfully appealed against by the Portsmouth AFC players.

Having found themselves three goals down through no fault of their own, the visitors battled to regain some pride after the break. The game as a whole became a calmer affair, though Pead was again the original Pompey's star.

'He gave some remarkably good examples of goal-keeping,' reported the *Portsmouth Times*. 'Once he saved in grand style from a melee when he was fairly surrounded on the ground.'

If only his forwards had shown the same class, the result might have been different. Dawson and Mee at the other end missed easy chances to put their side back in the game. The *Portsmouth Times* also hinted at dark tricks by Cowes to ensure their passage into the second round, just in case crippling the visiting keeper and scoring offside goals was not enough:

The grass was long and rough and Cowes were up to all its peculiarities. Individually, Portsmouth AFC were quite as good as they were.

Their departure from the Hampshire Senior Cup, for the last time, was not a sign that the original Pompey's influence on the competition had ended.

The Hampshire FA had imposed a new rule on competing clubs to ensure there could be no repeat of Caldecott fiasco which marred the competition the previous season when Bournemouth endlessly challenged his inclusion in Portsmouth AFC's side for their second round clash. The *Portsmouth Times* described Bournemouth's conduct as sharp practice when it gave news of the new regulation:

In the case of any player not being resident within the necessary radius of any club entered for the competition, a club wishing to play him must make application to the council at least twenty-eight days previous to the cup tie.

Players must be qualified by birth within the county, within ten miles of the playing ground of the club, or by continuous residence for at least eight weeks within ten miles of the playing ground.

They also must have played in the same season for the club for at least twenty-eight days previous to the match.

The intention of the change was spelled out by the *Portsmouth Evening News*:

Revised rules this year make careful provision for competitors being bona fide members of the club for which they are entered and to ensure only those connected with Hampshire should take part in the contests.

CHAPTER SIXTY-EIGHT

The change for the cup had also been joined by a new look, literally, for the Portsmouth Senior Cup. A new trophy was to be purchased by the Portsmouth FA, its committee announced as the first round draw was made.

This paired Portsmouth AFC with the RMA at the Eastney Barracks. The tie was sandwiched in between the civilians' county cup ties on the other side of the Solent. A replay was also needed in the Portsmouth cup game with the first game at Eastney ending all square at 2–2.

The teams met again straight after the original Pompey's exit from the Hampshire contest to make it four cup matches in a row as 1894 drew to a close. Portsmouth AFC's work in holding the Marines to a draw in their initial encounter earned rare praise from the *Portsmouth Times* for its unexpected outcome:

The most sanguine of Portsmouth AFC's supporters could hardly have expected them to draw against RMA, who have been going very strongly, and at Eastney too.

Still, they did, and even yet there may be hope that the hard-working French may turn out a side which will do credit to the old club.

That hope proved to be forlorn when the replay took place at Stamshaw on December 1st 1894.

The sides went into the rematch knowing the winners would face Eastleigh at home on February 15th. It was to be the Marines looking forward to that game. They sent the original Pompey out of the competition by a margin of three goals to one.

The Marines' inside-left, Daly, did the damage with a hat-trick. He followed his first-half opener with a brace after the interval. The civilian scorer was unidentified, though the club were once more let down by their players. They staggered through the first forty-five minutes with just ten men, to handicap their chances of making progress with a home tie in the next round at stake.

The latest defeat prompted a further bout of gloom from the *Portsmouth Times* as it returned to its previous depressed thoughts:

Portsmouth AFC are now out of everything and, unless they show some improvement, are likely to remain out. However, it is very unEnglish to kick a man when he is down, though it is much safer than when he is up, and everyone will hope Portsmouth AFC will finish the season in more successful style than they have begun it.

The paper assured those fans who were still loyal that the remaining fixtures would be fulfilled. But its description of Portsmouth AFC as luckless proved apt the following week when the first visit to Bournemouth since the cup furore exactly a year earlier ended in a further defeat.

The town club could only muster nine men for the lengthy railway journey to the resort but managed to struggle on during the opening half to turn round just 0–2 down. Their makeshift defence, with substitutes Brooks and Colbran making up the numbers, held out for twenty minutes before Bournemouth could open the scoring, in spite of the home side notching up five corners in as many minutes at one stage.

Even then, Grant had an excellent chance to equalise when his run took him past the home defence only to send his shot ballooning over the bar with the goal at his mercy. Bournemouth piled on the pressure and went 0–4 ahead early in the second half before Portsmouth AFC rallied and Sampson beat home keeper Stokes with a clever shot.

It was never going to be enough to make a comeback and Bournemouth dominated the rest of the match to add yet another goal. The *Portsmouth Evening News* was unimpressed with the entire ninety minutes:

There was very little life in the game all through, both sides taking matters very easy.

CHAPTER SIXTY-NINE

The year 1894 was slipping away and sliding downhill for the original Pompey and the few weeks left proved no more kind to them. The dire straits which surrounded their fortunes were amply demonstrated by the make up of the team for the next recorded match – a Boxing Day fixture away to Ryde. Only Street, one of the backs, had appeared

in the Bournemouth game. He was marooned among ten different players on each occasion. Fielding a team of strangers is a recipe for failure. So it proved with Portsmouth AFC returning home across the Solent after a 2–4 defeat. The *Portsmouth Evening News* was pleased in spite of a seventh defeat in ten games for the town club: 'Portsmouth AFC played a capital passing game and the backs did sterling service.'

One of the absentees from Portsmouth AFC's side – half-back Lear – had been selected for the first Portsmouth FA representative match against Brighton on January 2nd 1895. Significantly, he was the only player from the club to be chosen, reflecting its rapidly fading status.

FOOTBALL ON SKATES.

An amusing and exciting entertainment was football match on skates played at the Victoria the Hall, Southsea, on Wednesday evening, between teams from Portsmouth and Southampton. A large attendance of spectators displayed great interest in the game, which was played in accordance with Association rules, and hailed with enthusiasm the final victory of the home team. There were six players on either side, all being equipped with roller skates, which were marvellously manipulated, some of the players performing wonderful gyrations while in chase of the leather. Portsmouth kicked off, and after one or two scrambles and a lot of noise, Southampton registered the first goal. Then the contestants became excited, and the fun commenced. Every other minute, the ball went amongst the spectators, and many received a smart whack, or one of the players, unable to stop his mad rush, went plump into somebody's lap. It was also very funny to see a player skate after the ball and glide gracefully by it, unable to pull himself up. Although much the lighter team, Portsmouth, after about ten minutes, had the best of the game, although on several occasions there was a heap of swaying arms and legs round their goal that looked rather dangerous. Once "hands" was given against the home team about a foot from their goal, but they saved, and a minute after Bailey shot a goal for Portsmouth. Then in quick succession Bailey scored again, and a third goal was rushed through. In the second half play was fast and furious, but nothing further was scored, although each goal was in turn in danger, and once Portsmouth missed a good chance. When time was called the home team glided from the hall the victors by three goals to one. The visitors have previously beaten Portsmouth twice at Southampton. Teams :—

Portsmouth—Goal, Eager ; backs, Ash (captain) and Taylor ; forwards, E. Bailey, Johnson, and Shepperd.

Southampton—Goal, Senior ; backs, V. Smith and C. Smith ; forwards, Roberts, Fry, and T. Roberts.

Mr. E. H. Andrews, captain of the Portsmouth Rugby F.C., acted as referee ; and Messrs. Arnold (Portsmouth) and Gubbings (Southampton) linesmen.

How football on skates arrived in Portsmouth in January 1895 as reported in the Portsmouth Evening News.

Further proof of that, if any was needed, arrived in the ominous form of St Mary's in 1894's last game. Portsmouth AFC were given the footballing equivalent of a hangover with a blistering nine-goal avalanche from the Saints. Tellingly, the overwhelming win in windy conditions at the Antelope Ground in Southampton, was inflicted by a team described in a post-match report as the reserves of the Southern League outfit. The *Hampshire Post* said tersely:

From the start, Saints had things all their own way and scored five goals before half-time against the wind.

The *Portsmouth Times* was lost for words. It could only ascribe the stunning defeat to the absence of Portsmouth AFC stalwart Grant because his wife had given birth on Boxing Day. The congratulations for his family could only be joined by commiserations for the painful death of a once successful football club, with just one win to its name that season. 'The combination of the Saints Reserves enabled them to pile on goal after goal, ' the paper reported.

On the same day, Southampton's first team were second in the Southern League. Portsmouth AFC were nowhere, in footballing terms. News of the defeat was joined by a rare tribute to the behind-the-scenes work of an official at the town club: loyal John French was lauded for his efforts to keep the club alive: 'He has worked for Portsmouth AFC night and day,' commented the *Evening Mail*. 'He has hunted for players from Hilsea to Point and from Milton to the Pontoon. He has borrowed steam launches but the team is as disappointing as ever.'

Lear, meanwhile, helped the Portsmouth FA to a 4–3 win in that inaugural fixture with Brighton alongside four RA players, four from the King's Own and two from the 15th Company RA. As the military dominance of football in Portsmouth strengthened, so great was that power that the club's involvement in fundraising for a private ground for Portsmouth AFC was seen as crucial to the campaign's success:

The club are still working hard to secure a private ground for the next season and it's understood a benefit match will be played on behalf of the club's funds...

advised the *Portsmouth Times*.

King's Own, Portsmouth RA and other crack clubs have promised their assistance but what will be the date of the game or the composition of the sides is presently undecided.

The civilian club was so poor they had to cancel the scheduled home return with Bournemouth and arrange to play the game away in return for a promise of half the gate money. The result was unrecorded, if the repeat away match ever took place, but one fixture which has survived into the 21st century was the only form of football at which Portsmouth AFC could still beat Saints – soccer on skates.

The Wednesday evening fixture on January 23rd 1895 at Southsea's Victoria Hall ended in a 3–1 win for the home team. A large audience was present to watch an amusing and exciting entertainment which was a world away from football although played in accordance with the association rules.

The *Portsmouth Evening News* was tickled by the diversion from the problems which beset the original Pompey as it spoke of the 'wonderful gyrations' some players performed to reach the ball. It wasn't all laughs for the fans:

Every other minute the ball went amongst the spectators and many received a smart whack or one of the players, unable to steady his mad rush, went plump into somebody's lap.

It was also very funny to see a player skate past the ball and glide gracefully by it, unable to pull himself up.

Although the lighter team, Portsmouth had the best of the match after the initial ten minutes. Southampton scored first but the home side were 3–1 up by half-time and that was how the score stayed. The winning team was: Goal – F Barber; backs – EW Ash (c), W Taylor; forwards – E Bailey, C Johnson, F Shepherd. Portsmouth RFC provided the referee in the form of its captain, EH Andrews. The umpires were Portsmouth AFC's Arnold and Gribbings of Southampton.

The occasion was so popular it was quickly followed by a repeat at the same venue on February 13th. Southampton proved the winners by a single goal in the return.

The second-half goal came amid a fast and furious display from both sides. Portsmouth's team on that occasion was: Goal – F Barber; backs – EW Ash, W Taylor; forwards – C Johnson, E Bailey, F Shepherd.

Elsewhere, Saints' power in Hampshire football at the expense of every other club in the county was seen when Hampshire FA had to re-arrange the Hampshire Senior Cup semi-final to avoid a clash with St Mary's fixtures. The *Evening Mail* was unimpressed:

This means Southampton have become 'boss of the show'. Their matches have been such an attraction they over-ride everything else and the Hampshire FA must fix dates so they do not clash with the professional ones. We do not begrudge Saint their popularity. They have worked for it, but why not hold an important match at Portsmouth with the 15th Company RA and the King's Own engaged in a semi-final and likely to meet in a final. They are likely to get a bigger gate in Portsmouth than in Southampton for the game.

CHAPTER SEVENTY

Portsmouth AFC were as far from being able to boss the Hampshire FA around as it was possible to be. They were not even affiliated to the organisation, an administrative task which even the likes of Spartan FC and Havant Eclipse had managed to achieve.

A total of twelve clubs were in the Portsmouth division of the association. Eight of them were military outfits. The Portsmouth FA had a further seventeen clubs on their books and junior organisations such as Kent Road Athletic, Buckland Victoria, St Simon's Institute and St Mary's Gymnasium had achieved a form filling exercise beyond what was supposed to be the town's premier club.

How Portsmouth AFC could skip membership and still take part in competitions such as the forthcoming six-a-side tournament was never explained. But the club joined those in the draw for the first round of the fifth of the annual contests.

They were lucky for once with a bye for the opening game alongside nine other entrants in the senior section. Among those also sitting out the initial stage were RA-B, North End-B and Southsea Rovers-A. Six ties were to take place in the opening round to get the action underway at the North End Recreation Ground on March 2nd.

Six pitches were laid out to enable the organisers to cope with forty-nine entries – such as Southsea Rovers-A, -B and -C and North End-A and -B – in the junior and senior categories. The four-strong sub-committee of the Portsmouth FA was again led by the indefatigable Grant. He was assisted by Wood, French, Norris and Colour Sergeant Johnson, of the King's Own Royal Lancashire Regiment.

They had arranged for the medals to go on display at JB Jackson in Palmerston Road, Southsea, who had made and designed them. The original Pompey opened their quest for them in their first of the twenty-minute matches with a win over Southsea Rovers by two corners to nil in a close game.

A corner was worth a point and a goal four points. But any hopes of further progress were wrecked by the mighty RA. Even the soldiers' B-team, though it perversely seemed to comprise the corps' best players of Reilly, Phillips, Patterson, Hanna, Williams and Jardine, was too strong for the likes of Brown – goal; Walsh, Lear – backs; Dawson, Windust, Atkins – forwards. Moving into the third round with a three goals to nil victory, the Artillerymen's A-side went on to win the tournament – in which the strength of many sides was affected by an illness – in a final with the A side of the 15th Company RA.

Portsmouth AFC went into the popular tournament boosted by reports that their elusive private ground could be much nearer to fruition at last. The *Evening Mail* announced the possibility with a tantalising report on February 26th:

It's probable Portsmouth AFC will be proud possessors of a private ground next season. Negotiations are pending but have yet to reach the stage when full publicity can be given.

The article concluded with details of the club's first match for what was likely to be more than two months. As that game at Weymouth took place on March 9th 1895, the gossip was in overdrive about the town club's future. The *Portsmouth Times* commented:

...it may be bigger things are in store and rumours of a private ground up at Fratton still fill the air.

Whatever the future for Portsmouth AFC, it had to be better than the present. The preview of the Weymouth match had included an offer for any spectators interested in watching the game to contact John French at Somers Road for the secretary to arrange transport for them.

That should have been players the club was appealing for. A considerable amount of difficulty, according to the *Portsmouth Times* had been caused simply raising a team for the clash:

The Portsmouth side included six from the King's Own and McGuire, of HMS Excellent. *The latter is by no means a youngster but he plays capital games and when he shoots he shoots hard and straight.It was rather a miscellaneous team to represent the chief civilian club in Portsmouth...*

The ragbag collection, however, overcame their unfamiliarity with each other and a pitch like a quagmire to put Weymouth firmly in their place. The 4–2 triumph was the first for the original Pompey for a remarkable five months, and only their second of a dire season. The home side was reckoned to be a crack team but Rogers put the visitors ahead after just two minutes with a shot from a neat pass from Grant. Weymouth soon equalised only for McGuire to unleash one of his special shots to give the visitors the lead again. Weymouth equalised once more to ensure half-time was reached with the score at 2–2.

A fast-paced second half saw the original Pompey go in front for a third time through an own goal. A fourth goal, by Windust, sealed their unlikely, if welcome, victory. It was as hollow a victory as it was possible to get.

CHAPTER SEVENTY-ONE

Portsmouth AFC's remaining fans could only look on with envy the following week when close to 4000 people watched the 1894/95 Portsmouth Senior Cup final between the King's Own Lancaster Regiment and the 15th Company RA. The US Men's Ground was the suitably military setting for the occasion, won 3–0 by the King's Own.

But the choice of venue was never far away from controversy in the football world of 1890s Portsmouth. The *Evening Mail* reported that the number of paying spectators – at 1501 – was less than half the total attendance. Most of the crowd was composed of naval and military personnel who took advantage of their entitlement to free admission. For the privilege, the Portsmouth FA had to hand over half the gate money which was collected to the ground's authorities in keeping with the practice of previous years:

...the time has, we think, arrived for the Portsmouth FA to consider whether it would not pay them better to play the senior final at Stamshaw.

There may be fewer persons, as far as actual numbers go, but 60 per cent of free passes is rather a lot.

It would be more satisfactory to hire a ground for some reasonable sum for a day though, of course, there would be the risk of wet weather to be considered.

The stiff charge for the Men's Ground still allowed the Portsmouth FA to bank £37.10s.6d from the match. This enabled the body to end the season with the tidy sum of about £20 in hand when the proceeds of the semi-finals were taken into account as well, and after the cost of the new trophy and the medals had been deducted.

The season's closing weeks brought no action for Portsmouth AFC. The club obviously decided to end on a winning note. Yet plenty of evidence existed of their fall from footballing prominence. The Hampshire FA played Kent and won 8–1 with no trace of the town club among its team of four RA players, two from Cowes and one each from Freemantle, Eastleigh, Royal Engineers, St Mary's and 15th Company RA.

The county repeated the overall mix for the following match with Middlesex. This helped Hampshire come second in its south east grouping with three wins from five games, scoring nineteen goals in the process with twelve conceded.

The association had also hosted the Hampshire Senior Cup final on April 3rd at the County Ground, Southampton, where 3000 fans had watched St Mary's thrash 15th Company Fareham 5–0.

The county showpiece game ended the season, with the exception of two lingering service games. The *Evening Mail* struggled to reconcile the potentially bright prospects for football in Portsmouth with the present reality:

That there is growing interest in football in Portsmouth is undoubtedly true and a really strong civilian club with a private ground in any accessible part of the town would soon have a large following and sound finances.

Yet the reality could not be denied, the paper admitted, as it agreed that 1894/95 had been a poor a season for lovers of the sport:

Portsmouth AFC, starting with a programme the length and magnitude of which was almost alarming, practically stopped playing at Christmas.

And the only other powerful civilian club, Southsea Rovers, though undoubtedly a strong side, did not do as well as anticipated.

With the junior clubs, there has been some keenness in their play, but there are so many of them that there is not much hope of any of them approaching first class strength.

CHAPTER SEVENTY-TWO

For Portsmouth AFC there was one well-known barrier to success – the lack of a ground. 1895/96 began with a repeat of a refrain from no less a person than Grant. The Portsmouth FA's secretary had concentrated solely on the paperwork after he played his last game in the surprise 4–2 win at Weymouth the previous March. He had turned out for Portsmouth during eight seasons in a football career which had lasted fourteen years from the tine he first laced up his boots at Battersea College which he had attended away from his Portsmouth birthplace.

He knew more about the game in Portsmouth than anyone else. He was reported in the *Portsmouth Evening News* as early as August 30th 1895 to 'be making things shipshape for the coming season.'

But his words in an interview with the *Evening Mail*, which carried more weight than those of most people, were entirely accurate in their forecast of the season ahead. He said the main interest would be provided by the military teams in Portsmouth:

As far as civilians go, senior football in the town will never be good until we can secure a ground and we get the benefit of the gates.

If this drawback were removed, football in Portsmouth would improve considerably.

He explained that Portsmouth AFC made every effort the previous season to obtain a ground but a lack of money, among other problems, meant they failed to succeed. The absence of facilities had limited the size of the new junior league which the association had formed for 1895/96.

The eighteen applicants had to be almost halved to ten to fit the pitches which were available.

Mr Grant expected the league to be the main source of interest for junior clubs in Portsmouth. For the seniors, the Portsmouth Senior Cup would once more provide a competitive feel to the campaign.

THE ENGLISH FOOTBALL ASSOCIATION.

TO THE EDITOR OF THE TIMES.

Sir,—The Rugby Union is threatened with civil war on account of a grave difference among its members on a matter of principle ; but the English Football Association is stirring up a rebellion from mere wantonness. For several years a six-a-side football competition has been played on the Hants County ground, which has caused very great interest and has done much to promote football among smaller clubs. It has been managed by a committee of the Hants Football Council, and there has never been a whisper of any evil resulting from it. This has lately been prohibited by the English Association without any reason being given, without permitting us to defend ourselves, with no regard to our strong protests. Now if these competitions are football, it is the business of the English Association to regulate them : if they are not football it has nothing at all to do with them. It proposes at present by a most high handed and arbitrary act to disregard the unanimous protest of a body representing 146 clubs and a vast number of players, and because these competitions may or may not do harm in some parts of England to prohibit them in parts where they have done the greatest good, and where by training young players they have produced some of the best amateurs in Hants. Even Parliament would not interfere with the liberty of large numbers of people in such a way without giving them a full hearing, and would certainly allow districts where public opinion is unanimous and which are well governed to decide for themselves. Yours faithfully,
C. G. ELLABY, President Hants F.A.
Wadham College, Sept. 2.

CG Ellarby goes national in The Times *about the FA ban on the popular six-a-side tournaments.*

The competition had attracted a same-again sixteen entries as the previous year.

Portsmouth AFC were included in the entries alongside RA, HMS *Excellent*, HMS *Vernon*, RMLI, RN Depot, and Geneva Cross. The presence of the military sides reinforced Mr Grant's view. Though, once again, the original Pompey were puzzlingly absent from the list of affiliated clubs to the Portsmouth FA.

Nineteen outfits were included in a *Portsmouth Evening News* report about the matter. They included such lesser footballing lights as Portsmouth Quick Star, with their secretary in Oyster Street; Portsmouth Hornets, based in Powerscourt Road; Blue Company from St Mary's vicarage and the Mornington Crescent-based Baystar from Landport.

The poor state and uncertainty around civilian football in the town contrasted with a report in the same paper about the football craze which was sweeping northern and midland areas of the country. The enthusiasm for the game was causing severe problems for employers, apparently.

So serious, in fact, that a group of Birmingham manufacturers had called a meeting to discuss how businesses could stop the football season interfering with their work routines. Several factory owners complained that the Monday start of the new season for the mighty West Bromwich Albion led to shops being deserted as the club' fans flocked to their grounds: 'Although the furnaces were burning as usual, many factories had to close their doors after dinner time, being quite deserted,' the report concluded.

Nationally, the 1895/96 season would see Aston Villa become Football League champions for the second time in three years with Derby County the runners up. The Second Division was won by Liverpool.

The Wednesday made it a good year for Sheffield by winning the FA Cup. In Scotland, Celtic became champions for the third time as Hearts became the cup holders. England also staged the latest of their games with Scotland, Wales and Ireland.

But football in Portsmouth was dealt a hammer blow by the Football Association just as the season was about to get underway. The game's rulers banned all six-a-side tournaments.

CG Ellarby, Hampshire FA's president, said no reason was given for the prohibition, and there was no chance to protest and to defend the tournaments.

The Portmouth Evening News was outraged by the move:

In Portsmouth, the action of the FA will cause no end of disappointment for the annual six-a-side tourna-

ment at the Stamshaw ground was one of the most popular features of the season.

The FA decision is a most arbitrary one for competitions out of the direct control of county and district associations might well have been left undisturbed.

Mr Ellerby added that the competitions produced some of the best amateur players in Hampshire. Undaunted by this setback, Portsmouth AFC continued on.

Mid September saw the club's name appear seven times among the season's fixtures which were to take place at the North End Recreation Ground. The matches began on November 2nd 1895, against Stubbington, continued with Fareham (November 30th) and Southampton St Mary's (December 17th) before they entered 1896 with games with Havant (January 18th), Chichester a week later and Eastleigh on February 22nd, before the final match on March 7th when Cowes were to be the visitors.

CHAPTER SEVENTY-THREE

The list proved another example of wishful thinking by the officials of the town club. Those matches could not be fulfilled as the outfit lurched from crisis to crisis. The season began, fittingly enough, with an away 1–2 defeat at Havant on October 5th 1895. Equally fitting, and entirely in accord with the recent past of the original Pompey, they played one man short throughout the curtain-raising game.

That same weekend brought news of the club's fate in the Portsmouth Senior Cup first round. It had been five years since the blue shirts could claim the competition as their own.

The draw ensured it would be another year at least, if the club could survive any longer, before they would be able to enjoy any further success.

They had been handed the worst possible draw of the other fifteen clubs, challenging for the cup with a tie against RA, who had rapidly emerged as the strongest team in Portsmouth. The mis-match was set for November 23rd 1895.

The luck of the draw also deserted Portsmouth AFC in the Hampshire Senior Cup. They were paired alongside Cowes, one of their bogey sides, on or before November 2nd.

Evening Mail columnist AN Other saw some light through the darkness which appeared to envelop the club's future. He reported that Bernard Pares, the long-time friend of the club, had returned from the continent and joined forces with the hard-working secretary Mr French to revive the struggling organisation:

Every effort will be made to bring it up to a standard worthy of the representative club of a town like Portsmouth.

There must be ample good material for a really good side and I hope that the mistakes of playing local men in the ordinary matches and dropping them in cup ties for 'star' performers will not be repeated.

To the adoption of this policy in the past, I attribute the gradual decline in the Portsmouth Cup.

The journalist returned to the refrain the following week with a justification of the opening day defeat at Havant.

'True to tradition', in his words, the original Pompey had turned up two men short and lost 2–3, by his reckoning. 'Still, I fancy they will pull through,' he wrote, 'and as I said last week, there must be ample material in Portsmouth for a rare good side. It only wants working up and I believe it can be done if the committee go the right way to work, playing the same team every week and civilians only.'

That might have been the case but that day saw the original Pompey facing just the reserve side of the Dublin Fusiliers.

So low had the town club's reputatation slumped that they were rated too poorly to take on the military side's first XI.

Even against the second string, Portsmouth AFC failed to dominate at Governor's Green. They won 3–1 through goals by B Pares (presumably Bernard), Norris and Dawson.

The *Portsmouth Evening News* was distinctly unimpressed with the display:

A rare link with the glory days of the original Pompey was provided by SR Pike as the club slipped out of existence.

There is nothing much to say in praise of either team. Pares and Dawson did the best work for Portsmouth AFC but there was nothing brilliant in the performance of their team.

CHAPTER SEVENTY-FOUR

Good news for Portsmouth AFC could be found in its rejoining the list of affiliations of the Portsmouth FA. The returnee, Bernard Pares, was given as the contact at Westfield, Clarence Parade, Southsea, as well as Mr French at his usual address of 16, Somers Road, Southsea.

Sixteen senior clubs were affiliated. The others were RN Depot, RMLI, RA, 15th Company RA, HMS *Excellent*, HMS *Vernon*, RMA, Southsea Rovers, 5th Fusiliers, Freemantle, Havant, Gosport Red Star, Geneva Cross, Portsmouth Grammar School and Dublin Fusiliers. All were entered for the Portsmouth Senior Cup.

There were nine other clubs in the junior league, including Southsea Rovers Reserves and Gosport Red Star Reserves, though no second team of Portsmouth AFC. A further twenty-two outfits were affiliated to the Hampshire FA.

Portsmouth AFC struggled back to life on October 26th when the services of two substitute backs and one stand-in left-sided forward enabled them to turn out against Royal Naval Depot at a US Recreation Ground more used now to hosting RA and their growing ranks of supporters. The borough club lost to a single goal scored by the Depot's left-winger after holding out during the first half. The *Portsmouth Evening News* was critical of the fare on offer, to continue the *Evening Mail*'s theme of the previous month:

Throughout, the game was keenly contested, although from a scientific standpoint the display of football was not of a brilliant description.

The paper had already made up its mind about the fixture in its preview comment:

Although the football fields in Portsmouth will be busy tomorrow, the matches will not be of a very important character.

This lowly assessment was explained by RA's visit to the mighty Tottenham Hotspur, which they won 2–1, US Rugby Club's trip to Holland and the journey by Portsmouth RFC to Southampton to take on Trojans.

In footballing terms, the respective attractions of Spurs or Royal Naval Depot was no contest. The

previous week had also seen RA travel to the already well-established Reading for a 1–3 defeat, while Portsmouth AFC were idle.

The officials at the original Pompey must then have realised they were wasting their time trying to keep the club going. What was once a group of pioneers had become a group of has beens, sadly.

November arrived, and matters got worse for the town club. They were barely functioning. The listed fixture with Stubbington at the North End Recreation Ground failed to make it into the match report roundup, unlike nine other Saturday games in Portsmouth and three Wednesday fixtures reported in the relevant issue of the *Hampshire Telegraph*. More seriously, the blueshirts' home tie with Cowes in the Hampshire Senior Cup first round was scratched to disappear without trace for the want of a borough team.

The cancellation of the major game came straight after the news that the Portsmouth Senior Cup match with RA was no more. The *Portsmouth Evening News* broke the story in its report of the Portsmouth FA meeting on November 4th:

An application had been sent in to change the date of their cup tie with Portsmouth AFC but, as the latter had scratched owing to their inability to raise a team, the matter fell through.

CHAPTER SEVENTY-FIVE

How the news must have saddened Portsmouth FA officials Grant and Bernard Pares, who had worked so hard to help the town club to survive. The *Evening Mail*'s AN Other took up the story in his 'On the Ball' column in mid-November, a week after the no show against Cowes and a week before Portsmouth AFC were to hand RA a walkover in the Portsmouth Senior Cup on a day when the civilians again failed to appear in the fixture list:

Poor old Portsmouth AFC. The first football match I saw in Portsmouth was played some years ago in a meadow at Alderman George Kent's farm. They were a poorish side then, but now they seem to be no side at all.

They scratched to the RA because they could not get a qualified team for the Portsmouth Senior Cup and, presmably, they failed to meet Cowes in the Hampshire Senior Cup on Saturday for a similar reason.

No doubt they are handicapped by not having a ground but I must express the opinion it would be better to disband the club, if there is any of it left with the exception of substitutes, than to scratch half the matches and lose the rest.

The blunt-talking journalist commented that the steady sales of the paper's Football Edition proved there was a lot of interest in football in Portsmouth:

There's plenty of keenness about and, if we are only in the fortunate position of a private ground or two, I am convinced a good association club could easily draw satisfactory 'gates'.

But November 23rd 1895 arrived and RA were duly awarded their first round tie with Portsmouth AFC. The club was still alive, just. They returned to action the following week against yet another military team – who else in the Portsmouth footballing scene of the late 1890s? – and the result was a 1–2 defeat to Northumberland Fusiliers at the North End Recreation Ground. Not content with one defeat, the club was also facing Shanklin on the same day of November 30th, according to the *Portsmouth Evening News*, and being trounced 1–5 by the island side. The demise of the town club was rapidly becoming more probable than possible. Confusion surrounded its status, or lack of it. The *Hampshire Telegraph* was sure the answer to the lack of a strong Portsmouth team lay in achieving the unity of the local sides to the Portsmouth FA. It believed links between affiliated and non-affiliated clubs would soon be barred:

…it is hoped before long there will not be a single club which has not thrown in its lot with the association.

When all are combined, the executive may find it possible to pick a town team.

For its part, the *Evening Mail*'s Ariel columnist was still pondering about the issue of the ground as November progressed:

It has been a standing grievance among the football clubs of Portsmouth that it was impossible to get good matches here owing to the faact there's no ground where a gate can be taken.

But I learn there's just a chance this difficulty may be removed. A proposition has been made in influential quarters that the Men's Recreation Ground should be closed on a certain number of days a year for gate money matches and that, on those occasions, soldiers and sailors should be charged half price.

The home team would, of course in such matches, be military or naval, but the sportsmanlike way in which the Officers' Recreation Ground was given up for a challenge cup match last season and let for the use of Portsmouth FA v Brighton FA on New Year's Day

---

The dire state of civilian football in Portsmouth in 1896 can be gauged by the excitement generated by the town's first women's soccer match. The game was billed as THE local Easter attraction that year. Some 4000 people, as many as ever watched Portsmouth AFC, turned up to see the clash between the skirted players who represented the North and the South. The fixture had been eagerly looked forward to since late January when a doubtful *Southern Daily Mail* revealed it would take place:

Lady footballers, I hear, have accepted the terms offered by the rugby club and will play at North End on Easter Monday.

That they will draw a good crowd there could be no doubt, though whether they exhibition will be edifying will be another thing. Twenty-one [correct] ladies in bloomers and smalls are not as a rule football material from which one anticipates a good game.

The *Hampshire Telegraph* had no such qualms reporting on the match and the enthusiasm which greeted its staging on April 6th. Crowds started to gather at the ground fully 90 minutes before the 3.30 pm kick off. Both teams were composed of northern ladies.

Eleven of them wore red jerseys and eleven blue. The North won 7–3 after a tremendous struggle. The Hampshire Telegraph reporter among the vast crowd was suitably impressed by what could only be described as a mild-mannered version of the game:

Both sides went to work in a business-like manner but their spirited play was softened with gentleness and consideration.

There was no charging and, if one lady saw that an opponent really wanted to kick the leather, she placed no impediment in her way.

The ball was never headed. All the work was done with their feet.

Most of the players wore short skirts but one or two took to the turn in loose knickers which enabled them to outstrip their skirted sisters in the frequent runs after the ball.

The spectators decided not to treat the game seriously from the outset. They were out of an afternoon's fun and they got their full measure with little scientific football thrown in.

dispels the notion that the service club is in any way hostile to promoting high class sport in this town.

CHAPTER SEVENTY-SIX

Whatever high class sport there was, it certainly wasn't going to come from Portsmouth AFC. The 'On the Ball' column of the *Evening Mail* reported on December 14th that a letter had been received from Mr French which contained a glowing account of the formation of a new club, Portsmouth United FC, of which he was the secretary at his house in Somers Road and ready to accept challenges from opponents. A Mr Shaften was to be the captain of the new club, with a Mr Berry as his vice-captain.

'Whether this combination is to be a continuation of the luckless Portsmouth AFC, or whether that still exists, I know not,' the columnist commented. 'Be this as it may, I wish the new club well. It's little short of a scandal that in a town the size of Portsmouth there should not be a strong senior club.'

Not for the first time, enthusiasm for football was growing around Portsmouth and nationally, as Portsmouth AFC ebbed away. A rise in the number of affiliations to the local football association had taken the total of members to sixty. The large figure was welcomed by the *Hampshire Telegraph*:

This is how it should be for the game can never be properly controlled until the clubs are under the governing power of a central body.

To make it easier for that to happen, it was decided by football's rulers in Portsmouth to allow clubs who were based within six miles of Cosham railway station to affiliate. This decision, and the results in the same edition of the *Hampshire Telegraph*, showed how little Portsmouth AFC were being missed – Southsea Rovers beat Freemantle 1–0 in the Portsmouth Senior Cup, RMLI defeated the RN Depot 3-2, while the RMA and Dublin Fusiliers drew a goal apiece and HMS *Excellent* handed out a 4–2 drubbing to Portsmouth Grammar School.

Portsmouth AFC might have been absent but at least one of their players carried on. Lear was chosen as a Portsmouth FA half-back for its established January 1st fixture with Brighton FA. More than half his team mates in the representative side were to come from the new footballing force in Portsmouth of RA. Six of the artillerymen were chosen along with two players from the 15th Company RA. Only a pair of other civilians were selected – one each from Southsea Rovers and Freemantle.

Lear was made the captain for the clash on the first day of 1896 which resulted in a resounding five-goal success for the home side at the US sports ground. The venue would not be hosting a Hampshire Senior Cup semi-final, though, according to the Southern Daily Mail. The paper's optimism of just a few weeks earlier had proved misplaced.

As for Portsmouth AFC, their condition remained uncertain. Their name appeared in fixtures against RMLI, Havant and Chichester during January 1896 but no match reports have survived, to make it seem unlikely that the games were fulfilled. Lear was one familiar name which did gain another mention in print

Portsmouth AFC were obviously without a game on January 4th 1896 in spite of the fixture list, and the half-back captained Southsea Rovers in their ill-fated Portsmouth Senior Cup tie with the mighty RA. The result was a foregone conclusion, a 0–6 defeat for the civilians to give the Gunners as good as a second walkover in that season's competition.

The *Southern Daily Mail* saw the result coming, along with every football fan in Portsmouth:

As expected, Southsea Rovers were easily knocked out of the Portsmouth Senior Cup.

Rovers were without several of their most prominent players and, though reinforced by the old Portsmouth AFC captain, Lear, they were never in the hunt with the Gunners.

Meanwhile, the uncertain fate which continued to surround Portsmouth AFC again showed how far behind football was in Portsmouth as the modern game took shape. The FA had brought in the penalty kick and the *Portsmouth Evening News* used its edition of January 18th to include a brief explanation by Mr Pickford, the Hampshire FA secretary, about the change – four years later.

The previous problematic law had allowed a referee to award a goal if he saw a certain score prevented by handling but the offence could not take place close to the goal. The new law changed all that. Penalty kicks were proposed in 1891 after a suggestion by the Irish FA to the game's internal rule-makers. The kicks were the first way to punish those players and teams who deliberately stopped goals being scored.

But the early penalties scored by Portsmouth AFC and their contemporaries were far different from those seen in the 21st Century. The kicks could be taken from any point twelve yards from the goal-line under the following conditions:

All players with the exception of the player taking the kick and the opposing goalkeeper – who could not advance more than six yards from the goal-line – had to stand at least six yards from the ball.

Goal markings at the time consisted of two semi-circular goal areas. Not until 1902 were drastic alterations made to form the markings recognisable today. Rectangular goal areas arrived along with the penalty area of current dimensions and shape with a fixed penalty spot.

The increasing need to rationalise the laws of football were also seen around Portsmouth as its football association secretary, Mr French, raised the possibility of a referees association in the town. His idea in November 1894 was dismissed by the *Portsmouth Times* as favouring those officials competent in taking tests rather than those good at making decisions on the pitch.

Making them sit exams would also be sure to make the already difficult job of finding a good match official harder, the paper reasoned, though it had every sympathy for them:

A member of Portsmouth AFC gave up his own match to referee an Army Cup tie at the Men's Recreation Ground.

The rain came down in torrents, the unfortunate referee was drenched through, and when the game was over the representatives of the competing teams did not even say thank you. It is, indeed, a thankless office.

CHAPTER SEVENTY-SEVEN

Portsmouth AFC were in no need of having to appoint match officials or a penalty taker. The club was disintegrating by the week. At the end of February, Bernard Pares resigned from his role as a vice-president of the Portsmouth FA, his work with the town club exhausted. His place, symbolically, was taken by Sergeant Richard Bonney of the club's usurpers, RA.

Yet another phantom fixture for the town club occurred around the same time – on February 22nd 1896 – with Eastleigh, before the final mention of any game to do with Portsmouth AFC, a supposed home meeting with Cowes at Stamshaw on March 3rd 1896.

Elsewhere, RA had made it through to the Hampshire Senior Cup final to face St Mary's Reserves which the Portsmouth-based team won 3–0 for their only success in the competition. The Gunners were involved on April 11th in the last act of the season when they were defeated by the 15th Company RA in the Portsmouth Senior Cup final. The match report in the *Portsmouth Evening News* read as if Portsmouth AFC had never existed, though

The Royal Dockyard Football Club played its first match on Saturday, beating the Naval Depot by two goals to nil. Whether the new club rises from the ashes of the old Portsmouth Club or whether it is a new organisation I don't quite know. At any rate they have the advantage of the help of the old Portsmouth secretary, John French, and have certainly begun well in starting with a win. There is certainly room and equally certainly material for a strong civilian club in Portsmouth. I hope the Dockyard F.C. will fill the vant.
A. N. OTHER.

The debut of Royal Dockyard FC as a short-lived successor to the original Pompey as reported in the Southern Daily Mail *in February 1896.*

its ghost could be remembered in the closing words of its footballing round-up:

With the competition for the Portsmouth town cup on Saturday, the football season in Portsmouth, which has been unexampled for the good number of matches played, was brought to a close.

In 1894/95, it may be remembered that we had a compulsory suspension of football owing to six weeks' frost but since September there has not been a single break in the fixture lists through adverse weather, though a few clubs have created disappointment failing to complete their engagements.

Not so, the Royal Dockyard FC. The club sprang from nowhere in February 1896. The presence of John French as their secretary indicates they took over from Portsmouth United which never got off the ground.

With Shaftoe as their captain and Berry also in the side, Royal Dockyard strove to fill the gap created by the demise of Portsmouth AFC and become the leading civilian club in Portsmouth, although the name was far from being the cleverest for a side without any military links.

It was a military side which they faced on their debut. Naval Depot were swept aside 2–0 on February 15th 1896. AN Other, of the *Evening Mail*, used his role as the leading football commentator in Portsmouth to predict a way forward for civilian outfits once more.

He wrote, though he was no wiser about Portsmouth AFC's fate than he had been three months earlier with the outfit in a state of flux:

Whether the new club rises from the ashes of the old Portsmouth AFC, or whether it's a new outfit I don't know.

At any rate, they have the advantage of the help of the old Portsmouth AFC secretary, John French, and

> Congratulations to Sergt. Bonney on his election as vice-president of the Portsmouth Football Association. The R.A. hon. sec. is as keen as mustard, and he will not only talk but work for the Association. The position was vacant on the retirement of Mr. Bernard Pares, who has also resigned his seat on the Hampshire Association Council. This, I take it, is due to the collapse of the Portsmouth A.F.C., which is now numbered amongst the departed. Since it was knocked out of the semi-final of the Hants Cup, four or five seasons ago, the Portsmouth Club has gradually faded away, and, groundless, friendless, and bankrupt, it has now ceased to exist.

This article contains the last-known contemporary mention of Portsmouth AFC's existence as reported in the February 29, 1896, edition of Southern Daily Mail.

have certainly begun well in starting with a win.
There is certainly room and equally certainly material for a strong civilian club in Portsmouth and I hope Dockyard FC will fill the void.

Further games were lined up by the still hardworking French with 5th Fusiliers, RA Reserves, Hilsea RA and HMS *Excellent* as the distinctly low-key opponents into late March.

CHAPTER SEVENTY-EIGHT

French's involvement seemed to be the sole remnant of the original Pompey in the new club. The first Royal Dockyard team line-up which was printed contained none of the borough club's players. They had disappeared from the football scene around Portsmouth as surely as the frost of the previous season. Perhaps that's hardly surprising given their frequent inability to turn up regularly for matches.

AN Other was certain about Portsmouth AFC's fate by the time February was about to give way to the March of 1896. He took Bernard Pares resignation from the Portsmouth FA, and also the Hampshire FA, to be the final move in the break-up of an outfit which had led the way in much of the previous decade to ensure football took hold in Portsmouth. Pares's decision to stand down from both positions could only be because of the demise of the original Pompey, the columnist reasoned:

...which is now among the departed. Since it was knocked out of the semi-final of the Hampshire Senior Cup four or five seasons ago, Portsmouth AFC has gradually faded away, and groundless, friendless and bankrupt it has ceased to exist.

It had done enough to show that football could survive in Portsmouth outside of the military, though it had failed to move forward as the game developed generally. Others in the town were determined to do just that. The *Portsmouth Times* of October 31st 1896, commented:

The old repugnance to professionalism is disappearing and, if only the ground difficulty could be solved, I am pretty certain Portsmouth would not be long before they possessed one [a professional club].

Eighteen months to be precise, as a group of businessmen and sportsmen met at 12 High Street, Portsmouth, to agree to the formation of the current Portsmouth FC.

Appendices

Statistics Relating to Portsmouth AFC 1884–1896

1884 – 1885

DATE	TEAMS	COMPETITION	VENUE	ATTENDANCE	RESULT	SMITH AC/W	RUSSELL P	ADAMES W/ADAMS	WILLIAMS C	POOLE FJ	VINCENT J	DANCER PJ/PH	McDONALD J	
08.11	ROYAL LANCASHIRE REGIMENT		NORTH END	some interest	W 4 - 3									1
15.11	HAYLING ISLAND		NORTH END		W 5 - 1	g	f-b	f-b	h-b	h-b¹	l-w	l-w	c-f	2
13.12	HAVANT		away		W 2 - 0 (2 -0)	g	c-f	b			r-w		c-f¹	3
20.12	MR PARES'S TEAM		NORTH END		L 0 - 3									4
27.12	COWES		NORTH END		D 2 - 2 (2 -1)	g		b			h-b	f	f (c)	5
03.01	FAREHAM		away		L 0 - 4 (0 -1)		b	b	l-w				c-f (c)	6
10.01	SOUTHSEA		NORTH END		W 2 - 1	scratch match - friendly								7
17.01	MR PARES'S TEAM, SUNFLOWERS		EAST HANTS GROUND SOUTHSEA		L 0 - 2	g	h-b	b					c	8
21.01	ROYAL ARTILLERY		away		L 1 - 2									9
24.01	HAVANT		NORTH END		W 7 - 2	g						r-w	f (c)¹	10
31.01	CHICHESTER		away		L 2 - 4	g	l-w¹	h-b					c-f (c)	11
07.02	HAYLING ISLAND		away		W 3 - 0 (1 - 0)	g	b	b				f	f (c)	12
14.02	SOUTHSEA		NORTH END		W 1 - 0	g		h-b					c-f (c)	13
07.03	FAREHAM		NORTH END		D 2 - 2	g	c-f	b				l-w¹		14
14.03	CHICHESTER		NORTH END		W 5 - 1		p	p		p			p(c)²	15
21.03	COWES		away	Crowd of excited onlookers	W 3 - 1	p		p				P	P	16
18.10	FIRST PRACTICE MATCH		NORTH END		3 - 1	McDonald's Team v Kent's Team								
22.10	PRACTICE MATCH		NORTH END		1 - 0	W Pates Team Won								
25.10	PRACTICE MATCH		NORTH END		1 - 0									
22.11	PRACTICE MATCH		NORTH END		3 - 1	McDonald's Team won v Russell's Team								
29.11	PRACTICE MATCH		NORTH END		result unknown	McDonald's Team v Dancer's Team								
14.01	SOUTHSEA		NORTH END		W	scratched – only six Southsea players turned up. Portsmouth AFC won easily.								

Notes: 21.03 COWES – Portsmouth Times gave the score as 3 -1, Hampshire Telegraph as 3 - 0

1884 – 1885

SIMPSON T/J	DAVIES RR/RE	HALLETT	DANCEY	HEMINGSLEY R	HUDDY T	LILLYWHITE W	KENT FE	HUDDY C	JONES RE	GILLHAM C	DAWE J	COOK H	ALEXANDER M	WILLIAMS J	MARSDEN	PARES REV NE	NUGENT T/WT	PARES GL	ARMSTRONG J	WILLIAMS W	SCOTT-CHAD T	PINFOLD CE	ALLEN LJ	KINDERSLEY AE	GREEN	
																										1
c-f²	r-w¹	r-w		own goal																						2
r-w			l-w	l-w	h-b	h-b	b				own goal															3
																										4
				f	b			f²	f	f	h-b															5
				h-b	c-f		h-b			r-w		g	substitute players used as a right winger and a left winger													6
																										7
l-w	r-w			h-b	r-w								b	h-b	c-f											8
																										9
l-w³	r-w			h-b	l-w¹	h-b										b	f²	c-f	12 players listed and played							10
r-w				h-b	r-w	l-w							b			b			c-f¹							11
f¹	f			h-b	f¹								h-b			b			f¹	h-b	12 players listed					12
l-w	r-w			l-w		no scorer given							b			b			c-f			b	h-b	r-w		13
	r-w			h-b	c-f	r-w										h-b		b						l-w¹		14
	p¹			p	p											p	p¹		p¹					p		15
p	p²			p	p								p¹											p	p	16

1885 – 1886

DATE	TEAMS	COMPETITION	VENUE	ATTENDANCE	RESULT	SMITH AC/HC	ADAMES WO/WV/WC	MOORE A	KENT FE	HEMINGSLEY R	RUSSELL P	WILLIAMS J	GODFREY CE	
03.10	HAVANT		away		W 3-0 (2-0)	g	f-b	f-b	h-b	h-b	h-b	l-w[1]	l-w	1
10.10	HAYLING ISLAND		away		D 3-3						p			2
17.10	HILSEA ARTILLERY RAMBLERS		NORTH END		W 2-0 (1-0)	b		c-f		b	c-f			3
24.10	ARGYLL & SUTHERLAND HIGHLANDERS, PARKHURST		away		L 0-8	b	b				h-b			4
07.11	CHICHESTER		away		W 4-1 (1-1)	f-b	h-b	g						5
14.11	STUBBINGTON HOUSE		NORTH END		W 3-0 (1-0)	g	b (c)							6
21.11	MIDHURST		away		W 3-2 (2-1)	b	h-b (c)			b	l-w			7
05.12	WIMBORNE	HSC 1	GARRISON BARRACKS GROUND	wretched weather but keen interest	L 1-2 aet 1 – 1 90 mins 0-0 h-t	f-b	h-b							8
09.12	HORNDEAN		NORTH END		W 4-1 (1-0)	b	h-b(c)					h-b		9
26.12 am	FAREHAM		away		W 2-0 (2-0)	g	h-b				b			10
26.12 pm	WORCESTERSHIRE REGIMENT		GARRISON RECREATION GROUND	large number of spectators	W 3-0 (2-0)	b	h-b	g			b			11
28.12	HAVANT		NORTH END		W 6-4 (6-0)	f-b	h-b	h-b						12
30.12	ROYAL MARINES LIGHT INFANTRY		away FORTON		W 10-0	p	p							13
02.01	SUNFLOWERS		NORTH END		W 2-0	f-b	f-b				f-b			14
09.01	COWES		NORTH END		D 2-2 (2-0)	f-b					f-b			15
25.01	93RD REGIMENT		GARRISON RECREATION GROUND		L 2-4 (2-1)	f-b	h-b				h-b			16
end 01	HILSEA ARTILLERY RAMBLERS		NORTH END		W 6-0	f-b	h-b(c)							17
30.01	HORNDEAN		away		W 4-0	b[1]	h-b	l-w[2]			g			18
13.02	STUBBINGTON LODGE SCHOOL		GARRISON RECREATION GROUND	large number of spectators	W 3-1 (1-0)	g	h-b							19
20.02	RMLI		away FORTON		W 6-0 (3-0)	f-b					h-b			20
27.02	HAYLING ISLAND		NORTH END		W 7-1	f-b	h-b(c)				h-b			21
06.03	PETERSFIELD		NORTH END		W 13-1 (3-1)	p	p(c)				p			22
13.03	PORTSMOUTH GRAMMAR SCHOOL		away		D 1-1 (0-1)	b					b			23
20.03	HMS MARLBOROUGH		OFFICERS' RECREATION GROUND		L 0-1	g	h-b(c)				h-b			24
27.03	PETERSFIELD				D 1-1	f-b	h-b(c)				f-b			25

Notes: Games against Worcestershire Regiment W 2-0 Wanderers D 0-0 Southsea Sunflowers W 2-0 listed but no further details given

16.01 Friendly match between teams captained by RE Davies and Harward. Harward's team won 4 - 1. Goals scored by Kindersley, Pinfold, JH Smith and Edmonds (2).

1885 – 1886

HUDDY T	DAVIES RE	KINDERSLEY AE	PARES L/GL	PEARMAN CT	POOLE FJ/T	GODFREY AH/AC	WILLIAMS C	PINFOLD CE/PENFOLD	YOUNG R	SMITH HJ	DONALD A	BROOKS H	NELSON Lt TM RMLI	DAWSON G	MURPHY	PARES REV NE	BOND	SMITH JH/AH	ARMSTRONG J	CARRELL AH	EDMONDS	ALEXANDER M	JONES A	THOMAS	HUDDY C	
r-w	r-w	c-f[1]	c-f			own goal				12 players listed																1
p[1]		p		p	p	p[1]				unnamed scorer																2
r-w	r-w				h-b	l-w[2]	g	h-b	l-w																	3
l-w	r-w	r-w			h-b	g		l-w		h-b	c-f															4
	r-w			l-w[1]	h-b	c-f							r-w[1]	l-w[1]	h-b[1]	f-b										5
l-w		c-f			h-b	c-f[2]		h-b					r-w	r-w[1]	l-w		b									6
r-w[1]					h-b	c-f[2]							r-w		l-w		g					only 10 players listed				7
r-w	r-w(c)[1]				h-b	c-f		h-b		l-w	l-w					f-b		g								8
		l-w[1]				r-w[1]														c-f[1]	r-w	l-w[1]	h-b	b	g	9
l-w	r-w	c-f			b																				h-b[1]	10
	r-w	l-w[1]			h-b															r-w[2]						11
r-w[2]						g																			c-f[4]	12
p[3]				p			p									p[3]									p[3]	13
	r-w(c)	r-w						h-b				c-f	no scorers given								l-w	only 10 players listed				14
	r-w(c)	f			f[1]							f		h-b				f[1]		f						15
l-w[1]	r-w(c)[1]	r-w			h-b	c-f[3]					g							f								16
					h-b	c-f[3]			l-w	r-w[1]						l-w[2]			r-w			only 10 players listed				17
	r-w	l-w			h-b	c-f[1]		r-w														only 10 players listed				18
l-w	r-w(c)	h-b			h-b	c-f[1]				r-w					f-b											19
					h-b	c-f[2]					g			r-w		r-w[2]										20
	l-w		r-w		h-b	c-f[2]	g[1]	l-w[3]						r-w		r-w						plus own goal - Hayling back				21
p[4]				p		p[5]				p	p[2]					p					p[2]					22
	l-w		r-w		h-b[1]	c-f															r-w	Edmonds listed on right and				23
•	l-w					c-f			r-w		r-w				f-b			h-b	l-w							24
f	f				h-b	f[1]	g																			25

1885 – 1886

PARES Basil	HARWARD CN/AN	McDONALD J	PARES Bernard	JONES RE	WHITE F	NICHOLSON	PETERS W	GIBBONS	PATE W	LEADER HJ	WILLIAMS H	HUDDY J	LIVERSIDGE	ALLAN LJ	TURNER	LEAHY PW	
																	1
																	2
																	3
																	4
																	5
																	6
																	7
																	8
																	9
h-b	r-w	l-w¹															10
c-f			l-w														11
	r-w	l-w		f-b	h-b	l-w											12
		p				p¹											13
							h-b	g									14
		only ten players listed						g									15
							f-b										16
							f-b		g								17
							b										18
	one scorer unnamed						f-b			l-w¹							19
							f-b				h-b	l-w²	l-w				20
							f-b										21
								g									22
	left wing								g					h-b			23
							f-b										24
*		f													h-b	f	25

1886 - 1887

DATE	TEAMS	COMPETITION	VENUE	ATTENDANCE		RESULT	SMITH AC	PINFOLD CE	BYLE/BOYLE/DOYLE W	POOLE FJ	ADAMES WO	LEAHY PW	
02.10	WOOLSTON WORKS		PORTSMOUTH		L		g	b	b	h-b	h-b	h-b	1
09.10	2ND WORCESTERSHIRE REGIMENT		GARRISON RECREATION GROUND		L	1-3	b		b	h-b	g		2
16.10	FAREHAM		GARRISON RECREATION GROUND		W	5-0	g	h-b	b	h-b			3
23.10	2-1 WELSH DIVISION RA		NORTH END		W	5-0							4
30.10	PETERSFIELD	PSC1	away		W	6-1 (2-0)	g						5
03.11	US MEN'S GARRISON		GARRISON RECREATION GROUND		L	2-3	f-b						6
06.11	WORCESTERSHIRE REGIMENT		GARRISON RECREATION GROUND		L	0-1 (0-1)	f-b			h-b			7
13.11	PORTSMOUTH GRAMMAR SCHOOL		away		W	5-2 (3-1)	b				g		8
17.11	ROYAL IRISH RIFLES		GARRISON RECREATION GROUND		D	1-1 (0-1)	b			h-b	g		9
20.11	HAYLING ISLAND		away		W	4-0 (1-0)				h-b	g	f-b	10
27.11	2-1 WELSH DIVISION RA		HILSEA		W	3-0	g		c-f³				11
15.12	BLANDFORD	HSC1	away	large attendance	W	3-2 (2-1)	f-b		c-f	h-b			12
18.12	PORTSMOUTH GRAMMAR SCHOOL	PSC2	GARRISON RECREATION GROUND		W	3-0	b		b		g		13
15.01	ROYAL IRISH RIFLES		GARRISON RECREATION GROUND		W	1-0 (0-0)	b		f				14
22.01	FAREHAM				W	2-0 (0-0)					g		15
26.01	HORNDEAN		GARRISON RECREATION GROUND		W	4-1 (2-1)					g		16
29.01	WIMBORNE	HSC s-f	away	several hundred spectators	L	1-3 (0-1)			f		g		17
05.02	FREEMANTLE	PSC s-f	US OFFICERS' GROUND		W	2-0 (0-0)	b		h-b		g		18
12.02	ROYAL IRISH RIFLES		US MEN'S GROUND		W	4-2	b		b				19
19.02	HORNDEAN		away		W	7-0 (4-0)					f¹		20
05.03	PORTSMOUTH GRAMMAR SCHOOL		away		W	5-1 (4-0)	b		f		f¹		21
10.03	ROYAL IRISH RIFLES		GARRISON RECREATION GROUND		W	5-1 (2-1)					g		22
19.03	PETERSFIELD		away		D	1-1	g		f				23
23.03	MR RICHARD'S GARRISON TEAM		US RECREATION GROUND		W	2-0 (1-0)	g						24
26.03	WOOLSTON WORKS	PSC Final	US MEN'S RECREATION GROUND	about 800	W	1-0 (1-0)	g		f				25
08.04	HMS MARLBOROUGH		US RECREATION GROUND		W	2-0	g						26

1886 – 1887

GODFREY AH	KINDERSLEY AE	HUDDY TB/TS	SIMPSON J/TJ	FINLAY J	HEMINGSLEY R	DAVIES RE	STIMPSON J	ARMSTRONG J	EDMONDS	PETERS J W	BOYLE J	PARES GL	BROOKS H	PARES Bernard	CARROLL AH/CARRELL	GRICE H	PARES REV NE	SARISBURY	MASON G	SEDDON FT/FJ/TJ SEDDEN	BENTLEY J/T	RAWLINGS	ROBERTS H	#
c-f	l-w (c)	l-w	r-w	r-w																				1
c-f	h-b (c)		l-w	r-w	h-b	r-w	l-w			no scorer listed														2
c-f	h-b (c)		l-w	l-w	b			r-w	r-w	no scorers listed														3
																								4
c-f[1]	h-b (c)		h-b	h-b	f-b					f-b	r-w[2]	r-w[2]	l-w[1]											5
l-w			l-w								c-f				g	f-b	h-b	h-b	h-b	r-w				6
	h-b (c)	r-w	l-w	f-b								h-b	l-w			g					r-w	c-f		7
l-w[2]	h-b (c)	l-w	h-b	b			h-b				c-f[2]	r-w[1]								r-w				8
c-f[1]	h-b (c)		l-w						b											r-w			h-b	9
c-f[2]	h-b (c)	r-w[1]	l-w									r-w[1]												10
r-w	h-b (c)		l-w	h-b	b									only 10 players listed						r-w				11
r-w	h-b (c)		l-w								f-b									h-b[2]	r-w			12
r-w	h-b (c)		l-w			No scores given					c-f									h-b	r-w			13
			h-b	g										only 10 players listed						h-b				14
f[1]	h-b (c)		b[1]	b																h-b				15
	h-b (c)						h-b					f[3]		b										16
f	h-b (c)			h-b										f						h-b				17
f	h-b (c)[1]									b										h-b				18
		f	h-b									f[4]									f			19
	h-b (c)			b			h-b			b		f[4]								h-b				20
	h-b (c)			g			b					f[4]								h-b				21
h-b		b						f[1]	f	b		f[3]								h-b				22
	f											f[1]								h-b				23
f	h-b									b		f[2]			f					h-b				24
	h-b(c)	f	b							b		f								h-b				25
			h-b							b		f[1]			f[1]		h-b							26

1886 – 1887

SMITH AH/JH	ROSS	LEADER HJ	WILSON	PLANT REV AW	ADAMES P	WARD	KENT FE	McDONALD J	PEARMAN CT	BISHOP	COLLIS W	NELSON Lt TM RMLI	SIMPSON W	CLARKE	LOWRY Lt JH RIR	BESANT	DIPLOCK S	EYNOTT L	BROOKS G	MILLER	THRING	YOUNG R	GRANT WE	#
																								1
																								2
																								3
																								4
				Simpson listed in two positions																				5
				no scorers listed																				6
																								7
																								8
r-w	l-w																							9
		f-b	h-b	l-w																				10
			b	l-w																				11
								g	l-w[1]															12
									l-w															13
				f						b	h-b	f[1]	f											14
													f	h-b	f	f	f							15
												f	b			f[1]		h-b	f					16
								f		b		f[1]	b											17
			f									f	f[1]				f							18
			f														f			g	f			19
																	f[1]	f				g	f[1]	20
																	f	h-b					f	21
																	f							22
												b					f							23
												h-b		f			f							24
																	f							25
h-b												b					f						f	26

141

1886 -1887

1886 – 1887

MACK H	PRICE	ASHBY P /ASHLY P	#
			1
			2
			3
			4
			5
			6
			7
			8
			9
			10
			11
			12
			13
			14
			15
			16
			17
			18
			19
			20
			21
h-b	f¹		22
h-b	h-b	f	23
h-b		f	24
h-b		f¹	25
	f		26

NOTES:

18.09	Scratch match played with HILSEA RAMBLERS. Drawn 1-1. McDonald kicked goal for borough team.
03.11	US MEN'S GARRISON – Hampshire Post has team : Johnson AC Smith WA Jupp FJ Seddon (capt) WE Grant W Boyle EC Prinsep Rev AW Plant E Seddon S Diplock FG Seddon. Team listed from Portsmouth Times.
20.11	HAYLING ISLAND – Portsmouth Evening News has scorers: GL Pares TS Huddy AH Godfrey + own goal. Score used from Hampshire Post.
14.01	ROYAL IRISH RIFLES – Southern Daily Mail has team: R Hemingsley AC Smith Bishop FJ Seddon J Finlay W Collis Lt TM Nelson L Eynott Rev AW Plant W Simpson. Only ten players listed. Team listed from Portsmouth Evening News.
26.03	WOOLSTON WORKS – Southern Daily Mail changes team to: W Boyle GL Pares S Diplock P Ashby TB Huddy for the forward line. Team listed from Hampshire Post.
08.04	HMS MARLBOROUGH – Hampshire Telegraph gives 2-1 score, 1-0 h-t. Score used from Hampshire Post. Scorer of second goal given in Hampshire Telegraph as the Rev N Pares, in the Evening Mail as Bernard Pares.

1887 - 1888

DATE	TEAMS	COMPETITION	VENUE	ATTENDANCE	RESULT	BOYLE W	EDMONDS	SEDDON FJ/SEDDAN/ SIDDON/SEDDEN SEDDOR	EYNOTT L	STIMSON/ STIMPSON AJ	#
01.10	PORTSMOUTH GRAMMAR SCHOOL		away		D 4-4 (2-1)	g	f-b	h-b (c)	h-b	f	1
22.10	HORNDEAN		away		W 5-0 (4-0)	b		h-b (c)		h-b	2
29.10	HILSEA RAMBLERS		MEN'S RECREATION GROUND		L 1-3 (1-0)		f-b	h-b¹			3
02.11	CHICHESTER G & AC		h		L 0-3 (0-1)		h-b	h-b (c)			4
05.11	HAYLING ISLAND		RECREATION GROUND PORTSMOUTH		W 5-1 (4-1)		h-b	h-b			5
12.11	ROYAL SCOTS GREYS		RECREATION GROUND		W 3-0 (0-0)						6
16.11	WINCHESTER		MEN'S RECREATION GROUND		L 3-6 (1-3)		h-b	h-b (c)	h-b		7
19.11	PETERSFIELD	PSC1 r	US RECREATION GROUND		W 3-1 (1-1)	f-b		h-b (c)			8
26.11	ROYAL IRISH RIFLES	PSC2	MEN'S RECREATION GROUND		D 2-2 (1-1)		h-b			h-b	9
03.12	ROYAL ENGINEERS	PSC2	MEN'S RECREATION GROUND	fairly large numbers	W 8-2 (4-1)		h-b			h-b	10
17.12	HILSEA RAMBLERS	PSC s-f	OFFICERS' RECREATION GROUND		D 3-3 (2-3)	f-b		h-b (c)			11
24.12	SUNFLOWERS		USRG		W 2-0		l-w¹	h-b		h-b	12
07.01	HILSEA RAMBLERS	PSC s-f r	OFFICERS' RECREATION GROUND		L 0-1 (0-0)	c-f		h-b (c)		h-b	13
25.01	HILSEA RAMBLERS	PSC s-f 2r	OFFICERS' RECREATION GROUND		L 0-4 (0-4)			h-b (c)			14
01.02	HORNDEAN	PSC s-f	US MEN'S GROUND	fair numbers despite keen east wind	D 1-1 (0-1)			h-b (c)	g		15
04.02	WOOLSTON WORKS	HSC s-f	BAR END CRICKET GROUND		L 0-1 (0-0)			h-b (c)		h-b	16
17.03	PORTSMOUTH GRAMMAR SCHOOL	PSC final	HILSEA RECREATION GROUND	large numbers	D 0-0 (0-0)			h-b		h-b	17
31.03	PORTSMOUTH GRAMMAR SCHOOL	PSC final r	HILSEA	large crowd of interested spectators	W 3-2 (0-2)						18

NOTES:

12.11	Royal Scots Greys also named Scots Greys. Score listed from Portsmouth Evening News. Also given as 3-2 in Southern Daily Mail.
17.03	Attendance given from Southern Daily Mail. Full description reads: "Large number of spectators, including several ladies." The Portsmouth Evening News stated: "Far more numerous (spectators) than could have been expected in the face of a bitter wind and threatening snow."

1887 – 1888

WOOD AH	LEADER HJ	GRANT WE	DIPLOCK S/A	PLANT REV AW	COOK	HEMINGSLEY R	THOMPSON	SIMPSON T/JT	KAVANAGH	DICKSON	SMITH AC/DOYLE AC	COOPER	POOLE FJ	SEDDON EJ/SIDDON	SEDDON C	ALLEN LJ	JOHNSON A	JUPP WA	PRINSEP EC	SEDDON GF	WILLIAMS	SPERANZA Lt RE	PARES GL	#
f	f	f	f	f	one player – a back – unreadable in newspaper. No scorers listed																			1
	f²	f¹			g	f-b	h-b	f¹	f	f¹														2
		h-b	l-w	l-w							f-b	g	h-b	c-f	r-w	r-w								3
		h-b	l-w	l-w							f-b			c-f			g	f-b	l-w	r-w				4
		l-w³	r-w¹	r-w¹				f-b									g				f-b	h-b	l-w	5
	l-w	c-f				f-b		f-b			g			h-b				r-w¹						6
f-b		r-w¹						f-b										l-w						7
	h-b	r-w	r-w		h-b			f-b		Plus unnamed scorer								l-w¹			h-b		l-w¹	8
		c-f¹	f					f-b										r-w				h-b		9
		c-f²		r-w				f-b					f-b					l-w					l-w⁵	10
	r-w¹	c-f		r-w				f-b														h-b		11
		c-f¹		l-w				f-b			g			r-w								h-b		12
r-w	r-w	l-w		l-w				f-b			f-b											h-b		13
	r-w	r-w			g			f-b			f-b											h-b		14
	r-w¹	c-f			f-b			f-b														h-b		15
			l-w	l-w				f-b			g							r-w					r-w	16
	h-b	l-w	l-w		f-b			f-b			g							r-w						17
																		r-w						18

1887 – 1888

	JUPP J	GLENNIE C/GLENNY	HUDDY TS/TB	WHITMARSH Lt JF	ARMSTRONG J	FINLAY J	JEFFKINS	WARD	PARES Bernard	ASHBY P	CALLAN	LEWIS	DURRELL CT	STIMPSON GAT	HAMPTON WE	SMITH H	LOOPE	DREWSON	PARES REV NE	SMITH JH	PARES LC	
																						1
																						2
																						3
																						4
	c-f																					5
		h-b	h-b[1]	l-w	r-w[1]																	6
		g	c-f[1]		l-w[1]											r-w						7
		g																				8
		g			f	f-b	r-w[1]															9
		g	r-w[1]					h-b														10
		g							l-w[1]	l-w						h-b[1]						11
											f-b	r-w										12
													g									13
	l-w	l-w												c-f		h-b						14
															r-w		g	r-w	r-w			15
			c-f																f-b	h-b		16
			c-f																		r-w	17
																						18

1887 – 1888

These games listed but no match reports or statistics found:

03.12	PORTSMOUTH GRAMMAR SCHOOL	HILSEA
07.12	CHICHESTER G & AC	away
10.12	PETERSFIELD	away
24.12	YMCA	GOVERNOR'S GREEN
28.12	CHICHESTER	home
31.12	WIMBORNE	SOUTHAMPTON
07.01	SUNFLOWERS	PORTSMOUTH
14.01	WINCHESTER	away
21.01	CHICHESTER	away
28.01	PETERSFIELD	home
11.02	HAYLING ISLAND	away
25.02	ROYAL IRISH RIFLES	RECREATION GROUND
03.03	PORTSMOUTH GRAMMAR SCHOOL	HILSEA
10.03	HILSEA RAMBLERS	HILSEA
17.03	ROYAL SCOTS GREYS	HILSEA
24.03	HMS MARLBOROUGH	RECREATION GROUND

November: Original PSC 1 match with Petersfield ended in a draw. Exact date and score unknown.

1888 - 1889

DATE	TEAMS	COMPETITION	VENUE	ATTENDANCE		RESULT	SEDDON FJ	SWEETENHAM FW / SWEETMAN T	JEFFKINS	ALLAN/ALLEN F	SMITH AC/DOYLE	GRANT WE/WS/WA	JOHNSON HW	
06.10	UNITED SERVICES		SERVICE REC GROUND		L	1-2 (1-1)	p	p[1]	p					1
13.10	ROYAL ENGINEERS (CHATHAM)		USRG		L	0-6				g	f-b	f-b	h-b	2
27.10	UNITED SERVICES		USMG		D	1-1	h-b[1]			r-w	f-b	h-b		3
01.11	SOUTH YORKSHIRE REGIMENT		USMG		W	2-0 (1-0)	h-b (c)	g[1]			f-b	h-b		4
03.11	US MEN'S TEAM	PSC 1	MEN'S REC GROUND	large numbers	L	0-3 (0-1)	h-b (c)				f-b	h-b	g	5
17.11	HAVANT		away		L	0-2 (0-2)		p				p		6
24.11	PORTSMOUTH GRAMMAR SCHOOL		HILSEA		L	0-1 (0-1)								7
08.12	PETERSFIELD		MRG	very sparse attendance	W	3-2 (2-1)	p[1]					p[2]		8
13.12	WINCHESTER		USMG		W	2-0 (1-0)	h-b (c)			r-w	f-b	h-b		9
19.12	FAREHAM		USMG		W	6-0	h-b (c)			g	f-b	h-b		10
22.12	UNITED SERVICES		USMG		D	0-0 (0-0)	h-b (c)				f-b	h-b		11
02.01	PORTSMOUTH SUNFLOWERS		GOVERNOR'S GREEN		W	1-0 (0-0)	h-b (c)					h-b		12
08.01	KING'S ROYAL RIFLES	HSC 2	ALDERSHOT		W	4-0 (3-0)	h-b (c)				f-b	h-b		13
12.01	HAYLING ISLAND		HILSEA		W	15-0	p[3]					p[2]		14
19.01	FAREHAM		away		W	3-1 (2-0)	h-b (c)				f-b	h-b		15
26.01	YORKSHIRE REGIMENT		MEN'S REC GROUND		L	0-1 (0-1)	h-b				f-b	h-b		16
02.02	YMCA		NORTH END		W	3-1	h-b (c)				f-b	h-b		17
23.02	PORTSMOUTH GRAMMAR SCHOOL	HSC s-f	MEN'S REC GROUND	large assembly	W	2-0 (0-0)	h-b (c)[1]				f-b	h-b		18
02.03	ROYAL ENGINEERS (ALDERSHOT)	HSC f	COUNTY GROUND SOUTHAMPTON	Several thousand spectators	L	1-5 (0-3)	h-b (c)				f-b	h-b		19
09.03	STUBBINGTON HOUSE & LODGE		away		L	1-2								20
13.03	PORTSMOUTH POST OFFICE		GOVERNOR'S GREEN		L	0-3								21
16.03	HAVANT		away		L	1-3 (1-2)	h-b (c)					h-b		22

SHERLOCK HOLMES WAS A POMPEY KEEPER

1888 – 1889

SHUTE T/SHUTTE FEN/FA	DIPLOCK S	EDMONDS FH/GH	SEDDON EH/GH	LOVETT QUARTER-MASTER SGT RA	SEDDON GF	PRINSEP EC/RC/AC/PRINCEP	COOPER	BOYLE B/W	POOLE FJ	PLANT REV AW	SEDDON C	SMITH JH/HJ	BROOKS H	JUPP WA	GRICE TH	PARES EF	FENNELL C	EYNOTT CJ	RICHARDS T	COX	DURELL TC	JONES H	SHORT GF	#
																								1
h-b	h-b	l-w	l-w	c-f	r-w	r-w																		2
	l-w		l-w				g	f-b	h-b	c-f	r-w													3
			c-f		r-w	r-w				r-w[1]		f-b	h-b	h-b										4
	r-w		c-f		r-w	l-w		h-b		l-w				f-b										5
p	p		p	p		p				p					p	p		only 10 players listed						6
										p														7
		p	p	p						p			only 10 players in side				p	p	p	p				8
			r-w		r-w					l-w		f-b					no scorers given				g	h-b	c-f	9
			l-w[1]							r-w[1]											f-b	h-b		10
l-w			l-w		l-w					r-w		f-b									g			11
			r-w		r-w							f-b						l-w			g			12
			r-w		r-w	l-w			h-b	l-w[1]											g			13
			p[1]		p[1]						p[2]													14
g			r-w[2]		r-w				h-b									l-w						15
g	r-w		l-w		l-w	c-f																		16
																								17
			r-w		r-w	l-w																	l-w	18
			l-w		l-w	r-w	'A substitute' listed on the right wing – could be Short																	19
																								20
																								21
h-b			r-w		r-w																			22

1888 – 1889

PARES Basil	WOOD AH	PARES Bernard	JONES J	PARES GL	HAMPTON WE	TAFT	OZZARD AH	KENDALL HS	LOVELL	ANDERSON H	GARRINGTON GA	McDONALD J	COOK AW	ALLEN AS/SL	FREESTONE J	McCOWEN J	FREESTONE E	STALLARD W	MOREY A	#
																				1
																				2
																				3
																				4
																				5
																				6
			p																	7
																				8
																				9
l-w	c-f[3]	r-w[1]																		10
			h-b	c-f																11
Goal scored by 'A Forward'					f-b	h-b		'AN Other' listed on the left wing												12
				c-f[3]	f-b															13
		p[3]	p[1]				p[2]													14
							l-w[1]	f-b	c-f[1]											15
				f-b	r-w					h-b										16
c-f[1]	l-w[1]						r-w				g	h-b	r-w			h-b				17
		g		c-f[1]	f-b										h-b					18
		g		c-f[1]	f-b										h-b					19
																				20
																				21
					f-b							g			f-b	l-w[1]	c-f	r-w		22

1888 –1889

13.10	ROYAL ENGINEERS (CHATHAM)	Team listed from Southern Daily Mail Hampshire Post team: Allen Smith Grant Johnson Prinsep FG Seddon Lovett Seddon Shutte Diplock Evans Hampshire Telegraph team: Allen Dr Doyle W Grant F Shutte EH Seddon (c) AN Other Diplock Edmonds GF Seddon Prinsep Only ten listed.
08.12	PETERSFIELD	Full description of attendance: 'very sparse attendance because of persistent downpour'.
22.12	UNITED SERVICES	Team listed from Hampshire Telegraph. Hampshire Post team: Durrell AC Smith JH Smith FJ Seddon J Jones WE Grant EC Prinsep Rev AW Plant GL Pares E Seddon Shutte
19.01	FAREHAM	Scorers listed from Southern Daily Mail. Hampshire Telegraph scorers : Lovell E Seddon Ozzard
23.02	PORTSMOUTH GRAMMAR SCHOOL	Dr A Conan Doyle given as AC "Smith" in Portsmouth Evening News preview. Attendance described in Portsmouth Evening News as "ropes lined with enthusiastic crowd, mostly partisans of the grammar school". Attendance listed from Evening Mail.
02.03	ROYAL ENGINEERS (ALDERSHOT)	Hampshire Post gave the score as 0-5 and venue as Banister's Park, Southampton. Score listed from Hampshire Telegraph.
20.03	STUBBINGTON HOUSE AND LODGE	Scorer given in Southern Daily Mail simply as Seddon.

1889 - 1890

DATE	TEAMS	COMPETITION	VENUE	ATTENDANCE	RESULT	GARRINGTON GA	PUGHE RR/PUGH/PUGHUE	COOPER Lt	SEDDON FJ	PAINE C/PAYNE	MacDONALD H/McDONALD	PRINSEP EC	DREW HRH	#
19.10	YMCA		home		W 4-1 (2-1)	g	f-b	f-b	h-b (c)	h-b	h-b	l-w¹	l-w²	1
26.10	ROYAL MARINES ARTILLERY		EASTNEY		W 4-2 (2-0)				h-b (c)		h-b	r-w	f-b	2
02.11	PETERSFIELD		away		W 3-0 (0-0)	g	f-b		h-b	r-w				3
09.11	CHICHESTER		USMG		W 4-0 (3-0)	g	f-b		h-b		h-b	r-w	f-b	4
16.11	KING'S OWN YORKSHIRE LIGHT INFANTRY	PSC 1	MEN'S RECREATION GROUND	Good number of spectators	W 1-0 (0-0)	g	f-b		h-b (c)		h-b	r-w	f-b	5
20.11	STUBBINGTON HOUSE SCHOOL		USMG		W 1-0 (0-0)	g			h-b (c)			r-w		6
23.11	FAREHAM		away		W 5-0 (5-0)		f-b		h-b (c)	only ten players listed				7
30.11	PORTSMOUTH GRAMMAR SCHOOL		HILSEA		W 6-0	g	h-b					f-b		8
14.12	UNITED SERVICES CLUB		MEN'S GROUND		W 5-0	g	h-b			h-b				9
21.12	COWES	PSC 2	away		L 0-3 (0-1)	g			h-b		h-b		f-b	10
28.12	ROYAL ENGINEERS (ALDERSHOT)	HSC 2	away	Large number of spectators	L 2-3 (1-1)	g			h-b		h-b¹			11
18.01	UNITED SERVICES CLUB		USMG		L 2-4 (2-0)									12
08.02	ROYAL MARINES ARTILLERY		MEN'S RECREATION GROUND		W 4-2 (2-2)		f-b	f-b						13
22.02	ROYAL MARINES LIGHT INFANTRY		USMG		D 1-1 (0-0)	g								14
	Other fixtures listed but no details:													
25.01	GENEVA CROSS		NETLEY											
15.03	ST MARY'S (SOUTHAMPTON)		away											
29.03	FAREHAM		away											

Notes:

23.11 FAREHAM – Team and scorers listed from Portsmouth Evening News. Scores given in Hampshire Post as JEFFKINS 2 ARTHY 1 GF SEDDON 1 R ALLEN 1

28.12 ROYAL ENGINEERS (ALDERSHOT) – Score listed from Hampshire Post and Southern Daily Mail. Given in Hampshire Telegraph as 0-2

1889 – 1890

WATTS W	EDMONDS W/FH/H/TH	ALLAN SL/ALLAN/AL	ALLEN RE/ALLEN	GRANT WE	ADAMS	SEDDON GF/GH/GE	DOYLE AC Dr	ARCHY W/ARTHY	PARES GL	LORING EM/LOVING HM	SMITH JH	GREEN H	JENKINS CSM/JEFFKINS	DURRELL FO	GREEN	DURELL TC	GRAHAM N	SEDDON EJ	BEEL GR	MILLER L	ALLAN G	BYNG A	#
c-f¹	r-w	r-w																					1
f-b	l-w²	c-f¹	g	h-b	l-w¹	r-w																	2
		c-f²	h-b	h-b	r-w¹	l-w	f-b	l-w															3
	l-w¹	l-w		h-b		r-w¹		c-f²															4
	l-w	l-w¹		h-b					c-f	r-w													5
	l-w		h-b			l-w	f-b	c-f¹			f-b	h-b	r-w										6
	l-w		r-w²	h-b		h-b	f-b	c-f¹						r-w²	g								7
	l-w		h-b²	h-b		l-w¹	f-b	r-w	c-f (c)²	r-w¹													8
	r-w	c-f	h-b			l-w			r-w							l-w	f-b	f-b					9
	l-w	c-f	h-b			r-w										r-w	l-w	f-b					10
		l-w				r-w¹	f-b	c-f	r-w									f-b	h-b	l-w			11
						h-b													g	f-b	f-b	h-b	12
		h-b				l-w¹										l-w				r-w			13
	c-f	h-b				l-w			l-w				r-w			f-b							14

1889 – 1890

PRIESTLY E/PRIEST	WHITMARSH JF Lt	WOOD AH	FRIAR	COOK AW	KENDALL HS	LUMSDEN Lance Corporal	GUNNER	TAFT	SHORT	EYNOTT CJ	ARMSTRONG J	#
												1
												2
												3
												4
												5
												6
												7
												8
												9
												10
												11
h-b	l-w²	l-w	c-f	r-w	r-w							12
						g	h-b	h-b	c-f³	r-w		13
h-b								f-b		h-b	r-w¹	14

1890 - 1891

DATE	TEAMS	COMPETITION	VENUE	ATTENDANCE	RESULT	ECKERSLEY HT/ JH ECKERSBY	ARBUCKLE BV	BAKER A	FOSTER	SEDDON FJ	TRINGHAM	WHITMARSH JF Lt	GRANT WE	#
14.10	ROYAL NAVAL COLLEGE	USOG			W 1-0 (0-0)	g	f-b	f-b	h-b	h-b	h-b	l-w	l-w	1
25.10	YORKSHIRE REGIMENT	USMG			L 0-3									2
08.11	GENEVA CROSS (NETLEY HOSPITAL)	PSC 1	HILSEA		W 2-1 (1-0)								h-b	3
12.11	STUBBINGTON		US REC GROUND		W 6-0 (2-0)									4
22.11	UNITED SERVICES	USMG			L 0-2 (0-1)			f-b					h-b	5
29.11	OXFORD LIGHT INFANTRY	USMG			not given								h-b	6
06.12	WINCHESTER	USMG			L 1-2 (0-1)	g							h-b	7
10.01	PORTSMOUTH NORTH END	PSC 2	HILSEA		W 9-0 (3-0)			h-b¹						8
15.01	OXFORD LIGHT INFANTRY	USMG			W 3-1 (2-1)									9
22.01	YORKSHIRE REGIMENT	USMG			W 4-2 (2-1)									10
24.01	SOUTHAMPTON NAVAL WORKS	HSC 2	WOOLSTON		L 2-3 (2-3)								h-b	11
31.01	NAVAL WORKS WOOLSTON	PSC s-f	USOG	about 300	W 3-2 (1-1)								h-b	12
07.02	FAREHAM		away		W 2-1 (2-0)	g							p¹	13
14.02	PORTSMOUTH GRAMMAR SCHOOL		HILSEA		W 2-1 (0-1)								h-b	14
21.02	HAVANT		MEN'S REC GROUND		W 3-1								h-b	15
07.03	OXFORD LIGHT INFANTRY	PSC f	USMG	very large numbers	D 1-1 (0-0)					h-b			h-b	16
14.03	OXFORD LIGHT INFANTRY	PSC fr	USMG	1200	D 0-0 (0-0) 90min + 40 min aet					h-b			h-b	17
28.03	OXFORD LIGHT INFANTRY	PSC f2r	USMG	very large company	D 1-1 (0-0) 90min + aet					h-b			h-b	18
18.04	OXFORD LIGHT INFANTRY	PSC f3r	USMG	about 4000 spectators	W 1-0 (0-0)								h-b	19

Notes:

	PSC final teams used from the Portsmouth Evening News. Line-ups in the Hampshire Post switched around the positions of one or two of the players in each game.
08.11	The s-f with Naval Works Woolston was originally described as the Hants Minor Challenge Cup fourth round. Also described as the Hampshire Junior Cup in the Portsmouth Evening News.
07.02	Score given in the Hampshire Post as 0-1.
07.03	Attendance listed from Hampshire Post. Given in Portsmouth Evening News as 'several hundred spectators'.
28.03	Attendance listed from Portsmouth Evening News. Given in Hampshire Post as 'very large company'.

1890 – 1891

PARES GL/EL	SEDDON GF	PIKE SP/SR/SL	GARRINGTON GA/CARRINGTON	SMITH JH	SIMPSON TJ	WOOD AH	PARES Basil	ALLAN RL	ALLEN RE/HE/E	COLLINS JH	ALLEN SL/FL/MFL	GRIFFITHS	TRISCOTT	LEVER D	JEFFKINS S	COOPER EF/ES	POOLE FJ	NEWELL REV CF	PRINSEP EC	OXFORD FM	MILLER EJE/ETE	COOK AW	PARES Bernard	#
c-f	r-w	r-w¹																						1
																								2
																								3
c-f	l-w	r-w¹	g	f-b¹	f-b	h-b (c)	h-b	l-w	r-w															4
p⁴											p¹													5
			g			h-b		l-w	r-w	f-b	h-b	l-w	c-f	r-w										6
c-f			g			h-b (c)		l-w	r-w							f-b	f-b	l-w	r-w					7
c-f¹			g			h-b (c)		r-w	l-w	h-b						f-b	f-b	l-w	r-w					8
c-f³	r-w	g	l-w²			h-b (c)										f-b	f-b				f-b	l-w²	r-w¹	9
c-f³	r-w					h-b	h-b				l-w										f-b	l-w	r-w	10
c-f²			g	l-w	l-w	h-b	h-b							f-b									r-w	11
c-f¹			g	l-w	r-w¹	l-w¹	h-b							f-b									r-w²	12
two substitutes on the left-wing, one substitute on the right-wing																f-b	ten players listed						r-w²	13
						other scorer given simply as Pares																		14
			g								r-w					f-b	f-b							15
c-f	r-w	g	l-w			h-b								f-b				r-w				l-w¹		16
c-f	r-w	g	l-w			h-b (c)	r-w							f-b								l-w		17
	r-w	g	l-w			h-b (c)			l-w					f-b¹								c-f	r-w	18
c-f	r-w	g	l-w			h-b (c)	h-b							f-b								l-w¹	r-w	19

1890 – 1891

PEAD W	THRESHER JF	BAKER RJ	PARES F	McDONALD H	UTTERTON JF/JA/JG	SHUTTE FEN	PAYNE S	JENKINS PG	BLURTON R	PEAD C	ROLLANDS	FLANNERY JF	#
													1
													2
													3
													4
													5
													6
													7
													8
g	f-b	h-b											9
													10
	f-b	r-w											11
				f-b	h-b								12
				f-b	h-b	p							13
													14
				h-b			h-b	l-w²	l-w	c-f¹	r-w		15
				f-b									16
				f-b									17
				f-b									18
				f-b								l-w	19

1891 - 1892

DATE	TEAMS	COMPETITION	VENUE	ATTENDANCE	RESULT	WOLFE ED	MILLER ET	COOPER ES Capt	GRANT WE	UTTERTON J	RICHARDS T	HALL G	COLLINGS JH/COLLENS	PEAD W	ALLEN RE	#
28.11	HMS EXCELLENT		USMG		L	0-1 (0-1)	g	f-b	f-b	h-b	h-b	h-b	l-w	l-w	c-f	r-w	1
30.12	OXFORD LIGHT INFANTRY		USMG		L	0-3		f-b				h-b					2
23.01	NORTH END		home		D	1-1 (1-0)						h-b		p		l-w	3
13.02	PETERSFIELD		away		W	4-2 (0-1)		p	p					p	p		4
12.03	PORTSMOUTH GRAMMAR SCHOOL		HILSEA RECREATION GROUND		W	2-0 (1-0)									p1		5
22.03	SECOND BATTALION SOUTH STAFFORDSHIRE REGIMENT		USMG		L	0-3 (0-0)		f-b	g	h-b							6
26.03	HMS EXCELLENT		USMG		D	1-1 (0-0)		f-b	g	h-b		h-b					7

Notes:	
23.01	Scorer listed from Southern Daily Mail. Given in Hampshire Post as Peade and in Portsmouth Evening News as Grant.

Other fixtures listed but no further details:	
02.01	WINCHESTER -away
06.01	CHICHESTER – away
09.01	ROYAL MARINES ARTILLERY - USMG
30.01	FAREHAM – home
20.02	HAVANT – away
27.02	OXFORD LIGHT INFANTRY - USMG
06.02	PORTSMOUTH POST OFFICE – cancelled owing to bad weather

1891 – 1892

ALLEN RL	GARRINGTON GA	COOK AW	WOOD AH	BAKER RJ	HARGREAVES J	EADES	GREEN	RICHARDS A	BAKER F	KENT	BURNBURY	PEARCE WG	PERKINS	WILLIAMS	GUNDRY	DAWSON H Lt/B	CHIGGAALL	DRUMMOND	KERWIN/KIRWAN	ECKERSLEY HT	STAITE	FIELD	ALLEN J	PEARCE	#
r-w																									1
	g	f-b	h-b	h-b	l-w	l-w	c-f	r-w	r-w															p	2
h-b1		plus two substitutes. Only ten players listed								g	f-b	p													3
p													p		goals scored by Collins and the Allen brothers										4
														p1											5
						other player listed as Allan										f-b	h-b	h-b	l-w	l-w	c-f	r-w			6
r-w1											f-b					h-b			l-w	l-w		c-f	r-w		7

SHERLOCK HOLMES WAS A POMPEY KEEPER

1892 - 1893

DATE	TEAMS	COMPETITION	VENUE	ATTENDANCE		RESULT	HUMBY EJ/EA/G/EH/ET	BAKER RJ	EARP E	SHEPHERD B/SHEPPARD	GRANT WE/WH	COOK AW/COOKE	PEAD HJ	WILLIAMS B/R	
08.10	PORTSMOUTH POST OFFICE		GOVERNOR'S GREEN		W	7-0 (3-0)	g	f-b	f-b	h-b	h-b	h-b	l-w	l-w	1
15.10	ROYAL MARINES ARTILLERY		EASTNEY		W	4-2 (3-1)	g				h-b		l-w²	l-w	2
22.10	HAVANT		GOVERNOR'S GREEN		D	0-0	g				h-b		r-w		3
29.10	1ST CO SOUTHERN DISTRICT ROYAL ARTILLERY				D	2-2 (0-2)	g		f-b				l-w²	l-w	4
29.10	19th COMPANY ROYAL ARTILLERY		USMG		D	3-3							p¹		5
05.11	ROYAL MARINES LIGHT INFANTRY	PSC 1	away	large numbers	W	4-0 (1-0)	g				h-b		l-w	l-w	6
23.11	CAMERONIANS (ALDERSHOT)		USMG		W	3-0									7
26.11	BOURNEMOUTH	HSC 1	STAMSHAW	good gathering	W	8-0 (1-0)	g				h-b		l-w¹	l-w³	8
10.12	HMS EXCELLENT		USMG		D	0-0									9
17.12	MEDICAL STAFF CORPS ALDERSHOT	HSC 2	STAMSHAW	numerous gathering	W	3-0 (1-0)	g	f-b			h-b	r-w	l-w	l-w	10
21.12	HAMPSHIRE REGIMENT		USMG		D	1-1 (1-0)		f-b	c-h	c-h		c-f		r-w¹	11
14.01	NORTH STAFFORDSHIRE REGIMENT	PSC 2	USMG	Large numbers	L	0-6 (0-2)	g	f-b	h-b	r-w	h-b	c-f	l-w		12
04.02	SOUTHAMPTON ST MARY'S	HSC s-f	COUNTY GROUND SOUTHAMPTON		L	0-2	g				h-b		l-w	l-w	13
18.02	PETERSFIELD				W	5-2 (0-2)									14
25.02	HAVANT		away		W	2-0 (2-0)					h-b		l-w¹		15
04.03	NORTH STAFFORDSHIRE REGIMENT		GOVERNOR'S GREEN		L	1-7 (0-3)	g				h-b	f-b	c-f¹		16
11.03	DEPOT ROYAL ARTILLERY		USMG		W	3-1 (1-0)	g		h-b¹			f-b	l-w		17
18.03	ROYAL MARINES ARTILLERY		GOVERNOR'S GREEN		W	3-1 (1-0)	g					f-b	l-w		18
22.03	SOUTHAMPTON		away		L	0-3									19

Notes:

15.10	ROYAL MARINES ARTILLERY – one of the Pead players scored at least two of the goals. Other scorers were unnamed.
	Likely to be the same game. The 2-2 score was given in the Portsmouth Evening News. For the Evening Mail, the score was 3-3.
05.11	Opponents listed in the Portsmouth Evening News as Forton, where the game took place.
26.11	Venue also given in Portsmouth Evening News as Public Recreation Ground, North End
07.12	Attendance listed from Evening Mail. Described in Portsmouth Evening News: "judging by the number of spectators who put in an appearance at Stamshaw Recreation Ground these cup matches are attracting an unusual amount of interest."
17.12	Team listed from Hampshire Post. Evening Mail gave GL Pares as c-f and Basil Pares as the r-w.
14.01	Team listed from Hampshire Post. Evening Mail has the forwards as: l-w Sheppard, Matson; c-f Cooke; r-w H Pead, Dawson. It also described the attendance as "a crowd of very considerable dimension in spite of the bad weather."
04.03	Team listed from the Evening Mail. Hampshire Post gave: Humby Cook Burks Waddington Dawson Gibbon Rundle Matson H Pead G Pead Grant. Portsmouth Evening News had another version with the last three players in the line-up listed as Grant H Pead G Pead

1892 – 1893

COLLINS JH	MATSON ST	RUNDLE CA	GREEN T	DAWSON H Lt/B	PEAD W	HUNT C	EARP AJ	WAITE MG	GIBBONS S	POOTE F	WOODS T	FRENCH W	FOSTER RH	GIVENS	GIBBINS RB	BURKE R/E	WOOD AH	PARES GL	PARES Basil	HARRISON	WILSON	PEAD G	PARES Bernard	
c-f	r-w	r-w	no scorers listed																					1
	r-w	f-b		h-b(c)	c-f	r-w	f-b	one of the half-backs listed as a substitute						other scorers not given										2
l-w	l-w					h-b		f-b	f-b	h-b	c-f	r-w												3
r-w	r-w			h-b				f-b		only ten players listed			h-b	h-b										4
p¹		plus own goal																						5
r-w	r-w			h-b(c)			h-b²	f-b					c-f		f-b	plus two unnamed scorers								6
																								7
	r-w			h-b(c)			f-b									f-b	c-h	c-f²	r-w²					8
																								9
				h-b			f-b									h-b	r-w¹	c-f²						10
l-w	l-w						f-b									c-h(c)			g	r-w				11
	r-w			l-w	h-b																f-b			12
				h-b(c)			f-b									f-b	h-b	c-f	c-f			r-w		13
																								14
	r-w		g										f-b							h-b				15
l-w	l-w			h-b(c)					h-b				f-b							r-w				16
l-w¹			+ own goal off a DRA back player							f-b								h-b						17
l-w			c-f¹							f-b								g						18
																								19

1892 – 1893

SPARKS W	TAYLOR J	FRENCH J	WADDINGTON F	WHITMARSH Lt JF	CLARKE	BUCKWRIGHT	GRIFFITHS	LEIGH R	PEAD C	
										1
										2
										3
										4
										5
										6
										7
										8
										9
										10
										11
										12
										13
										14
f-b	h-b	l-w	c-f¹	r-w						15
			r-w							16
		c-f			h-b	r-w	r-w			17
			r-w¹		h-b	r-w¹		h-b	h-b	18
										19

1893 - 1894

DATE	TEAMS	COMPETITION	VENUE	ATTENDANCE		RESULT	PEAD G	GRANT WE	COLLINS R	McKINLAY J	EARP AJ	#
07.10	HAMPSHIRE REGIMENT		NORTH END RECREATION GROUND		W	2-1	g	f-b	f-b	h-b	h-b	1
14.10	FREEMANTLE		STAMSHAW RECREATION GROUND		L	0-2 (0-1)	g	h-b			f-b	2
21.10	PORTSMOUTH GRAMMAR SCHOOL		HILSEA		W	3-2 (3-0)	g	h-b	h-b			3
28.10	DEPOT ROYAL ARTILLERY		USMG		L	0-4 (0-3)	g	h-b				4
04.11	POST OFFICE		STAMSHAW RECREATION GROUND		W	9-1	g	h-b¹				5
11.11	HAVANT		NORTH END RECREATION GROUND		W	11-0 (3-0)	g	h-b			f-b	6
18.11	SOUTHAMPTON ST MARY'S	PSC 1	STAMSHAW RECREATION GROUND	some 300	L	0-8 (0-6)	g	h-b			f-b	7
25.11	NUMBER ONE CO ROYAL ARTILLERY		USMG		L	5-8 (1-6)	g	h-b	h-b			8
02.12	CONNAUGHT RANGERS		USMG		W	2-0 (0-0)		h-b				9
09.12	BOURNEMOUTH	HSC 2	NORTH END RECREATION GROUND	very limited company	D	1-1 (0-0)	g	h-b				10
16.12	BOURNEMOUTH	HSC 2r	away	large attendance	W	1-0 (0-0)	g	h-b			c-f	11
13.01	BOURNEMOUTH	HSC 2 2r	COUNTY GROUND SOUTHAMPTON	large attendance	W	1-0 (0-0)	g	h-b				12
20.01	DEPOT ROYAL ARTILLERY				L	0-3						13
27.01	CONNAUGHT RANGERS		USMG		D	1-1 (1-1)	g	h-b				14
10.02	ROYAL ENGINEERS	HSC s-f	COUNTY GROUND SOUTHAMPTON	about 1000	L	0-2 (0-1)	g	c-f				15
17.02	CHICHESTER				D							16

Notes:

04.11	Team listed from Portsmouth Evening News. Evening Mail has the line-up: G Pead Poat Collins Lear Grant substitute W Pead H Pead Williams Matson Wild.
18.11	Attendance listed from Portsmouth Evening News. Added: 'Attendance cut by violent weather, otherwise likely to be record gate'. Given in Portsmouth Times as 'miserable knot of spectators'.
25.11	Lear given as Tear in Portsmouth Evening News line-up.
09.12	Attendance listed from Evening Mail. Full description reads: 'Very limited company in spite of it being an important match.'
27.01	Team listed from Hampshire Post. Portsmouth Evening News has Doyle and Wells swapping places with H Pead and C Williams.

Also listed but no further details given:

23.12	STAFFORD REGIMENT at NORTH END RECREATION GROUND
17.03	MEDICAL STAFF CORPS at NORTH END RECREATION GROUND

1893 – 1894

WOOD AH	PEAD HJ	WILLIAMS J	POATE S	MATSON ST	LAWTON W	HUMBY	DAWSON Lt B	WILDE W/WILD/WH/WYLD	PEAD W	GIBBON/GIBBONS RPH	LEAR BEC	CALDECOTT WE/CALDICOTT	COLLINS WE	DAWE J	EMERY W	POATE D/POAT	WILLIAMS C/G	BROWN	MARTIN S	BURKE P/G	EMERY D	MITCHELL	#
h-b	l-w¹	l-w	c-f	r-w	r-w	+ own goal																	1
h-b	c-f	r-w	r-w	l-w		f-b	h-b(c)	l-w															2
		c-f¹	r-w¹	r-w¹	l-w			l-w	f-b	f-b	h-b												3
	r-w			l-w					f-b		f-b	h-b	h-b	l-w	c-f	r-w							4
	r-w¹		+ two own goals					l-w¹	c-f¹		h-b¹		f-b		f-b	r-w¹	h-b	l-w					5
h-b	l-w¹			r-w¹			h-b	r-w²			c-f²		+ own goal			f-b	l-w⁴						6
h-b	r-w			l-w			h-b(c)	l-w			c-f					r-w				f-b			7
			l-w								h-b					r-w²				f-b	f-b		8
			l-w				h-b(c)	l-w¹								g	r-w¹				f-b		9
	r-w			l-w			h-b				f-b	h-b				c-f				f-b			10
+ unnamed scorer				l-w			h-b(c)				f-b					l-w				r-w			11
																r-w							12
																							13
	l-w										h-b					l-w						c-f	14
											h-b					l-w							15
																							16

1893 – 1894

PARES Basil	PARES SL	BROUGHTON P	SELLY A/SELLEY	HILL	PORTCH	PHILLIPS	DOYLE C	REID A/READ P	SELBY JR	HOOSE	HARGREAVES J	PARES GL	PARES Bernard	MIDDLEMASS/MIDDLEMAS W	SHEPHERD	TAYLOR J	WELLS	ELLIOTT	WHITMARSH Lt JF	WATSON F	#
																					1
																					2
																					3
																					4
		+goalscorer of Matson likely to be S Martin given in line-up																			5
																					6
																					7
l-w³	c-f	r-w																			8
		f-b	h-b	c-f	r-w																9
l-w							r-w¹														10
l-w		f-b					r-w	h-b													11
c-f¹								h-b	f-b	f-b	h-b	l-w	l-w	r-w							12
																					13
		f-b					r-w¹								f-b	h-b	r-w				14
		f-b					h-b			h-b				l-w				f-b	l-w	l-w	15
																					16

1894 - 1895

DATE	TEAMS	COMPETITION	VENUE	ATTENDANCE		RESULT	PAICE W	KING T	STREET G	DAWSON C	NELSON	GRANT WE	HAMILTON	PEAD HJ	
22.09	PORTSMOUTH GRAMMAR SCHOOL		HILSEA RECREATION GROUND		L	1-3 (1-1)	p¹								1
06.10	CHICHESTER		STAMSHAW RECREATION GROUND		W	2-1 (2-0)	r-w	g	f-b	f-b	h-b	h-b	h-b	l-w¹	2
13.10	HAVANT		STAMSHAW RECREATION GROUND		D	4-4 (1-1)	l-w		f-b	f-b	l-w			h-b	3
20.10	CONNAUGHT RANGERS		USMG		L	0-1	l-w			l-w		+ 'AN Other' full back		r-w	4
03.11	COWES		away	fairly good numbers	L	0-7 (0-6)				h-b		r-w			5
10.11	COWES	HSC 1	away	*abandoned h-t, heavy rain*		2-5						p			6
17.11	ROYAL MARINES ARTILLERY	PSC 1	away		D	2-2 (1-1)			f-b			l-w		h-b	7
24.11	COWES	HSC 1r	away	moderate crowd	L	0-2 (0-2)				p					8
01.12	ROYAL MARINES ARTILLERY	PSC 1r	STAMSHAW RECREATION GROUND		L	1-3 (0-1)			f-b	c-f		h-b			9
08.12	BOURNEMOUTH		away	fairly large crowd	L	1-5 (0-2)			f-b			l-w			10
26.12	RYDE		away		L	2-4 (1-2)			f-b						11
29.12	ST MARY'S RESERVES		away ANTELOPE GROUND		L	0-9 (0-5)									12
09.03	WEYMOUTH		away		W	4-2 (2-2)				h-b		h-b			13

Notes:

24.11	WEYMOUTH - STAMSHAW RECREATION GROUND – large number of spectators – **L 1-2** – The Hampshire Post listed team as: Reynolds Osborne Aston Arnold Hogg Hickenbottom Lt Phillips Burrell Roberts Lt Schreiber Daly – likely to be 2nd X1
24.11	COWES – score listed from Portsmouth Times. Given in Portsmouth Evening News as 1-3, without a Portsmouth AFC scorer.
04.03	WEYMOUTH – line-up listed from Portsmouth Evening News. Line-up in Southern Daily Mail: C Monaghan AW Street P Watts H Johnson WE Grant BC Lear G Rogers C Dawson H Windust G MacGuire A Ward. No scorer listed

Other fixtures listed without any further details given:

15.12	15TH COMPANY ROYAL ARTILLERY
22.12	LANCASTER REGIMENT
05.01	ROYAL MARINES LIGHT INFANTRY
12.01	CHICHESTER
26.01	PORTSMOUTH GRAMMAR SCHOOL
02.02	HAVANT
09.02	ROYAL ENGINEERS
16.02	ST MARY'S (SOUTHAMPTON) – NORTH END RECREATION GROUND
23.02	LANCASTER REGIMENT
02.03	COWES

A game was also advertised against BOURNEMOUTH at the NORTH END RECREATION GROUND for mid-January.

1894 – 1895

AYLING	WELLS T	NELLTHORPE F	PEAD G	HARVEY H	LEAR BEC	RADSHAW W / REDSHAW/RENSHAW	WOODS G	BORLAND	DUNN G	MEE F	PEW F	BOYCE G	KELLY	SELLY/SELLEY W	REID A	HAYLING	PRIEST	DAVIDSON C	PEAD A	SEELEY JR	SHEPHERD F	BRYANT G	
																							1
l-w	c-f¹	r-w																					2
r-w			g	f-b	h-b²	h-b		c-f¹	+ unnamed scorer														3
			g	h-b	h-b		f-b		h-b	c-f	r-w	r-w											4
			g	h-b	h-b			c-f		r-w			f-b	f-b	h-b	r-w							5
				h-b	p									p				f-b					6
			g	h-b	h-b					l-w									c-f	r-w	f-b		7
			g							p													8
r-w			g	h-b	h-b					l-w				f-b							l-w	r-w	9
				h-b																			10
																							11
																							12
				h-b(c)		+ own goal	+ Rogers not in line-up																13

1894 – 1895

REYNOLDS	BROOKS (substitute)	COLBRAN (substitute)	PATTERSON C	WALSH	WILLIAMS W	SAMPSON	JARDIN	HICKS	WOOD AH	COLLINS WE	SHUTTE FEN	JACKSON	KINGSMILL G	DEARDEN	FOX	McPHERSON	MIDDLEMISS	REILLEY	STREET AW	PHILLIPS G	HANNA F	WINDUST H	
																							1
																							2
																							3
																							4
																							5
																							6
+ 'AN Other' on right wing																							7
																							8
+ unnamed scorer																							9
g	f-b	h-b	h-b	l-w	c-f	r-w¹	r-w																10
									g	f-b	h-b	h-b	h-b	l-w¹	l-w	c-f	r-w¹	r-w					11
																							12
		h-b	l-w						twelve players listed									g	f-b	f-b	l-w	c-f¹	13

1894 - 1895

	McGUIRE G	CLARKE	
1			
2			
3			
4			
5			
6			
7			
8			
9			
10			
11			
12			
13	r-w[1]	r-w	

1895 - 1896

DATE	TEAMS	COMPETITION	VENUE	ATTENDANCE	RESULT	BLAIR	PRIEST	CLARKE	MARCHMENT/MAIDMENT	LEAR BEC	SERGEANT	PARES B	JERRARD	DAWSON C	NORRIS	
05.10	HAVANT		away		L	1-2	only ten men									1
12.10	DUBLIN FUSILIERS RESERVES		GOVERNOR'S GREEN		W	3-1	g	f-b	f-b	h-b	h-b	h-b	l-w[1]	l-w	c-f[1]	r-w[1]	2
26.10	ROYAL NAVAL DEPOT		UNITED SERVICES RECREATION GROUND		L	0-1 (0-0)				h-b	h-b		c-f	2 substitute backs, 1 substitute l-f			3
30.11	NORTHUMBERLAND FUSILIERS		NORTH END RECREATION GROUND		L	1-2											4
30.11	SHANKLIN				L	1-5											5

Notes:	
05.10	HAVANT – Score listed from Portsmouth Evening News. Given as 2-3 in Southern Daily Mail.
Other fixtures listed but no further details given:	
12.10	STUBBINGTON HOUSE SCHOOL - GOVERNOR'S GREEN
02.11	STUBBINGTON - NORTH END RECREATION GROUND
09.11	COWES HSC 1 - away
07.12	ST MARY'S SOUTHAMPTON - NORTH END RECREATION GROUND
18.01	HAVANT - NORTH END RECREATION GROUND
25.01	CHICHESTER - NORTH END RECREATION GROUND
22.02	EASTLEIGH - NORTH END RECREATION GROUND
07.03	COWES - NORTH END RECREATION GROUND

1895 – 1896

	PIKE SR	HARRISON	PAICE W	GARDINER B	McPHERSON	CLEGG	
1							
2	r-w						
3		g	h-b	r-w	r-w	l-w	
4							
5							

Also Available by the Same Author
GLORY GUNNERS
THE HISTORY OF ROYAL ARTILLERY (PORTSMOUTH) FC

Kevin Smith

This book details undoubtedly the best football club Portsmouth has ever seen. Until its publication, Royal Artillery had remained hidden from view for a hundred years.

Royal Artillery were an elite service sporting outfit that gave successful, organised football to the city. The Pompey Chimes and the Football/Sports Mail on Saturdays are the legacies of the Artillerymen as well as a series of national triumphs in a staggering six-year period of achievements.

But they also made headlines for the wrong reasons. Their fortunes were wrecked in a 'professionalism' scandal that reached the top of the football establishment.

Available from good bookshops, just quote ISBN 0 9534707 0 9, priced £8.50.

Or purchase direct from the author, Kevin Smith, at the following address:
34 Ledbury Way, Bognor Regis, West Sussex PO21 3JP
Priced £8.50 including postage and packing.